DATE DUE

Athletes Who Indulge Their Dark Side

Athletes Who Indulge Their Dark Side

Sex, Drugs, and Cover-Ups

Stanley H. Teitelbaum

PRAEGER
An Imprint of ABC-CLIO, LLC

A B C 🔖 C L I O

Santa Barbara, California • Denver, Colorado • Oxford, England

Library of Congress Cataloging-in-Publication Data

Teitelbaum, Stanley H.
    Athletes who indulge their dark side : sex, drugs, and cover-ups / Stanley H.
Teitelbaum.
        p. cm.
    Includes bibliographical references and index.
    ISBN 978-0-313-37756-3 (hard copy : alk. paper) — ISBN 978-0-313-37757-0
(ebook) 1. Athletes—Psychology. 2. Athletes—Drug use.
3. Athletes—Sexual behavior. 4. Doping in sports.
5. Compulsive behavior. I. Title.
    GV706.4.T42 2010
    796'.01—dc22   2009035331

ISBN: 978-0-313-37756-3
E-ISBN: 978-0-313-37757-0

13 12 11 10 9   1 2 3 4 5

This book is also available on the World Wide Web as an eBook.
Visit www.abc-clio.com for details.

Praeger
An Imprint of ABC-CLIO, LLC

ABC-CLIO, LLC
130 Cremona Drive, P.O. Box 1911
Santa Barbara, California 93116-1911

This book is printed on acid-free paper (∞)

Manufactured in the United States of America

To Jake, Max, Zoey, Will, and Ben—my personal dream team.

CONTENTS

ACKNOWLEDGMENTS

I owe a debt of gratitude to the many people who have contributed to my thinking, organizing, and shaping of this book.

Most of all I am forever appreciative to Leighsa King for providing the support, endless availability, sensitivity, and knowledge in facilitating the flow of the work.

I am grateful to Bill Minor, Marc Steger, Sue Macy, Debbie Goldbergh, and Cindy Sabella for helping me to navigate the process and for connecting me to key resources necessary to bring this book to fruition.

A big thank you goes to Lawrence Teitelbaum for his guidance and special input, and the support of family members Martin Cohen, John King, and Diane Teitelbaum.

I was inspired by the creative ideas from colleagues Henry Kellerman, Paul Elovitz, Peter Buirski, Alan Melowsky, and Dan Dervin, and the useful suggestions from Jim Gaspar, Joe Feldman, Diane Feldman, Gary Greenbaum, Al Pollock, Greg Rauscher, Pearl Wolf and Howard Geltzer.

Among the many others whose interest in my analysis of these sports scandals spurred me forward are Joan Erdheim, Andrea Corn, Carolyn Craig, Dan Sosnowik, John Hussey, Gene Carney, and Phil Harmon.

The staff at the New York Public Library, Lucille Bertram and the Teaneck, New Jersey, Public Library Staff, and Lily Dougherty-Johnson at the Amagansett, New York Free Library were consistently reliable in accessing research sources.

I gratefully acknowledge Dan Harmon and Debbie Carvalko at Greenwood Publishers and Rebecca Edwards at Cadmus Communications for their expertise in cultivating this project.

As always the insights, formulations, constructive critique, and encouragement from Sylvia Teitelbaum in moving the work along were beyond invaluable.

INTRODUCTION

Sports scandals have captured our interest for decades, and the public's appetite for these stories is increasingly insatiable. We love sports, we thirst for sports news, and we are incurably attracted to the constant parade of celebrity athlete downfalls. The modern-day landscape has shifted in recent eras, and we now are drawn to sports stars' off-the-field activities as much as we are drawn to what they do in the game. New scandals occur on an almost weekly basis featuring these athletes who cross the line, and the public is captivated by these incidents involving moral or legal transgressions.

In the context of intense media scrutiny and the "hero-ization" of gifted athletes, lapses in off-the-field behavior fuel constant headlines. These transgressions, many of them serious offenses, range from the illegal use of performance-enhancing drugs and other forms of cheating, to sexual misconduct, to gambling, to the illegal possession and use of weapons, and even to murder.

What prompts sports heroes to make pathologically self-destructive choices in crossing boundaries—choices that lead them to engage in activities that put their careers and their lives at risk? What goes on inside the minds of corrupt athletes, when they cross society's and sport's boundaries? What allows them to operate with unbridled hubris? What creates the climate that encourages them to view themselves as being above the system, and to expect a free pass when their corrupt actions come to light? Why do so many celebrity sports stars indulge their dark side in off-the-field misbehavior?

Simply put, they do it because they feel they can! Because their acquired distorted self-image, as a result of fan adulation and being pumped up by the media, conditions them to believe that they can cross these boundaries with impunity. Their immense wealth and exaggerated status make them ill prepared for the need to cultivate and to protect their image.

It is ironic to observe how frequently our star athletes, who seem to have it all, disregard the rules of society and indulge their dark side, with little concern about the implications for their careers or their lives.

In general, the realistic appraisal and anticipation of consequences for stepping over the line is a sufficient deterrent against the acting out of antisocial behavior. Such self-restraint is often absent in the lives of some celebrity sports heroes, who are conditioned to expect a quick fix in response to their needs and to indulge their wishes impulsively and even recklessly, without forethought and without regard for the repercussions. Past transgressions often have been treated lightly, which further encourages athletes to believe that they have a license to do whatever they want.

The culture of cheating in sports, which mirrors the scandals of deception in our society at large, has reached epidemic proportions; and collusions and cover-ups among the league, the owners, the coaches, and the players rule the day. As we become increasingly disillusioned in celebrities and investment managers who are exposed as fraudulent, and politicians and corporate leaders who are guilty of lying, cheating, hypocrisy, and deception, we are faced with similar situations in the world of sports. Barry Bonds, Roger Clemens, Marion Jones, Floyd Landis, and Michael Vick are merely a small sample of elite sports stars who have been tainted by scandals in the early twenty-first century. We are so flooded with these sports scandals that we have become jaded and inured to their impact on our culture. The continuing cavalcade of athletes' misconduct has become so expected and accepted that some sports scandals that once were viewed as shocking are now considered to be mundane and unimportant. A widespread sense of moral outrage has been replaced by reactions of numbness and indifference.

In many ways, sports represents the last frontier in which to establish solid values and commendable character traits in our children. Instead of solidifying this goal, we are seeing an erosion of character and integrity in many of our sports stars, which is being passed along to youths who are eager to emulate their heroes. As a result we are in danger of producing a corresponding preponderance of erosion of character and integrity in children. Along with the influences coming from parents, schools, and peers, elite athletes contribute to the task of molding youngsters to embrace values that lead to productive lifestyles. Correspondingly, young people look to their role models in sports to shape them in their journey toward adulthood.

The mantle of role model invariably comes with the territory of attaining prominence in sports. There is a serious side of sports celebrity status, which is to be mindful of how off-the-field demeanor affects the fans, and, hence, one of the most significant contributions to society that a star athlete can make is to recognize the responsibility and opportunity that accompanies success.

Others have subscribed to the position that it is not the province, nor the responsibility, of sports stars to serve as role models. Charles Barkley, a celebrity athlete, has been most adamant about renouncing this commitment. Barkley proclaims that being a role model is a task that must be embraced by parents and that it has become a burden that has been displaced improperly onto sports heroes.

When sports figures indulge their dark side and pursue shortcuts to performance, engage in gambling activities, or resort to violent solutions in dealing with conflict, they are setting a poor example and sending a message that condones cheating, domestic violence, disrespect of others, and a general disregard of the acceptable norms of society. Unfortunately, a substantial segment of gifted athletes who achieve a high level of success are abysmal failures as role models because of their proclivity to cheat to embellish their performance, or engage in lapses in off-the-field conduct. Sadly, too many of our adored sports figures are providing a model of corrupt behavior, rather than a model of integrity.

Our youths are prone to model themselves after their idealized sports stars. By indirectly encouraging them to learn to "drug up," to win at any cost, and to work around the rules and beat the system, celebrity sports heroes are endorsing a belief system that places performance above integrity and is indoctrinating our youths to feel like imposters. Performance resting on a foundation of deceit, dishonesty, and corruption creates a fragile and false identity. By contrast, athletes who take the high road toward legitimate success and operate off the field in a reputable fashion are paving the way for young fans to adopt a positive value system and a firm foundation for self-esteem. Young kids, especially, need to believe in the goodness of their heroes, before they are ready to accept and integrate the flawed sides of their role models. The gentlemen's agreement between athletes and sports writers to ignore negative stories about public figures, prevalent in an earlier era, has long been replaced by an intense scrutiny in which everything is examined and reported. Such transparency is commendable, but one downside is that it deprives young devotees from sustaining their unqualified admiration, and compels them, prematurely, to lose their starry-eyed regard for their heroes and forces them to relinquish their perfect world fantasy at an early age. The cautionary tale that accompanies the exploration of these sports scandals is not for prurient purposes nor to cast moralistic judgments, but rather to emphasize the position that we must not allow the growing reactions of cynicism, acceptance, and indifference to become the norm in reacting to the increasing number of scandals embracing celebrity sports figures.

This book is dedicated to highlighting the underbelly of prominent sports scandals and to contribute to a climate that inserts significant pause in the current cultural tilt toward acceptance and implicit endorsement of athletes who are prone to indulge their dark side.

CHAPTER ONE

The Steroids Scandal

A BRIEF HISTORY

The use of performance-enhancing drugs by elite athletes is not a new phenomenon. Such use dates all the way back to the ancient Greeks, who consumed dried figs and mushrooms to ratchet up their energy levels before playing their games. Professional sports has a long history of players relying on supplements to give themselves an energy boost and added strength to deal with the rigors of a long season. Even when dangerous side effects are publicized, athletes are prone to trade future health problems for short-term success. The threat of damaging health issues is generally easily pushed aside, with denial and rationalization, to pursue the dream. In sports, consistent with this mind-set, the pull to seek an edge to heighten performance, regardless of the consequences, is as old as sports' origins. This trend is exacerbated by the quick-fix mentality prevalent in today's society, in which it is the present that counts; gratification without delay rules the day, and the future will take care of itself.

Amphetamines

In past decades, the drugs of choice among athletes were amphetamines. It was widely accepted that these stimulants, also commonly referred to as greenies, helped players to sustain their stamina. In baseball, greenies often were passed openly around the clubhouse and even in the dugout before a player's next at bat. No rules governed against it, and it was not perceived as a form of cheating. The standard of accountability in large measure is influenced by society's value system at any given point in time, and our current culture is enmeshed in surveillance and scrutiny. In earlier eras, taking performance-enhancing drugs like amphetamines was viewed by the media and in the public eye as something that sports stars needed to do simply to boost their energy. There is a long tradition in sports to find ways to seek an edge over opponents. Recently, the New England Patriots, and coach Bill Belichick, were penalized by the National Football League (NFL) for videotaping their opponent's defensive signals so they would know in advance when to expect a blitz. In baseball, pitchers like Gaylord Perry and Preacher Roe allegedly owed their success to throwing illegal spitballs, and batters like Sammy Sosa, George Brett, and Lenny Dykstra supposedly hit home runs with the aid of corked bats. Some accounts confirm the rumors that, in the most famous game in baseball history, Bobby Thomson's walk-off home run, "the shot heard around the world," was assisted by a coach sitting behind the scoreboard with a telescope who stole the catcher's signs and relayed them to the batter. Taking performance-enhancing drugs became just another route to gain an edge.

The self-destructive aspect of stimulants became highlighted when supplements containing ephedra were implicated in the sudden deaths of NFL star Korey Stringer in 2001 and baseball prospect Steve Bechler in 2003. The day after he performed poorly in a preseason practice, Stringer, according to his Minnesota Vikings' teammates, took a supplement called Ripped Fuel, which contains ephedrine, and he collapsed and died during a practice session. Steve Bechler, a Baltimore Orioles pitcher, reported to spring training ten pounds overweight and was taking ephedra as a dietary supplement, when he collapsed from heatstroke during a workout and died the next day. Research studies have indicated that users of ephedrine, which can increase heart rate, elevate blood pressure, and intensify dehydration, "were 200 times more likely to suffer complications of the herb than people taking other supplements."[1]

In the wake of these tragedies, supplements containing ephedra were banned by the NFL and Major League Baseball (MLB), but athletes imbued with an image of their invulnerability and invincibility, and enmeshed in a syndrome of denial, were quick to attribute these deaths to poor judgment in the self-regulation of these supplements and to adopt an "it can't happen to me" strategy. Even when the Food and Drug Administration (FDA) banned the sale and use of ephedra products in 2004, after determining that they were linked to a higher risk for seizures, strokes, and heart attacks, professional athletes were not dismayed. By that time, many of them had discovered and entered the world of steroids.

Steroids

The appeal and pull toward performance-enhancing drugs can be compared in two groups of professional athletes. On the one hand, there are star players who are out to transform their careers from superior to Herculean greatness. In assessing Barry Bonds's metamorphosis to the all-time home run leader, Cory Lidle, a major league pitcher, maintained that, without steroids, Bonds probably was capable of hitting about 550 home runs. This would have placed him in an elite group of sluggers, but short of immortality. The implication is that talented players can become superstars with the help of steroids. On the other hand, there are the marginal players, or those who are trying to make it to the big leagues, who are often predisposed to turn to steroids.

Before the advent of steroids, when other sources of performance-enhancing drugs were in vogue, the drive for success at any cost dwarfed safety considerations. Former major league pitcher Bobby Ojeda summed it up by pointing out that many players, such as himself, in their quest to make it to the big leagues (that is, "the show" as it is called among ballplayers) are inclined to ignore or dismiss the dangers of using performance-enhancing drugs. These players will do anything they think will make them stronger and give them additional energy and an extra edge to help them make the team. In retrospect, Ojeda perceptively queried, "Did we cross the line of concern for our long-term health? When you are twenty-one and chasing a dream, there is no line."[2] Thus, it is one thing, as Ojeda suggests, to seek an advantage that propels you into major league status; but it is quite another to use steroids to transform yourself (a la Barry Bonds or Mark McGwire) from a superior player to a level of record-breaking greatness. When this happens, the long-standing benchmarks of excellence are threatened, and the entire sport becomes riddled with suspicions of cheating.

In more recent times, the use of performance-enhancing drugs has received scandalous attention, especially as it mirrors the widespread eruption of corruption and cheating at all levels of our society. In addition, the number of athletes who are under a cloud of suspicion for juicing with steroids to inflate their productivity has mushroomed. Many observers maintain that the primary threat to the integrity of sports is the steroids scandal, rather than the gambling episodes that the leagues are most vigilant in monitoring.

THE QUESTIONS OF WHO, WHY, AND WHEN

What are the factors that have tempted elite athletes to use steroids? First, there is the group contagion effect. When an athlete sees his teammates perform above their usual level and physical signs suggest steroids use, temptation to cross the line into illegal chemical assistance increases. If peers are inflating their power surge with the help of juicing, and getting away with it, there is a greater pull to join the group. Mike Schmidt, the Hall of Fame third baseman, was a straight arrow who played before the steroids era. In spite of his outstanding offensive records as a "clean" athlete, Schmidt acknowledges, "If I had played in the 1990s, I would have used steroids. Why? Because I'm human."[3] In effect, Schmidt is underscoring the power of a group norm, even if it crosses a line.

The second most important factor is greed. The explosive profitability of sports has generated enormous sums of money available to attract elite players. For many athletes, the lure of astronomical contracts and mega-million-dollar endorsement deals makes it an easy choice to use steroids to enhance their statistics, even if it jeopardizes their health.

A third factor relates to the dream of immortality—that is, basking in the glory of sports fans at whatever cost. If steroids bring the athlete to a higher level of productivity, then that is the ticket to everlasting fame. According to Victor Conte, the Bay Area Laboratory Co-Operative (BALCO) guru, Tim Montgomery, who became the world's fastest runner after using steroids supplied by BALCO, proclaimed that if he won an Olympic gold medal "it wouldn't matter if I died right on the other side of the finish line."[4] In simple words, to achieve that level of success would be worth sacrificing his life.

Other athletes have retrospectively taken a more remorseful stance on their steroids involvement. Lyle Alzado was a professional football hero who earned the NFL defensive player of the year award in 1977. Before his death in 1992 from a rare form of brain cancer, Alzado confided that his illness was connected to the many years of massive doses of steroids taken during his career. Steve Courson, an NFL offensive lineman from 1977 to 1985, was among the first former football players to acknowledge using steroids during his playing days to increase his size and strength. He went public about his steroids use in 1985 and was summarily released by the Tampa Bay Buccaneers, in what was a punishment for muddying the NFL image. Three years after his retirement, Courson developed a serious heart problem, which he attributed to his earlier steroids involvement. He became an early outspoken opponent of steroid use throughout the league and was critical of the inefficiencies in the NFL's steroid testing program, which began in 1986. And Johnny Davis, who played with the San Francisco 49ers in 1982, claims that the team was rampant with players using steroids while en route to their Super Bowl championship season.[5]

Although the testimonials of Alzado, Courson, and Davis relate to earlier eras, and the NFL was the first major sports league to implement a drug-testing policy, George Will adeptly points out that steroids cheating continues to abound throughout the league. Will observes, "It requires the willful suspension of disbelief to think that diet and strength training are the only reasons why the average NFL offensive lineman weighs 307 pounds."[6]

BASEBALL

Curiously, however, it is baseball, not football, that attracts the most glaring headlines about the influence of steroids. The reason for this inequity of attention is that the premier power hitters create an imbalance and threaten baseball's traditions, including its most hallowed home run record, whereas in football, the offensive and defensive linemen, the players most likely to indulge in steroids to augment their size and strength, neutralize one another. Football's marquee players, the quarterbacks, are less reliant on steroids, because it is their ability to read defensive alignments and to throw with accuracy that leads to their success.

Former baseball star Jose Canseco wrote in his book, *Juiced,* that 85 percent of professional baseball players used steroids. Canseco's claims were discredited throughout the major league community, by players and owners alike. He is most often viewed as a huckster out to make a quick buck by sensationalizing a controversial issue. Nevertheless, his revelations about himself and others, even if exaggerated, kept this scandal in the limelight. A similar bombshell came from Ken Caminiti, the National League Most Valuable Player (MVP) in 1996, who told *Sports Illustrated* in a 2002 article that his career year was attributable to steroids. Caminiti, who died in 2004 from a drug overdose, also maintained that steroids use had increased to 50 percent among active baseball players.

Caminiti was the first player to admit openly to taking steroids. Although his body broke down soon after his MVP year, probably reflecting the downside of juicing, he had no compunctions about using steroids and justified his actions on the grounds that many of his teammates as well as rival players were following the same path. In the aftermath of Caminiti's whistle-blowing about baseball's poorly kept secret, the players union and the franchise owners established a drug-testing plan. Although this move was woefully belated, it was the first of its kind in baseball.

The Rise and Fall of Mark McGwire

It was easy to admire Mark McGwire. Not only was he a prodigious long-ball slugger, but he seemed to have his priorities in order. During his rookie season with the Oakland A's in 1987, he belted forty-nine home runs, a record for a rookie; and he undoubtedly would have crossed the magic line of fifty were it not for the fact that he chose to miss a number of late-season games to be with his wife while waiting for the birth of their son. In subsequent seasons, he teamed up with Jose Canseco, and the awesome duo became known as the "Bash Brothers."

A little over ten years later, in 1998, McGwire was at the center of baseball's feel-good story, when he and Sammy Sosa threatened to eclipse Roger Maris's long-standing single-season home run record. No player had seriously challenged Maris's record of sixty-one homers since 1961. The baseball establishment was ecstatic. The McGwire-Sosa home run chase brought back a level of popularity to and interest in the sport, which had waned since the protracted strike in 1994, the eighth interruption since 1970. Fans were getting sick of these strikes and turning away from the sport. Although the love of baseball and the need for heroes and a feeling of connection eventually would bring angry fans back to the game, by 1997, attendance, while recovering, continued to be 10 percent below the prestrike level.

In August 1998, a sports writer, Steve Wilstein, happened to notice a strange bottle in McGwire's open locker. Perplexed, Wilstein first thought it was some kind of vitamin; but it turned out to be androstenedione, a testosterone booster. As noted by Fainaru-Wada and Williams in their investigative volume, *Game of Shadows* (2006),

> Andro was legal. But it had been banned by the International Olympic Committee, the NCAA, and the NFL. Olympic doping experts told Wilstein that Andro had the same muscle building effects as anabolic steroids, which Congress had outlawed in 1991. Andro was a steroid by another name. In the Olympics, using Andro was considered cheating. Users who got caught were banned.[7]

Wilstein was reviled for breaking this story. At this point, McGwire was well on his way to surpassing Maris's record, and the writers, the fans, and the baseball establishment were eating it up. With Sosa not far behind McGwire, it became an exciting horse race. The fans wanted to remain in blissful denial, not to have their bubble burst in the midst of their love affair with the affable gigantic slugger. In a fascinating twist, the outrage about these revelations was directed at Wilstein. He was perceived as the villain, a reporter out to make a name for himself by publicizing this exposé. It is a psychological phenomenon that many people need to hold on to their illusions even when reality stares them in the face. Thus, resentment was directed toward Wilstein, the messenger, who dared to puncture the bubble and made the fans uncomfortable with the truth, which they were not ready to face. The need for a sports hero to connect with, to relate to, to identify with, and to supply a source of hope is so strong that many people are reluctant to acknowledge the misdeeds of beloved athletes. Only gradually, and long after McGwire had broken the record by hitting seventy home runs in 1998, did the masses acknowledge their disappointment in McGwire. As the realization reached a crescendo that McGwire's onslaught of the record was fueled by androstenedione, his dwindling fan base reacted with disillusionment and resentment toward the slugger. How dare he fail us and not be the legitimate superman that we needed him to be. But this sentiment took time to develop.

In spring training in 1999, after he set the new home run record, McGwire was still perched on the Herculean pedestal. Most sports writers had played down the Andro story, and they were eager to pump him up as the new champion. For his part, McGwire—aware that hero-worshiping kids were trying to emulate him and were stocking up on Andro—declared that he would no longer use this steroid precursor, which had made him bigger and stronger. Meanwhile, young athletes across the country were emulating McGwire, and sales of androstenedione had increased more than fivefold in the year following revelations about McGwire's drug use. Nevertheless, when a writer at a press conference had the audacity to ask McGwire about his admitted use of androstenedione, and the message it sent to adoring kids, the reporter was treated like a pariah, as if he was disrespectfully daring to question royalty.

For a long time, the writers, the baseball establishment, other players and the players union, and the fans were in collusion to distance themselves from the unpleasant truth, that long-standing home run records were being assaulted by cheaters, that the heroic feats we wanted to latch on to and experience vicariously were a sham, and that the well-loved game we trusted to supply legitimate excitement was now under a cloud of suspicion. Commissioner Bud Selig remained mum, because he was afraid to jeopardize the revival of baseball excitement, thanks to the tainted feats of the McGwires and Sosas.

Years later, after his election to the Hall of Fame, Tony Gwynn voiced support for McGwire, stating, "I know he's a Hall of Fame player,"[8] while simultaneously pointing an accusatory finger toward everyone who had ignored the steroid era as it was evolving. "We knew. Players knew. Owners knew. Everybody knew. And we didn't say anything about it."[9]

When Mark McGwire retired after the 2001 season, he was still considered a lock for election to the revered Hall of Fame. His career total of 583 homers over sixteen seasons was his chief credential. Still in effect, however, was the collusion of enablers who dumbed down their vision and their speech by creating a conspiracy of silence and turning a blind eye toward the connection between bigger physiques and the power surge that had been going on in baseball. McGwire was certainly only one of many players who were posting inflated power numbers with the help of steroids, but his production became emblematic of the artificially enhanced hero. Meanwhile, the steroids issue in sports was attracting political attention. President George W. Bush expressed concern in his 2004 State of the Union address that too many athletes were setting a poor example for the youth of America, who were all too ready to emulate their sports heroes. Bush warned that "the use of performance enhancing drugs like steroids in baseball, football, and other sports is dangerous, and it sends the wrong message—that there are shortcuts to accomplishment, and that performance is more important than character."[10] And later that year in a Senate Commerce Committee hearing, John McCain cited medical evidence that indicated that the negative by-products of steroid use included enlarged heads, shrunken testicles, and, most alarmingly, an increased frequency of heart attacks and strokes. McCain demanded that the players union institute a more stringent program of steroid testing and penalties, or face the prospect of congressional intervention.

Indeed, congressional hearings on steroids in sports were scheduled for March 17, 2005, and high-profile athletes, including McGwire, Sammy Sosa, Rafael Palmeiro, Jose Canseco, Jason Giambi, Bill Romanowski, and Steve Courson, were called to testify. It turned out to be the undoing of Mark McGwire. When questioned about whether he had used perform-ance-enhancing drugs, the mighty hero repeatedly replied, "I'm not here to talk about the past."[11] McGwire was probably following poor advice from his inept legal team, but his response conveyed a refusal to deny that he had used steroids, and, in effect, it was viewed as an implicit admission that he had. In a huge swing of the pendulum by those who had adored him, McGwire was crucified by the media for his stonewalling testimony; and he paid the price the next year when he became eligible for induction into the Hall of Fame. McGwire has never openly admitted that he juiced, but it is now widely accepted that he was cheating. In failing to defend his record, he essentially dug his own professional grave.

Rafael Palmeiro was the most outrageous witness of the congressional hearings. With great emphasis, he brazenly lied through his teeth when he dramatically set the record for insincerity and pointed his finger at the committee chairman and declared, "Let me start by telling you this: I have never used steroids. Period."[12] Palmeiro was still an active player at that time and the fact that he had consistently produced big power numbers made him a potential Hall of Fame candidate. He was exposed as a fraud later in the 2005 season, when he tested positive for the steroid stanozolol and was suspended. Upon his return after his suspension, he was an inef-fective shadow of his former athletic prowess, undoubtedly weighed down mentally by the impact of his disgrace, and soon thereafter he retired.

The congressional hearings served the purpose of shaming and forcing the powers of baseball, that is, the owners and the players union, to adopt a stronger drug policy and sanctions. The message from Congress to MLB was police yourself or face up to additional congressional intervention. And so it was that a new joint drug agreement was reached in which a player would receive a 50-game suspension for a first positive test and a 100-game suspension following a second drug offense. For those who failed three tests, a lifetime expulsion was ordered. Significantly, for the first time, sanctions for amphetamine use also were set in place.

When the Hall of Fame ballots were tallied in 2006, Mark McGwire's first year of eligibility, he received a staggeringly low total of only 23.5 per-cent of the votes. The standard for admission is 75 percent, so Big Mac with his 583 career home runs was definitively shunned by the writers in what amounted to a steroids backlash referendum. Most of the writers who failed to endorse him acknowledged that they were influenced by the sus-picion that he had used steroids. The avoidance and obfuscation were just too much. Our society can be forgiving toward athletes who fess up to their mistakes, but we do not respond kindly to being deceived. This sentiment was being expressed by the Hall of Fame voters. The baseball Hall of Fame is replete with alcoholics, drug abusers, wife beaters, and even Klansmen, but in the modern era, players are judged by their character and integrity as well as by their on-the-field performance. The consensus among the sports writers was that McGwire was shot down not only because he was perceived as a steroid user, which made his records fraudulent, but also for his pathetic performance at the congressional hearings, which reflected his poor character and lack of integrity.

Many of the writer-voters, who take the ballot quite seriously, felt the need to explain and justify their newfound negativity toward McGwire. Most of them took the position that they opted not to endorse him because of his stonewalling testimony. Some suggested that they might have voted for him, if he had come clean on the steroids issue.

Was the paltry 23.5 percent vote an overkill? Given the belief that many other ballplayers on steroids never came close to banging seventy home runs in a season, and given the fact that McGwire had not violated any rules within baseball at the time, the vote should have been a lot closer. Although the nonendorsement of McGwire may be valid, the vast majority of the writers also projected their anger at themselves for having ignored the obvious and functioned as a group of enablers. Thus, they chose to humiliate and reject McGwire instead of acknowledging their shortsightedness. Those who voted for him, the loyalists and apologists, who believed his rejection was an overreaction based on self-loathing within the ranks of the writers, point out that a player should be judged by the standards existing at that time, and that when Big Mac hit his barrage of homers, a drug-testing program had not yet been established and steroids were not banned from baseball.

By voting him down, the writers were guilty of ignoring the fact that they were applying a later standard to McGwire's era, and were appeasing their culpability for their earlier inattentiveness. Would Ty Cobb, a notorious racist who once tried to kill a man, or other inductees who have spent time in prison, be denied entry if they were on the ballot today? Feeling belatedly duped and betrayed by McGwire after they had bought in to the feel-good story of his seventy home run record, the sports writers were flexing their muscles and using McGwire to transmit the message that athletes who cheat their way to record-breaking accomplishments will be treated harshly. It was a late wake-up call, but McGwire had brought this shabby treatment onto himself by his insipid "I'm not here to talk about the past" testimony at the congressional hearings on steroids. By virtue of his taking the equivalent of the Fifth Amendment, many believe that he implicitly admitted that he had used steroids. Like many scandals in our government, for example, Watergate, Monica Lewinsky, and so on, the transgressors are crucified more for the attempted cover-up than for the misdeed itself.

In our present culture of corruption scrutiny, elite athletes need to be mindful of their image, not only during their playing years, but also after retirement from the game. The glare of the incessant media spotlight brings down numerous athletes who engage in immoral or illegal activities. Undoubtedly, McGwire was following the advice of his attorneys in his stonewalling testimony before Congress, and thereby protecting himself legally, because it was illegal to use steroids without a prescription. But, in so doing, he did not protect his image, and he miscalculated the scope of the backlash. This was a serious lapse of judgment that cost McGwire his shot at enshrinement. It seems likely that on future ballots these writers will continue to deny his entry into the Hall of Fame, because psychologically they may need to keep scapegoating McGwire to displace their feelings of guilt about wearing blinders during his home run odyssey.

Our society is more forgiving toward celebrities who make a mistake and show remorse, and we often are ready to make room for a second chance, but we can be harsh and unforgiving about being deceived. Mark McGwire has put himself in the position in which he has become the easy target for the disappointment, resentment, rage, and disillusionment against all athletes who are under suspicion of using steroids.

McGwire would have fared better if he had explained himself as follows:

> I did use a form of steroids as a performance-enhancing drug during the second half of my career. I knew it was illegal to do so without a prescription, but baseball did not have a drug policy at that time; so I was not violating any rules of the game. I found that the drug enabled me to recover more quickly from injuries, and that it allowed me to maintain and add strength and energy during the wear and tear of the long season, especially as I got older. All athletes are perennially seeking a competitive edge, and I know that lots of other guys were also using drugs. I was just one of the many, and I know that that doesn't make it right; and so I am deeply regretful for whatever way I have contributed to tarnishing the integrity of baseball.

Such a statement of ownership and contrition would have elicited compassion and a greater readiness to forgive. Waffling was the worst course of action. Even if he had made an adamant denial about ever using steroids, a la Rafael Palmeiro, he might have been received with greater acceptance.

Like many sports stars who share the toxic athlete profile of grandiosity, arrogance, and entitlement, McGwire miscalculated that his celebrity status as a home run king would exempt him from opprobrium and provide him with a free pass to the elite Hall of Fame, despite his outrageous nontestimony. In the final analysis, his statistics were insufficiently compelling, and on the dimensions of character and integrity, he has failed abysmally.

Ken Caminiti

In 2002, Ken Caminiti was featured in a *Sports Illustrated* story in which he admitted that his 1996 MVP award season was infused with steroids; and he estimated that 50 percent of active players were using steroids to add power to their game. Caminiti's revelations triggered a wake-up call to sports writers and others who, in the aftermath of Barry Bonds's record-setting year in 2001, began to seriously question and speculate about the power surge in baseball.

The good news was that as a result of the Caminiti story, MLB was pressured to include steroid testing as a provision in the new labor agreement that was negotiated in 2002. The bad news was that it was a conspicuously weak plan, sort of a let's-see-what-happens policy, which was set in place for the 2003 season. The policy indicated that anonymous testing would occur, and if more than 5 percent of the ballplayers tested positive, a more stringent plan would be drafted. Thus, the initial drug-testing policy was introduced into MLB. Selig gave lip service to safeguarding the integrity of the sport, but, even if he was sincere, he was handcuffed partially by the players union, which resisted stringent regulations and sanctions against the cheating athletes.

In the shadow of the BALCO steroids scandal in 2003, which identified cheating athletes in track and field, football, and baseball, the MLB establishment initially downplayed the revelations about the rampant steroids use throughout professional sports; however, eventually it was forced to implement a tougher policy. A new drug-testing plan was adopted in 2005 in which first-time offenders would face a ten-day suspension, and players who tested positive four times would receive a one-year expulsion. Selig and Donald Fehr, his player's union chief counterpart, sought to take credit for cleaning up the game, but in reality, it was the pressure from politicians in the wake of the BALCO investigation that forced the revisions toward a tougher plan.

Barry Bonds

Barry Bonds is the most compelling symbol of the steroids era. He is the all-time home run leader, a record set in 2007, which is tainted because of the widespread belief that in the second half of his career, his numbers were inflated significantly by his use of steroids. While Bonds has never tested positive for steroids, the circumstantial evidence against him is impressive. Bonds had looked like a lean marathon runner in his early years with the Pittsburgh Pirates. His magnificent offensive production after age thirty-five has created a large cloud of suspicion about artificial enhancement. The statistics tell the story. In his first thirteen seasons, before he allegedly began using steroids in 1999, Bonds averaged a home run every sixteen at bats and thirty-two homers per year. Astoundingly, from 1999 through 2007, he has attained the unprecedented ratio of a home run every nine at bats. And, remarkably, this occurred between the ages of thirty-five and forty-three. This level of production in his late thirties and early forties was unreal. According to a study by the Society for American Baseball Research, the peak age for leading home run hitters is twenty-seven, with a protracted decline commencing after age thirty. Defying baseball history and all the studies, Bonds at age thirty-five and older was hitting the ball more prodigiously than ever.[13]

It is well documented that Barry Bonds's physical appearance has changed dramatically in ways that are consistent with steroids use. Since joining the San Francisco Giants in 1993 his uniform jersey has expanded from size forty-two to fifty-two, his shoe size has increased from ten and a half to a thirteen, and visual comparisons of his head size then and now suggest significant expansion. Bonds would have us believe that these are the results of hard work with his trainer, but only the totally naïve and those who are heavily invested in denial seem to buy in to that formulation. There is a kernel of truth in Bonds's assertion that many steroids, such as HGH, "make you ridiculously able to train," according to Jim Warren, who had been one of his personal trainers.[14]

Jay Canizaro

Jay Canizaro, a former Bonds teammate, who has admitted using steroids, reflected,

> It [steroids] doesn't help you make contact, but the power you have is enhanced tremendously. On steroids, at the end of the year you're still playing like it's spring training. And you just feel so alive. . . . You're just a maniac. And you know that the steroids are giving you that surge, and you're that much more confident. When it all comes together it's like you can't do anything wrong.[15]

HGH increases muscle mass and hastens recovery, and it works best in conjunction with other performance-enhancing drugs. It is considered a designer steroid because it is undetectable in urine or blood testing.

In 2003, the BALCO scandal exposed Victor Conte as the proprietor who created and supplied performance-enhancing drugs for elite athletes. In grand jury testimony, it was disclosed that Bonds had been a heavy consumer, receiving his supplies from Conte through his trainer and lifelong friend, Greg Anderson. In a news scoop, the *San Francisco Chronicle* reported that Anderson had supplied Bonds with HGH and other steroids for several years, including 2001 when he bashed seventy-three home runs to eclipse McGwire's single-season record. Other baseball stars, including Gary Sheffield and Jason Giambi, along with the NFL's Bill Romanowski, were also named as BALCO clients. Prosecutors in the BALCO case have declared they possess two documents that verify that Bonds tested positive for steroids in November 2000, during the off-season before his record-breaking seventy-three home run year, and the drugs were supplied by Anderson.

In related developments that augur favorably for Bonds, two other high-profile sports figures pursued in the BALCO investigation were let off easy. Tammy Thomas, a former elite cyclist, was convicted of lying to the BALCO grand jury and was sentenced to only six months of house arrest. Similarly, Trevor Graham, the track coach for Marion Jones and Tim Montgomery, also was convicted of making false statements to a federal agent, and he received a lenient sentence of one year of house arrest and five years of probation. Victor Conte, the founder of BALCO, received a four-month prison term, and Patrick Arnold, his collaborator, was given a three-month term in prison.

The perception among professional athletes was that many players were taking some substances to remain energized and maintain strength in dealing with the grueling schedule. So why not me, too, just to keep my edge? Sports mirrors our society, and our society is rampant with corruption. In such a climate, it becomes a matter of being smart enough and lucky enough to stay under the radar and avoid getting caught. If the mound of circumstantial evidence (his gargantuan physical changes and his late-career power surge) implicated Bonds, he certainly was clever enough to use performance-enhancing drugs in a way that circumvented detection. When Bonds was summoned before the BALCO grand jury and confronted with testimony connecting him with the use of steroids, however, Bonds went too far in outsmarting himself. Although he admitted using "the clear," a designer steroid, and "the cream," a testosterone steroid, which he received from Anderson, he claimed that he believed he was using flaxseed oil and an arthritic cream. This explanation more than strains the limits of credibility, especially because Bonds is known to be extremely attentive to every detail of his life. Many observers believe that his testimony before the BALCO grand jury borders on perjury, and the question remains as to whether Bonds made statements that can be proved false. Bonds's attorney, Mike Rains, attempted to cover the legal loopholes by stating that his client's "position was that he had never taken steroids, although it was remotely possible he had taken them unknowingly."[16]

In a fascinating study conducted in Sweden on drug doping, which has received far too little attention, it was discovered that a common genetic anomaly can interfere with the conversion of testosterone into a form detectable in urine analysis. In the research study, fifty-five male subjects were injected with testosterone and were later administered a standard urine test. Surprisingly, seventeen of the men, almost one-third of the sample, tested negative, because they were missing both copies of a gene that metabolizes testosterone into a substance that dissolves in urine. The implications for the world of sports are profound, and might explain why some sports stars whose enhanced performance has aroused suspicion of steroid use have routinely tested negative. Rather than struggling with the suspension of disbelief about Bonds's involvement with steroids, we need to consider that he may be a prime example of the false negatives depicted in the Swedish study.

Fame can be a great corrupter of morality when elite athletes acquire a distorted self-image that prompts them to cross boundaries. The triad of grandiosity, entitlement, and arrogance fuels what I have previously referred to as "the toxic athlete profile,"[17] and Bonds appears to be enmeshed in each of these personality dimensions.

Bonds's flaxseed oil fable was the height of arrogance in insulting our intelligence. He would have fared better if he had explained that he did use "the clear" and "the cream" to help him recover more quickly from injuries, and that it was not against the rules of baseball at that time for him to do so. He would have received a more compassionate response in many quarters, but compassion was not his game.

THE CASE AGAINST STEROIDS

The term steroids in sports has become synonymous with cheating, fraudulence, and artificially inflated performance. Is this simply an expression of massive hysteria in response to the latest version of performance-enhancing drugs discovered by athletes to give them a competitive edge? MLB union chief Gene Orza has opined that steroids are "not worse than cigarettes,"[18] and naysayers have argued that, when taken under medical supervision, the physical problems associated with steroids are considered to be relatively mild. Is the vociferous antisteroids furor an extreme swing of the pendulum after years of denial about the obvious connection between bigger bodies and increasing power surges in baseball? Aside from Lyle Alzado's statement that the massive doses of steroids he had taken were a causative factor in his rare form of brain cancer, there have been no reports of professional athletes who have died from steroids. This statistic is in stark contrast to the number of fatalities in the professional athlete population related to alcohol or substance abuse (for example, Steve Howe, Ken Caminiti, Josh Hancock, and others).

Personal Health

Despite the fact that few reports of death have resulted from steroid use, several legitimate concerns do justify the demonization of steroids in sports. First, there is the compromised health issue. Considerable research documentation indicates numerous side effects from unsupervised and prolonged steroid use. These include acne, baldness, enlarged heads, shrinking testicles, mood swings, explosive anger, and sexual inhibition, as well as more serious conditions such as heart and liver damage and prostate cancer. HGH, another performance-enhancing substance that increases muscle mass and accelerates recovery from injury, is often taken by athletes in combination with steroids. The appeal of HGH is that it strengthens the joints that can support the steroid-acquired muscle mass. In fact, HGH is frequently the drug of choice because it is undetectable— that is, no established test can detect its use. The potential dangers associated with HGH are plentiful, including hypertension, diabetes, abnormal organ enlargement, and advancement of cardiovascular conditions. Other damaging side effects include the alteration of facial features, increased head size, and changes in the body's configuration. Steroids are illegal without a prescription because of these dangerous side effects. And if elite athletes are eager to cross the line to try anything that provides them with a performance advantage, perhaps they need to be protected from themselves.

The Integrity of the Sport

The second case against steroid use involves the impact of steroids as an affront to professional sports. This argument pertains to fairness. The assumption of a level playing field is jeopardized when some players are juicing and others are not. A big part of the appeal of professional sports is that it is built on statistics and records as measurements of success, and the legendary accomplishments of heroes. This is especially true in baseball, where Babe Ruth's home run record and then Roger Maris's record each stood tall for more than three decades as the barometer of power performance. Then along came Mark McGwire, Sammy Sosa, and Barry Bonds, who crushed homers with alarming frequency. Belatedly, suspicions were aroused about these slugging performances. Even players like Shawn Green and Brady Anderson, not routinely thought of as sluggers, posted monster home run seasons. Bonds is seen by some admirers as the greatest hitter in the history of the game. More often than not, however, he is viewed as a great hitter whose record-breaking statistics were inflated by steroids. Bonds purportedly admitted to the BALCO grand jury that he had unwittingly taken steroids, even though he never tested positive. As the sports steroids scandal has mushroomed, the unfairness aspect of gaining a significant performance advantage increasingly has been emphasized. *Newsweek* columnist George Will summed up this sentiment by noting that, "Cold covert attempts to alter unfairly the conditions of competition subvert the essence of sport, which is the principle that participants shall compete under identical rules and conditions."[19]

The Larger Human Toll

A third major concern regarding steroid use is their effect on children, who are prone to emulate their artificially enhanced sports heroes. Children identify with the behavior of their heroes, and if steroids are in the mix, it becomes a recipe for danger for these hero-worshiping youth. The most emotional testimony at the 2005 congressional hearings came from Ray and Denise Garibaldi who described the saga of their son, Rob, a premier college baseball player who admired Mark McGwire and Barry Bonds. Convinced that gaining the advantages of steroid use was a prerequisite for getting to the major leagues, Rob Garibaldi began using steroids when he started college by injecting himself with the popular substances Deca-Durabolin and Sustonon. He continued to use for five years, and, when confronted by his parents, he angrily acknowledged that he was copying his athlete role models, Bonds and McGwire. Shortly thereafter, in the throes of what was believed to be a steroid-induced depression, he committed suicide by shooting himself in the head. Retrospectively, his parents attributed previous episodes of violence and depression to his attempts to discontinue his reliance on steroids.

In a similar scenario Taylor Hooten, a seventeen-year-old Texas high school pitcher, hanged himself in his room, while combating the depression associated with steroid withdrawal. Hooten had been bulking up on steroids for about a year, had suffered from mood swings, and was exhibiting aggressive behavior. His parents, who have since dedicated themselves to a foundation whose purpose is to educate the public about steroids use, blame coaches who directly and indirectly encourage young players to make themselves bigger and stronger via the steroids route. In a public relations gesture, MLB czar Bud Selig provided $1 million to establish the Taylor Hooten foundation.

After years of looking the other way when his stars were getting grotesquely larger and home run production was soaring, Selig finally acknowledged steroids as a problem. In launching the foundation, he sanctimoniously declared that baseball had a "social responsibility" to address this issue. Was he merely appeasing a guilty conscience for putting revenue ahead of the physical well-being of his players and preserving the purity of the game? Previously, Selig had moved at a snail's pace, first ignoring the steroids problem and later addressing it only with lip service. In 1999, after the Andro controversy that surrounded Mark McGwire, Selig pledged to conduct a medical study, but nothing much came of it. Selig's administrative style and modus operandi has been to avoid dealing with controversial issues, rather than to confront them head on. He has succeeded in keeping Pete Rose on the hook for more than fifteen years with this approach. In 1998–1999, Selig's nightmare scenario was that the Andro revelations would snowball into a major scandal that would turn off the home run happy fans and destroy the MLB attendance resurgence. Like a bad dream, he hoped it would just go away.

REACTIONS

The Sports Writers' Reactions

When the leaks from the BALCO investigation became public, the sports writers seized the opportunity to impugn Bonds, as payback for his long-standing shabby treatment of the media. His attitude and demeanor toward reporters as well as fans have been routinely experienced as rude, surly, scornful, contemptuous, dismissive, patronizing, and insulting. Moreover, the writers were resentful for first having been duped into glorifying the McGwire-Sosa circus and then having applauded Bonds's assault on the home run record as a legitimate feat. Now they sought to highlight his clay feet and transform Superman into Clark Kent. The press gleefully launched into relentless rounds of attacks on Bonds as a tainted juicer and a gigantic fraud, who blatantly operated without integrity and who more than anyone else had put an indelible stain on the national pastime.

Jeff Pearlman, who was snubbed by Bonds while he was writing a biography of the hero, branded him as a chronic liar who outrageously twists reality whenever it suits him.[20] Reporter Gary Peterson, of the *Contra Costa Times*, excoriated Bonds in observing that "Bonds treat[s] people as if they were put on this planet specifically to annoy him."[21] And Rick Reilly sarcastically wrote in *Sports Illustrated*:

> I believe Bonds never knowingly took steroids. I believe Bonds—a man who won't eat buttered popcorn unless he knows its saturated fat content—would put anything into his body that his trainer, Greg Anderson, told him to do. I believe Bonds . . ., a man who studies his own body the way a rabbi studies the Talmud—really thought he was using "a rubbing balm for arthritis" as he told the grand jury, not a steroid. . . . And I believe reindeer fly, President Clinton did not have sexual relations with that woman, and Rogaine really can re-grow your hair. Now if you'll kindly move out of the way, I believe I'm about to get sick.[22]

Writers have considerable influence on the public perception of sports stars. They can pump them up or devil them down. Some writers in their zeal to discredit Bonds have gone overboard and crossed the line into wild journalism. Bob Klapisch, a New Jersey columnist with a large following has labeled Bonds a sociopath.[23] This is a serious misunderstanding and misuse of a psychiatric diagnosis without much evidence to support it. The hallmarks of sociopathy are a failure to accept social norms with respect to lawful behavior and a persistent violation of the rights of others. This term generally applies to people who engage in antisocial and criminal activity and it does not accurately capture

Bonds's personality. Klapisch is doing his readers a disservice by portraying Bonds this way. The aspects of Bonds's personality that coalesce around grandiosity, arrogance, an exaggerated sense of entitlement, haughty attitude, and a lack of empathy are more consistent with what mental health practitioners describe as narcissistic personality disorder. By using a psychiatric label inappropriately, Klapisch encourages readers to misconstrue the native of Bonds's Pathology.

Among Bonds's loyalists is *New York Times* reporter William Rhoden, who maintains that Bonds is the scapegoat for the performance-enhancing drug problem in baseball. In his view, Bonds is the victim of a witch-hunt and is being selectively vilified by the media people whom he has alienated. Rhoden points out that Bonds is only one of many big-name major leaguers under suspicion, that he has never tested positive, and that he should be judged as innocent until proven guilty. According to Rhoden, the real culprit is MLB for ignoring the growing drug problem in its own house, and the press for unfairly targeting Bonds.[24] Rhoden, however, seems guilty of selective inattention in neglecting to consider the overwhelming circumstantial evidence surrounding Bonds. A more parsimonious appraisal might be to observe that if it looks like a duck, walks like a duck, and quacks like a duck, then probably it is a duck.

Fan Reactions

As Bonds approached the all-time home run record in 2007 amid the ongoing steroids allegations, the reactions among baseball followers became increasingly diverse and polarized. Interest ranged from excitement to cynicism, and feelings gyrated from indifference to outrage. His strongest bastion of support came, of course, from the hometown fans who continued to adore him, in spite of the scandal, because his prodigious accomplishments allowed them to fulfill the wish of feeling affiliated with something special. In an informal poll conducted in the stands of SBC Park of 100 people, 92 percent said they believed that Bonds used performance-enhancing drugs. Astonishingly, only 24 percent of those interviewed said that they cared, and most of those who did not care rationalized that Barry was only doing what other athletes were doing—in other words, "what's the big deal?" The poll suggests that Bonds's devotees are not so much in denial of reality, as much as that they are willing to overlook, minimize, and dismiss it to maintain their allegiance to one of their own. It is akin to protecting and demonstrating loyalty to a corrupt family member who acts like he is being maligned by the system. In another poll taken by ABC News and ESPN shortly before Bonds broke the record held by Hank Aaron, 52 percent of the interviewees said that they were rooting for him to fail. Furthermore, in an interesting racial divide, the poll indicated that just one-third of black respondents said they believed Bonds had knowingly used performance-enhancing drugs in contrast to three-quarters of the white respondents who believed so.

The media is invested in inciting negative reactions to the use of performance-enhancing drugs among athletes in general, and toward Barry Bonds in particular, but it can be extrapolated from these polls that a substantial segment of the fan base is indifferent.

These fans view sports primarily as entertainment. Some feel guilty because they recognize that the media indirectly has told them to feel agitated and deceived, yet what they most feel is indifference. Others may harbor a degree of uneasiness because they secretly identify with the desire to gain an edge in certain aspects of their lives. In other words, many people would like to gain the advantages that come with cheating, especially if they knew they would not get caught, and it makes them uncomfortable to recognize this dark side of themselves.

Curiously, when the Giants play on the road, even though Bonds usually is seen as the enemy, the fans resent it when he is not in the lineup. Despite their distaste for him and desire to see him flounder, they also want to see him hit home runs and witness significant baseball history. Because sports increasingly are viewed as entertainment, the live-and-die nature associated with the plight of a team has become less urgent than in previous eras. In spite of the voluminous negative publicity about athletes and steroids (or perhaps because of it), MLB set an attendance record for the fourth consecutive season in 2007. This level of interest suggests that the fans are less concerned about players taking steroids and staining the game, and more interested in seeing sluggers hit home runs.

Although the press continues to sensationalize the steroids problem, and arouses the public's passion about blemishes on the integrity of the game, many people who come to the ballpark do not care about the media's spin on fakery. They just want to enjoy an entertaining event, and they go home disappointed if they do not get to see the long ball. We are becoming increasingly accustomed to being exposed to corruption at all levels of society, so why not in sports as well? Tom Verducci of *Sports Illustrated* maintains that "[s]teroids did to baseball what Watergate did to the presidency. They ended what had been an organic trust in the institution, and there is no going back."[25] In response to scandals of dishonesty and unscrupulous behavior in our politicians and business leaders, society has become more cynical, suspicious, and distrustful. This attitude extends to our sports heroes, many of whom are all too ready to cross the line into cheating or get involved in off-the-field misadventures.

We are both fascinated and repelled by Bonds, and, as noted by writer Michael Sandel, "When the role of chemical enhancement increases, our admiration for the achievement decreases."[26] Perception often carries great weight, and the general perception is that Bonds has avoided testing positive only because some steroids are undetectable. Because he is tainted, Bonds deprives us of the opportunity to embrace him. The part of us that needs heroes that we can admire and identify with and that provide hope for success and accomplishments is disappointed, disillusioned, and derailed by Bonds. It is reminiscent of the legendary eight-year-old boy who confronts Shoeless Joe Jackson on the courthouse steps during the Black Sox scandal, pleading "say it ain't so." Fans hope not to lose those exhilarated feelings that accompany their personal love affairs with sports heroes and their imagined connection to greatness.

Athletes' Reactions

Barry Bonds has steadfastly denied that he has knowingly used performance-enhancing drugs, and he refutes any and all suggestions that his late career power production has been artificially inflated. When he surpassed Hank Aaron on the all-time home run rung, he quickly proclaimed, "The record is not tainted at all. At all. Period."[27] In a previous interview, when he was asked about steroids in baseball, he disingenuously commented, "I don't know what cheating is. I don't know if steroids are going to help you in baseball. I just don't believe it. I don't believe steroids can help you— eye-hand coordination—technically hit a baseball, I just don't believe it and that's just my opinion."[28] This is an exasperatingly misleading statement designed to confuse, deceive, and obfuscate the truth. What Bonds conveniently glosses over is that for major leaguers, who by definition already have superior eye-hand coordination, performance-enhancing drugs make them stronger and enable them to hit a ball harder and longer than they otherwise would have.

Bonds maintains that his bad-guy image as unresponsive to the fans is an inaccurate invention of the media. To the extent that his disrespect toward the fans is exaggeratedly portrayed, his protest substantiates the belief that the media have enormous influence over the way fans perceive their sports stars. There can be no mistake, however, about Bonds's antipathy toward the press. He claims that reporters present him as a caricature to enhance their own popularity. In his tempestuous relations with the press who bombard him with questions about using steroids, he takes the route that the best defense is a good offense, and he accuses them all of spinning lies about him in their stories. "Should you guys have an asterisk beside your name?" he quips.[29]

Bonds seems to have a narcissistic indifference about cultivating his image; and he welcomes being portrayed as an antihero. He appears to thrive and gain strength from negative publicity, which intensifies his desire to show up his critics with more home runs. From the beginning of his career, he was determined not to squander his talent—as his father, Bobby Bonds, had—and, to his credit, he resolved not to smoke or drink, and he developed a work ethic that did not take things for granted. His goal was to become a baseball deity, which drove him to win multiple MVP awards and home run records. It is worth noting that Bonds had achieved Hall of Fame–worthy statistics before he allegedly started using performance-enhancing drugs in 1999. He was already the only player in baseball history with both four hundred home runs and four hundred stolen bases. But being great was not enough for Barry Bonds; he needed to become the greatest.

As part of the BALCO probe, Bonds's personal trainer, Greg Anderson, spent three months in jail; he was charged with distributing steroids and money laundering. Subsequently, a grand jury convened to determine whether Bonds should be indicted for perjury in his BALCO testimony and for tax evasion. The case against Bonds was weakened by Anderson's refusal to talk about supplying performance-enhancing drugs to Bonds, and he was remanded back to prison for contempt of court. Anderson's stand in not testifying against his lifetime friend is viewed as heroic and loyal in some quarters, but it appears to be motivated mostly by his rage at being betrayed by federal prosecutors who reneged on promises they made to him. The government has come under attack for excessively pursuing Bonds because he is a big fish. The arrogance of these hubristic authorities is a factor in this scandal that is considered by the defenders of Anderson, Bonds, and other high-profile athletes, and it needs to be recognized as a distraction from the validity of the allegations.

Reactions of Other Players

In the fraternity of ballplayers, it is generally accepted that Bonds and others have relied on performance-enhancing drugs. Former teammates Andy Van Slyke and Jeff Brantley have conveyed their belief that Bonds has used steroids. Van Slyke has gone so far as to assert that Bonds "unequivocally has taken (steroids). I never saw Barry as a fifty-home-run hitter. He was too thin and too light. It's like he went from being a Marlboro Light to a Camel unfiltered."[30] Former Yankee slugger Reggie Jackson expressed his distaste as follows: "There is a reason why the greatest players of all time have 500 (home runs). Now all of a sudden you're hitting 50 when you're 40."[31] Dick Pound, chairman of the World Anti-Doping Agency (WADA), cited the obvious in saying, "Look at before and after photos of Barry Bonds. I mean, hello?"[32]

MORE RECENT EXPOSÉS IN THE STEROIDS SCANDAL

Jason Grimsley

While pitching for the Arizona Diamondbacks, Jason Grimsley came under suspicion by federal authorities. Thirteen agents raided his home on June 7, 2006, after tracking a delivery of HGH. Grimsley admitted using steroids, amphetamines, and HGH during the last few years, and under the threat of more punitive action by the government, he identified other major leaguers as performance-enhancing drug users. According to a *Los Angeles Times* report, the players named were Roger Clemens, Andy Pettitte, Miguel Tejada, Brian Roberts, Jay Gibbons, and David Segui. Extensive denials were issued by these high-profile players, but suspicions continued. MLB did not add HGH to its list of banned substances until 2005, so a timeline has to be considered when identifying cheaters. Grimsley was suspended for fifty games based on his possession of drugs and his admissions, and he subsequently retired.

Gary Matthews

The lure of mega-million-dollar contracts is a dominant motivator for those athletes who use performance-enhancing drugs. After posting a career season in 2006, Gary Matthews became a free agent and negotiated a five-year, $50 million contract. Before the start of the next season, the *Sports Illustrated* Web site alleged that Matthews has received shipments of HGH from a pharmacy conducting sales on the Internet. When confronted, Matthews categorically denied ever taking HGH. A cloud of suspicion continues to float over Matthews, especially as there is no reliable test for detecting HGH and *Sports Illustrated* is generally considered to be a reliable source of information.

Kirk Radomski

A former New York Mets clubhouse assistant, Kirk Radomski admitted supplying performance-enhancing drugs to dozens of current and former MLB players during a ten-year period from 1995 to 2005. Under investigation by the federal authorities overseeing the BALCO case, Radomski pleaded guilty on April 27, 2007, to distributing steroids and money laundering. Agents discovered twenty-three checks by players made payable to Radomski between 2003 and 2005 after the MLB drug-testing plan was set in place. Radomski could receive up to twenty years in prison for his participation in illegal distribution of steroids. A condition of the plea agreement was for him to cooperate with the Mitchell Commission investigation initiated by commissioner Selig. An alarm bell ran through the baseball community in anticipation of new names and revelations to be disclosed by Radomski. In addition to the potential public relations disaster and the black eyes for individual players involved, sanctions could be imposed by the MLB. Players do not have to test positive to be disciplined. If the baseball authorities have the checks paid to Radomski and can connect the dots in establishing that they were for illegal drugs, then, according to the drug-testing policy, they could issue suspensions. In February 2008, Radomski was given a lenient sentence of five years' probation.

Bonds and Amphetamines

Barry Bonds proudly and vehemently reminds us that he has never tested positive for steroids, and argues that he is the victim of a media witch-hunt designed to bring him down. Nevertheless, according to a *New York Daily News* report, he did fail a test for amphetamines during the 2006 season. Always quick to externalize his problems, Bonds initially cast blame on a substance he got from teammate Mark Sweeney's locker. Sweeney refused to cover for Bonds, and Bonds later retracted the connection to Sweeney and did not deny the story. There was no penalty administered to Bonds, since this was a first positive test. Under baseball's drug policy, a second positive test for amphetamines results in a twenty-five-game suspension.[33]

Signature Pharmacy

Historically, federal stings and investigations into illegal sales of steroids have pursued the suppliers rather than the athletes involved. Recently, however, the major sports leagues have stepped up and been more aggressive in dispensing punishments to the identified players. Signature, an Orlando, Florida-based pharmacy, was exposed in September 2007 for illegally distributing performance-enhancing drugs to sports figures. Among the casualties were NFL suspensions to Rodney Harrison, the New England Patriots safety, and Wade Wilson, the Dallas Cowboys quarterback coach, for purchasing HGH shipments. In baseball, Rick Ankiel allegedly received a year's supply of HGH, Jay Gibbons was supplied with HGH and testosterone, and Troy Glaus with the illegal steroid substances nandrolene and testosterone. MLB, already reeling from the continuous onslaught and weight of the numerous steroids scandals, withheld disciplinary action pending further investigation.

Pitchers and Steroids

There is a general misconception that in baseball it is the hitters, who are bent on augmenting their long-ball power, who are the primary steroids cheaters. This is because the lion's share of publicity has centered around the increased home run production of players like Bonds, McGwire, and Sosa and the increasing number of players who are surpassing the 30 home runs in a season plateau. Moreover, except for the Jason Grimsley revelations, no marquee pitcher, until Roger Clemens was outed in the Mitchell report, has been seriously suspected of steroids use. In truth, the data covering major league and minor league players indicate as many pitchers test positive as all of the other position players combined. This is a curious and consistent trend.

It is the accelerated recovery time associated with steroids that appeals to pitchers. Tom House, who candidly admits trying steroids while pitching in the major leagues in the 1970s, explains:

> Steroids are attractive to pitchers because they enable them to bounce back quickly and pitch again. It's about recovery. Anything that has to do with competition, you want to prepare, compete, and repair. Whatever you can do to facilitate improvement in any of those areas, someone is going to do it.[34]

In a public relations effort, Rob Manfred, baseball's executive vice president for labor relations, presented statistics that demonstrated a significant drop from 2005 to 2006 in the number of players who failed a drug test. He attributed this shift to stiffer penalties set in place after 2005, in which the first positive test for steroids now results in a fifty-game suspension, a second offense carries a 100-game suspension, and a third positive test brings a lifetime ban. It is likely that the awareness and fear of consequences is serving as a deterrent for those athletes who are inclined to use steroids. However, an equally plausible explanation is that more and more ballplayers are staying one step ahead of the curve, simply by switching to HGH or other designer steroids, for which there is no reliable test.

THE MITCHELL COMMISSION

After the fiasco of the 2005 congressional hearings on steroids in sports, MLB was under pressure to address and repair its tarnished image. Surprisingly, a double standard exists in which Congress treats baseball more harshly than football. Interestingly, baseball was ahead of the other sports leagues in adopting sanctions for players who received performance-enhancing drugs, even in the absence of a positive test result. MLB fronted funds to develop a blood test for HGH before the NFL did so, and baseball was obliged to examine its history of performance-enhancing drugs use, whereas the NFL has been spared any such inquiry despite the ever-increasing size of its players. MLB has been applauded for having the most stringent drug-testing policy among the major sports leagues.

Politically speaking, the key objective for baseball was to perpetuate the renaissance of fan interest and keep the turnstiles ticking, while at the same time creating the impression that the league was dedicated to fixing the steroids problem that was threatening the integrity of the sport. In addition to negotiating with the players union to establish a somewhat tougher drug-testing plan, in March 2006, Bud Selig appointed George Mitchell, a well-respected former senator from Maine, to head an investigation into steroid use in baseball. Mitchell's mandate was to uncover players who had used steroids after such substances were banned in the 2002 collective bargaining agreement. Mitchell's team did not have subpoena power, however, and it was unrealistic to think that the fraternity of ballplayers would break the wall of silence.

Mitchell wanted to get current and former players to provide information about steroid use, and he requested interviews with forty-five players; however, in view of the obvious concern about legally incriminating themselves for using steroids without a prescription or facing disciplinary action within MLB, the group refused to meet with Mitchell. Los Angeles Dodgers star Nomar Garciaparra described Mitchell's request as a waste of paper, and Curt Schilling, the usually outspoken Boston Red Sox pitcher, summed up the prevailing sentiment by pointing out, "it's easier to say nothing."[35]

Many sports insiders believed it was simply a public relations move to demonstrate that MLB was serious about the steroids problem. Indeed, for a long while, the Mitchell group appeared to function like a dog chasing its tail, as none of the forty-five players who were invited to talk to the committee responded to the request.

In May 2007, New York Yankees slugger Jason Giambi revealed in a *USA Today* interview that he had used steroids and HGH. In a statement of contrition and sincerity, Giambi confessed, "I was wrong for doing that stuff. What we should have done a long time ago was stand up—players, ownership, everybody—and said, 'We made a mistake.'"[36] Under the veiled threat of disciplinary action, Selig urged Giambi to confer with the investigator. Giambi thus felt compelled to cooperate with Mitchell, because he had violated the law by using steroids without a prescription, although it was not against baseball rules to do so at that time. Feeling compromised, Giambi agreed to talk about his own use of steroids, but not about other players or his suppliers. This may have looked like a step forward for Mitchell's committee, but essentially, Giambi revealed the same information that he gave to the BALCO grand jury in 2003. A breakthrough occurred for Mitchell with the Kirk Radomski case in which thirty-six players were named as recipients of drugs supplied by Radomski. In his plea agreement, Radomski was ordered to cooperate with the Mitchell investigation. The players Radomski named did not respond to the allegations, and Mitchell was impotent to force them to talk. His only leverage would have been to bring the issue to Congress, which does have subpoena power, and that scenario would have created a public relations disaster in exposing baseball's dirty secrets.

In sanctimoniously seeking to protect the image of the game, Selig, who must have known about steroids use before he appointed Mitchell, basically was trying to establish his own image as a hard-line commissioner in the Kenesaw Mountain Landis tradition, out to clean up the game. Selig must have been contending with powerful feelings of envy toward Roger Goodell, the NFL law-and-order commissioner who is well respected for penalizing NFL players and coaches for violations on and off the playing field.

Roger Clemens

The Mitchell Commission issued its report in December 2007, and Roger Clemens was the highest-profile player identified, among the ninety who were named. Brian McNamee, Clemens's former trainer, was the source of the revelations about Roger "The Rocket." Clemens responded with outrage, and he vowed to clear his name of these charges. Along with other players who had declined to be interviewed by Mitchell out of fear of legal repercussions, Clemens stated that if he had known that his name would be cited, he would have moved quickly to meet with the Mitchell Commission to present his side of the story.

Clemens went on the television program *60 Minutes* to plead his case, and he vehemently reminded the audience that in this country you are guilty until proven innocent. His performance raised doubts for many people about his truthfulness, and many observers felt that Mike Wallace, who had a longstanding friendship with Clemens, was soft in how he conducted the interview. Clemens may have felt empowered by the fact that one year earlier he had been erroneously cited as a steroid user in a Los Angeles newspaper story regarding the affidavit submitted by pitcher Jason Grimsley when Grimsley's home was raided for illegal steroids.

In the midst of his outrage, Clemens placed a phone call to Brian McNamee in which Clemens's handlers were taping their conversation. Roger inquired about the health status of McNamee's ten-year-old son who had celiac disease (a digestive system disorder), and then went on to express his angst and anger over these charges. The gist of McNamee's reaction was to offer something along the lines of "What do you want me to do, Roger; I'll do anything for you, even if it means going to jail," which could be interpreted as an oblique reference to Barry Bonds's trainer, Greg Anderson, who spent many months in jail for refusing to testify about Bonds and steroids. Clemens responded with, "I just want someone to tell the truth." Interestingly, McNamee never said, "I did tell the truth, Roger." In analyzing McNamee's statements, some people felt that he had turned on Clemens because he was taping their conversation, and was reacting to the mistreatment of him by Clemens, the man he had idolized. Others believed that McNamee was implying that if Clemens paid him off, he would recant his statements and risk being sent to jail because he had illegally distributed steroids to Clemens and others. McNamee's interest in money was illuminated when less than two months later he placed his collection of Roger Clemens memorabilia on auction with eBay, with an estimated value of $75,000.

The next step pursued by Roger Clemens in his name-clearing campaign was to request a new congressional hearing, and to use this venue as a platform to express his righteous indignation before a wide audience. His emotional reactions were fueled by his anger at MLB and Commissioner

Bud Selig for not protecting him and sparing him the humiliation. His primary thought process probably veered in the direction of "Is this any way to treat a titan, after all that I've done for the game?" To be knocked off the sports hero pedestal was undoubtedly experienced as a lethal blow and must have created unthinkable anxiety about the loss of his image, the loss of admiration for his accomplishments, his tarnished reputation, and the setback to his future chance for enshrinement in the Hall of Fame. Like most star athletes, Roger Clemens was accustomed to being catered to, getting things done his way, and being accommodated with special conditions reserved for sports royalty. For example, he was granted permission to not travel with the 2007 Yankees on road trips in which he was not scheduled to pitch. Clemens was fearful that in the climate of antipathy toward sports celebrities, he would be brought down like Marion Jones, Floyd Landis, Barry Bonds, and Rafael Palmeiro; all of whom had emphatically claimed that they were innocent of any involvement with performance-enhancing drugs, and who later were exposed as frauds.

Clemens's modus operandi had always been to intimidate others, and he was determined to utilize this approach and aggressively take command of the situation, even if his denials were unconvincing to many people. Before the congressional hearings, Roger made the rounds in visiting members of the committee to present his side of the story. This was an entirely legal maneuver on his part, but symbolically, it also represented a new way to get an edge.

At the House of Representatives Oversight Committee hearings, Clemens's portrayal of his innocence in regard to steroids was severely undermined by Andy Pettitte, a fellow teammate and friend, whose deposition revealed that Clemens had discussed with him his use of steroids and HGH. Pettitte's reputation as a sincere and honest straight shooter was impeccable, and his account was widely perceived as believable. Clemens handled this dilemma by testifying that Pettitte must have misheard or misconstrued their past conversation about steroids. Many of the congress members indicated that it would have required a willful suspension of credibility to accept the proposition that Pettitte had simply misheard Clemens on the steroid issue. In an interesting sidenote, one of the congressional members asked Clemens, "Can I look at my children and say Roger Clemens always played the game with honesty and integrity?" True to form, Roger retorted, "You can tell your boys I did it the right way, and I worked my butt off to do it."

In some respects, these hearings became a political football in which Republican congress members were receptive to Clemens's explanations and suspicious of McNamee's integrity, whereas the Democratic members were more inclined to accept McNamee's side of the story and were more challenging in their approach to Clemens. Subsequent to the hearings, the Federal Bureau of Investigation (FBI) launched a probe into whether Roger Clemens had committed perjury before the committee. In an extension of the political divide, several Republican congress members declared that Clemens had been truthful about many points, to which McNamee's lawyer intimated that they had been pushed to take that position by Republican higher-ups.

In speculating about what may be inside the mind of Roger Clemens regarding his adamant stance of denial of steroid use, three distinct possibilities stand out. One is that he is innocent, which means that McNamee is fabricating and Pettitte is distorting the truth. While anything is possible, this is an unlikely scenario. A second possibility is that Clemens knows that he is guilty, but to salvage his reputation, he vehemently denies these accusations. He is gambling that any probe would fail to reveal incriminating evidence; and that even if he is indicted and then convicted of perjury, it would be viewed as a travesty of justice that would invite widespread public support. The third scenario is that Clemens is suffering from a delusional disorder in which he has distorted the nature of his injections administered by McNamee, that he has convinced himself that steroids and HGH injections never happened, and that he is being falsely accused. Under conditions of extreme stress, such a twisting of reality can occur in which black becomes white or vice versa.

If he was in the throes of a delusional disorder, Clemens had to choose between a pathway of righteous indignation (a la Clarence Thomas, Floyd Landis, and so on) or craft a creative apology. Clemens, being who he is, opted for the first path; however, if he had adopted the second route he would have fared better in the court of public opinion. Sports fans are traditionally open to restoring their faith and admiration for sports heroes who admit to their transgressions and humble themselves a little bit.

Andy Pettitte was embraced with open arms after he admitted to experimenting with HGH, and if Clemens was apologetic, he probably would have received the same kind of support. His statement could have been similar to the following:

> When I was named as a steroid user by the Mitchell Commission, there was an avalanche of negative publicity in which I was being portrayed as a sinister fraud. Immediately, I was the poster boy for all that was bad in baseball. My first reaction was to feel extremely hurt and betrayed. After all that I had done for baseball in my long career, which was primarily a result of devoting myself to the necessary hard work involved in maintaining my skills, I felt suddenly and sadly unappreciated. When the Boston Red Sox severed their ties to me in 1998 and indicated that my career was in decline, I felt rejected and frightened. To a large extent superior athletic performance is based on self-confidence, and my belief in my abilities was shattered by the Boston organization's mistreatment of me, so I succumbed to the temptation of allowing Brian McNamee, my trainer, to inject me with steroids and HGH, along with B12 and lidocaine. The truth is that I was in a

different mental state at that time, imbued with my celebrity status, fearful that my talent was eroding with age, and desperate to gain an edge that would allow me to maintain my superior level of pitching. The goal was to accelerate recovery from the minor nagging injuries acquired during the long baseball season. In all honesty it did not add anything to my fastball, but what it did do was make me feel fully healthy, and it restored my confidence in myself. I know that this does not justify my inappropriate actions. I convinced myself that since it was widely known that many players were using steroids to gain an edge and enhance their performance, and since there was no restriction within Major League Baseball against doing so, that I too could benefit from such assistance. After Major League Baseball initiated a drug testing program in 2003, I never again sought any steroids or HGH.

I did not respond to the Mitchell Commission's request for an interview on the advice of my lawyers. I felt unfairly targeted and scapegoated as the one most accused of creating a stain on baseball, the game I love. Most of all I felt vulnerable, and my instinctive response was to fight back, which is what I have always done when I feel threatened. I now fully realize that it was wrong for me to take steroids and HGH, which cheapened my successful career. It was doubly wrong to deny it when the truth came out. I am most ashamed of my failure as a role model for all the kids that looked up to me, and if there is one thing to convey to kids about this, it is that cheating may be tempting, but it is wrong; the truth always comes out in the end and the advantage in gaining an edge is far outweighed by the shame and permanent black eye you get when you are exposed. My fervent hope is that young people will learn from my strengths as well as my weaknesses.

A Gallup poll revealed that 57 percent of the respondents believe that Roger Clemens had lied about using steroids, and 62 percent believe that, nevertheless, he should get into the Hall of Fame.[37] In contrast, only 46 percent believe that Barry Bonds should be admitted to the Hall of Fame. How might we understand this discrepancy in which Bonds's design on baseball immortality was so unpopular? Three factors might best inform our understanding of this bias: (1) Bonds's unlikeable personality characteristics, (2) a racial bias, in which Bonds is penalized as an African American, and (3) the pending results of Bonds's perjury indictment (at the time of the Gallup poll, no decision had been made regarding Clemens's testimony).

Alex Rodriguez

In February 2009, while MLB was licking its wounds from the accumulation of steroids scandals, its premier player, Alex Rodriguez, was exposed as a steroid user. This was the last thing baseball needed for its already severely tarnished image.

After thirteen years as an outstanding player, Rodriguez had amassed more than five hundred home runs; he was expected to become the all-time home run king after his total inevitably eclipsed the 762 slugged by Barry Bonds. A-Rod, as he was affectionately known, was perceived as the "clean" alternative to Bonds, whose record wavered under a steroids cloud of suspicion.

When Mark McGwire received the lion's share of attention for his seventy home run season in 1998, Bonds devoted himself to outdistancing McGwire, which he did three years later; when he set the new season record with seventy-three homers. In a similar vein, Rodriguez—although he smashed fifty-two home runs and had 135 RBIs (runs batted in), an amazing offensive performance for a shortstop—was hardly noticed amid the excitement over Bonds's feat. A-Rod then embraced a mission to become better than Bonds.

A-Rod's meteoric rise to the top was dismantled by a *Sports Illustrated* article in February 2009, which outed him as having tested positive for Primobolan, an anabolic steroid that was illegal without a prescription, during his tenure with the Texas Rangers from 2001 to 2003. He was one of 104 players who had tested positive during a survey testing program in 2003 to determine whether more than 5 percent of MLB players were steroid users. The results (7 percent tested positive) ushered in baseball's first mandatory drug-testing plan the next season, with penalties for those who would test positive. No penalties were in place when Rodriguez's positive test findings emerged.

Rodriguez was cunning in his selection of Primobolan, which is a steroid designed to improve strength and to maintain lean muscle with minimal bulk development. In this way, he circumvented the obvious profile of a huge cartoonish body makeover, generally associated with steroids. He could rely on the ongoing perception that he was the clean contrast to the steroid-infusing cadre of professional ballplayers.

In response to being fingered in the *Sports Illustrated* exposé, A-Rod issued the obligatory apology in which he attributed his poor judgment to being young, stupid, and naïve. Interestingly, he directed his apology to the fans of the Texas Rangers, rather than to the millions of kids who identified with him, emulated him, and now had to deal with the disillusionment of being deceived by their hero.

We must wonder why someone blessed with so much talent would risk being scorned and discredited as a steroid user, and being mocked as A-Fraud. The dispositional-situational-systemic paradigm, which is useful in understanding how a cluster of factors can coalesce in precipitating a dark-side indulgence among professional athletes, can offer some clues in this direction. Dispositionally, Alex's eagerness to gain an edge is reflected in his purportedly tipping pitches to opposing players in lopsided games.[38] The purpose, according to biographer Selena Roberts, was not to fix games, but rather to engender reciprocity, which could lead to his getting some extra hits and inflate his batting average. Such a practice creates a stain on his character and integrity. Situational components can be seen in the pressure to excel, emanating from his new lucrative $252 million contract, and the pressure to maintain his level of performance in the wilting heat of the Texas summers. The systemic factor arises from the prevalence throughout MLB in that era of players using performance-enhancing drugs. Thus, a group contagion effect operated to push A-Rod and many others to succumb to the appeal of steroids.

On Narcissism

Alex Rodriguez frequently has been portrayed by the media as narcissistic. The term narcissism is used in many different ways in our culture, but two primary trends are readily apparent. In one definition, a narcissistic individual can be described as a person who is self-absorbed and is oblivious to the presence, needs, and feelings of other people. In another definition, a person who craves affirmation and admiration from others to feel worthy or special also may be classified as narcissistic. One or the other of these characteristics may be a dominant personality dimension, or they can operate in combination with one another.

A-Rod's personality seems consistent with both sides of the narcissistic spectrum. To the extent that he is excessively fixated on his body and his batting statistics, he can be viewed as self-absorbed. The extent to which he repeatedly seems to need to be admired and affirmed suggests an insatiable need to feel validated and loved.[39] The problem with this latter type of narcissistic fix is that it is unquenchable—that is, the supplies received have a short shelf life, analogous to a good meal followed by the next day's hungry appetite.

In Defense of Narcissism

Alex Rodriguez is the best player in baseball, but his detractors suggest that regardless of how good he is (he has won three MVP awards), his preoccupation with how he looked to others while he was on the field has led to his underperformance in clutch situations. In other words, his narcissism has created a significant impediment to sustaining his excellence. Simply viewing him as "an adulation junkie"[40] is to consider narcissism only from a pejorative and offensive perspective, rather than as a personality syndrome that needs to be understood in depth. U.S. society has little tolerance for narcissistic behavior, and such individuals are generally judged in a negative light. But narcissism can be seen as a double-edged sword. In A-Rod's case, the very quality that has at times undermined his productivity is the same quality that has driven his ambition toward greatness. While his quest to be and to be seen as the best player in the game may be fueled by his narcissism, at the same time he legitimately can be admired for his devotion to training and his overall exemplary work ethic.

A Sense of Cause

MLB needed a face-lift after the damage of the 2004 strike, and Mark McGwire became the designated hero. The trajectory of his adoration and decimation directly reflects the mood of our culture at different points in time. We were ready to be enchanted by McGwire's record-breaking feat in 1998, and, in contrast, after the pervasive denial of artificial performance enhancement was punctured and no longer tenable, he became the representation of all that was corrupt in the world of sports.

Although we quickly enshrined him during and after his prodigious power season (1998), we later needed to punish him rather than ourselves; when it became clear that our yearning for a baseball hero allowed us to be duped about what was really going on.

Sports writers, in particular, first heralded McGwire as the new Babe Ruth, and subsequently they discredited him as a deceitful villain who tarnished the image of baseball purity. This disdain was seen in their insipid lack of endorsement when the time came to cast Hall of Fame ballots.

The emphatic denial of steroids use by Palmeiro, Bonds, Landis, Clemens, and others, despite damaging indications of their respective involvement, can be grasped as a hubristic commitment to the "listen to what I tell you, rather than to what you see or hear" philosophy, which is prevalent among many sports stars.

Although it is supremely self-destructive to jeopardize their careers, and their place in sports' history when the truth comes out, the expectation among these high-profile athletes is that society's love for them will prevail and that they will be quickly forgiven for any misconduct.

In recent times the legal system, spearheaded by prosecutors who are eager to embellish their status, increasingly has become vigorous in pursuing and punishing corrupt sports figures—a cultural tilt that prompted Roger Clemens to declare that people in the United States are now deemed guilty before they are proven innocent.

The interaction between an athlete's dispositional proclivity toward crossing boundaries, and the role of society in creating the soil that conditions and encourages him to do so, is the engine that fuels many of our sports scandals. Fame often corrupts morality and may be a precursor to the choices and decisions that become self-destructive or corrupt. Star athletes frequently step over the line into moral or legal transgressions. Our society has conditioned these athletes to acquire a distorted self-image that propels them to indulge their dark side and to function with a belief system in which they can underplay the consequences.

OUTSIDE THE BIG FOUR

Golf

Concerns about steroids have permeated all sports. Even golf, a world in which an honor code among athletes has long prevailed, has embarked on developing a new testing program, which was scheduled to be in place for the 2008 season. The issue was highlighted at the 2007 British Open, when Hall of Famer Gary Player told reporters that to his knowledge at least one professional golfer was a steroids user.

Tim Finchem, chair of the World Golf Foundation, astutely pointed out that the world of sports, as a reflection of the world at large, is infested with corruption and cheating. In initiating the drug-testing program, Finchem proclaimed, "We're going to be proactive in light of the realities that are happening in sports. We are where we are because of the state of the world."[41] In banning substances that parallel the list covered by the WADA, which monitors Olympic testing, the World Golf Foundation is taking a preemptive strike before a drug scandal erupts in golf.

Cycling: Floyd Landis

When Landis tested positive after a miraculous run-from-behind victory in the 2006 Tour de France, many of his admirers held on to the hope that he was the victim of a flawed French laboratory system. Landis had carefully sculpted his image as a sincere, serious, religious, likeable American hero and we wanted to believe in him. For these followers, it did not matter that doping allegations were commonplace in other sports. It was more comfortable to hold onto illusions about Landis's purity, which we could latch onto and identify with, than to face the disillusionment of the demise of a much-needed hero. As noted by sports writer Adrian Wojnarowski, "It's fascinating how little cynicism runs through the minds of a public burned over and over, how they still want to believe in fairyz tale dashes-through the Alps."[42]

Landis vehemently proclaimed his innocence in spite of the finding that his urine sample revealed a testosterone-to-epitestosterone ratio of eleven to one, which was excessively beyond the acceptable four-to-one limit established by the WADA. The results indicated that traces of synthetic testosterone (not produced by his body) were contained in his urine. Landis presented a bunch of lame explanations to account for this discrepancy. His excuses ranged from the alcohol he drank the night before, to his thyroid medication, to dehydration; most of all he blamed flaws in the lab's testing procedures.

When a more precise analysis of his urine B sample confirmed the initial report, Landis was outraged. He described the case as a witch hunt and railed against the U.S. Anti-Doping Agency (USADA) and the French lab. He expressed his venom in his book *Positively False: The Real Story of How I Won the Tour de France*, in which he repeatedly denied that he had ever used performance-enhancing drugs, and asserted that the USADA officials offered him leniency if he shared information about Lance Armstrong's doping. Armstrong had faced years of suspicion about drug use, but had always tested cleanly. Landis adopted a "prove it" defense and spent close to $2 million in legal fees attempting to exonerate himself, his title, and his reputation.

An arbitration hearing upheld the findings of the test that indicated that Landis had used synthetic testosterone, and they stripped him of his title and imposed a two-year cycling ban. The arbitration committee determined that while the French lab procedures were indeed flawed, nevertheless, evidence was sufficient to rule against Landis. He was ordered to pay $100,000 in reimbursements to the WADA for its costs in dealing with the appeal. The one (out of three) dissenting arbitrator maintained that because the lab's documents were so flawed Landis should have been exonerated—that is, he should be cleared not because he did not cheat, but because of errors in the system. That had been the hope of the Landis defense team—that by attacking and discrediting the system, their client would be spared the ignominy of being declared a cheater.

Psychologically, it is possible to convince yourself that you are innocent of a wrongdoing, even though another part of you knows that you are guilty. This is the process of compartmentalization and dissociation. Deny, deny, deny, and externalize the problem by blaming the system for victimizing you, and you might start to believe in your innocence. If he is guilty, Landis may be operating under such a cloud of self-deception. What would have prompted him to cross the line to illegal steroid use? Money and the quest for glory are two motivators that lead some sports heroes to abandon good judgment. In Floyd Landis's case, perhaps he was emboldened by the Lance Armstrong situation, in which Armstrong, his hero, was tested repeatedly, amid drug accusations, but never tested positively.

Devastated by the arbitration ruling, Landis, true to form, blamed the trigger-happy antidoping authorities, the blood-thirsty media, and the jaded public, which in his mind made it impossible to get a fair hearing.

A GLANCE AT THE FUTURE

In spite of the persistent negative attention devoted to athletes who use performance-enhancing drugs, the steroids crisis appears to be spreading. It seems like a new scandal is emerging almost every week. To compound the problem, many sports stars have learned how to beat the testing system by discovering substances that are undetectable in the standard urine test. A research study conducted in Sweden indicates that 32 percent of men injected with testosterone have a genetic composition that conceals their doping with the hormone.[43] These men are missing both copies of a gene that converts testosterone into a form that dissolves in urine and enables them to test negative; thus, they are essentially given a license to cheat. This raises the question whether some of our star athletes, who are suspected of using performance-enhancing drugs but have never tested positive, fall into this category. How did we get into this messy state of affairs? The culpability for this corruption in sports lies in four directions: (1) the franchise owners who thrive economically on the popularity of their sport, (2) the players who know what is going on, but are loath to rat out their own brethren, (3) the sports writers who sensationalize the stories without productive solutions, and (4) the fans who have become indifferent or lethargic and who do not want to see their heroes fall from the pedestal. So what can be done to stem the tide?

Proposed Solutions

Following are some proposed solutions:

The deterrent effect

Greater transparency, exposure, and consequences are needed for athletes who test positive. It is commendable that the WADA is pursuing a reliable blood test for HGH. Athletes have turned increasingly to HGH, because it provides similar advantages to other banned substances and has been undetectable. The fear of being caught often serves as a deterrent to crossing the line and violating society's standards. A blood test for HGH would have to be endorsed by the players unions in the major sports leagues. These unions must be pressured, against predictable opposition, to enter into a collective bargaining agreement on this issue. To move away from their role as enablers, professional football and baseball unions have contributed funds for the development of a reliable urine test for HGH (they already have urine samples tested for other substances), but experts predict that such a test is still many years away. The blood tests developed by the WADA were available in 2008, and they represent a quicker and more direct approach to the problem, but the program was not implemented because the respective players unions remained opposed to blood testing. Moreover, the accuracy of such texts has come into question.

With regard to other performance-enhancing drugs, sanctions need to be tightened uniformly across the board in all sports so that offending athletes will be penalized not only for a failed drug test, but also for purchasing, receiving, or distributing banned substances. The heightened activity of federal investigators in pursuing pharmacies that distribute these drugs without prescriptions can facilitate this process.

Player admission

Many players will acknowledge the widespread use of steroids in their sport, but they hide behind the blue wall of silence when it comes to stepping forward with relevant information. A groundswell of peer pressure is needed to convey to the rank and file of professional athletes that it is to everyone's advantage to rid their sport of the poisonous effects of performance-enhancing drugs. Some high-profile stars such as Jason Giambi and Keyshawn Johnson have spoken out against steroids, and more athletes need to take the lead in registering their complaints with their players union.

Educational initiatives

These initiatives should include (1) ongoing seminars for athletes about the dangers of performance-enhancing drugs, which emphasize the themes of choices, decisions, and consequences; (2) ethics and morality programs integrated into the elementary school curriculum, and extended into the high school curriculum where adolescents are rebellious and antiestablishment in their attitudes; (3) mandatory seminars about performance-enhancing drugs for parents of kids who are in organized sports programs; (4) greater oversight by the National Collegiate Athletic Association (NCAA) of recruitment practices in attracting and rewarding players who attend their universities; (5) restrictions on booster and alumni involvement with college athletes; and (6) congressional pressures on the major sports leagues to improve how they monitor and police their own house. Such congressional pressure should include (1) penalties for team coaches and general managers who are complicit in players' involvement with performance-enhancing drugs, and (2) sanctions against franchise owners whose players are violating antisteroids regulations. Other initiatives could require every team to have a mental health practitioner and establish a policy in which conflicts between the collective bargaining advocates pertaining to new proposed regulations (for example, the players union versus the league administrators) shall be resolved by an impartial committee dedicated to promoting standards that will reduce the impact of performance-enhancing drugs as a stain on the game.

Organized fan strikes and protests

Instead of trusting their heroes to be clean until proven guilty, sports fans must demand that they perform free of steroids. The large segment of fans who care about the artificial enhancement of their heroes needs to organize a fans' strike, in which a day is designated for people to boycott the sport. The media can assist in publicizing a fan unappreciation day. Such a display would result in a drop of attendance, even if for one day.

With accompanying causative publicity, this effort would push the franchise owners to push to the forefront the need to do more than public relations initiatives to clean up their game. Fans also need to acquire a stronger voice. They could forge an alliance of protest, together with the media, to stage planned demonstrations about the dishonesty in sports.

Surely, these actions could hasten the path toward change. A significant step in the right direction occurred when the fan who purchased Barry Bonds's 756th home run ball opened a Web site and invited fans to vote on whether the ball should be adorned with an asterisk, should not be changed, or should be shot into space. In an amazing display of interest, more than ten million online responses were recorded, and 47 percent voted for the asterisk. It is encouraging to see that when their voices were solicited, millions replied. It is also meaningful that the Hall of Fame accepted the asterisk-branded ball for display at their museum.

THE WHATEVER SYNDROME

In dealing with the preponderance of performance enhancing drugs in sports, during the last decade the court of public opinion has transitioned through five phases of reactions. These phases comprise what I have coined "the whatever syndrome," and can be described as follows:

- Phase I: Blissful innocence—Suspicions about artificial enhancement are overridden by the need and wish to believe in the talent of our heroes. Denial is a major component in this stage of the process, and it is dismantled only gradually.
- Phase II: Acceptance of Reality—The evidence and media reports compel us to recognize that many of our cherished sports stars have cheated their way into the record book.
- Phase III: Anger—The necessity of relinquishing our belief in the unequivocal goodness of our idolized sports heroes generates resentment and anger. The loss of the bubble of our imagined connection to untarnished greatness can be painful.
- Phase IV: Apathy—A large segment of the public has become numb to the prevalence of corruption in sports. Many fans no longer care and react with indifference to new scandals surrounding athletes and performance-enhancing drugs.

It is imperative to regain a landscape in which sports are honest, clean, and transparent. The accomplishments that our heroes achieve must be achieved via a level playing field.

CHAPTER TWO

The Dangers of Invincibility

It is striking to observe how sports icons can blithely play Russian roulette with their careers, their image, and even their lives. Recently, scandals involving off-the-field misbehavior among sports stars have been increasing at an alarming pace. Even some of our most cherished superstars, who have attained record-breaking feats on the field, have morphed from hero to antihero when their misguided steps into immoral or illegal territory come to light.

We all have a dark side that is tempted at times to violate boundaries; generally, however, respect for society's standards and good judgment prevail. In addition, the realistic appraisal and anticipation of consequences for stepping over the line is sufficient to serve as a deterrent against the acting out of antisocial impulses. Such restraint is often lacking in the lives of celebrity sports heroes who make pathological and self-destructive choices that lead them into corrupt activity. What goes on inside the mind of these corrupt athletes? What are they thinking when they cross the barrier into corrupt transgressions? All too often, a part of the problem is that they are not thinking things through, but simply are indulging their appetites. They operate with unbridled hubris and have acquired a distorted self-image that allows them to do whatever they want without regard for the repercussions. They view themselves as above the system, and when they are caught in their corrupt actions, they expect to get a free pass. Frequently, past transgressions have been treated lightly by the legal system or the sports league, which reinforces the belief that athletes can follow their own rules and symbolically rely on acquiring and utilizing a get-out-of-jail-free card. Ultimately, a more serious scandal, fueled by self-sabotaging actions, may emerge.

Pete Rose, Denny McLain, Art Schlichter, and Jack Molinas represent superstars in different sports and different eras who are linked by their compulsive affinity for gambling, the ultimate sin in the sports establishment, which, in each case, led to self-sabotaging behavior. Their readiness to take liberties in ignoring, dismissing, or violating the rules of the game, or the standards of society, put them at risk in their careers. Their corrupt activity led to their removal from the hero pedestal, ruined lives, and the disgrace of a prison term.

PETE ROSE: A SPORTS ICON FOR THE HALL OF SHAME

Pete Rose was a sure bet for election to Cooperstown—home of the baseball Hall of Fame—until his self-destructive arrogance landed him in the Hall of Shame. Pete Rose is a disgrace. Pete Rose permanently should be denied entry into the Hall of Fame. He could have been the greatest baseball player of his era, but his corrupt inclinations did him in. This assessment will seem unfair to many who believe that his on-the-field record speaks for itself in establishing him as one of the all-time outstanding players in baseball history. It is true that his performance as an active player was unblemished, and that other legendary stars such as Ty Cobb and Babe Ruth had tarnished off-the-field reputations. Cobb assaulted a heckling fan who was physically disabled, and allegedly attempted to murder a man who had tried to mug him. Cobb and Ruth, the earliest Hall of Fame inductees, were elected solely because of their superior baseball performance, and they were judged in an era when integrity and character were not taken into consideration. Not so for Rose. A vast majority of fans are indifferent or forgiving toward his gambling activities while he was manager of the Cincinnati Reds; indeed, at Old Timers Day festivities, he receives ovations while Commissioner Bud Selig draws boos. Nevertheless, as unfair as it seems, MLB, in snubbing Pete Rose, is serving the greater good in sending the right message to the youth of America who admire his athletic accomplishments and yearn to follow in his footsteps. The core of the message is that in addition to talent, integrity and character do count, and that even superstar athletes with big egos, which are encouraged and reinforced by adoring fans, are accountable for their transgressions.

In his playing days, Pete Rose was something special. His zest for the game, his energy level and drive to win earned him the affectionate nickname of Charlie Hustle. His scrappy style of play was a throwback to earlier eras when overachievers like Billy Martin and Eddie Stanky made the most of their limited talent and constantly looked for an edge to win at any cost. His durability was exceptional as he gradually marched toward Ty Cobb's record of most career base hits. At the time, Cobb's feat was thought to be insurmountable. Surely, one of the most glorious moments of Rose's life occurred in September 1985, when he smashed hit number 4,192 to eclipse Cobb. His son Pete Jr. rushed out of the dugout to greet him, and Rose looked up to the sky and envisioned his deceased father watching over him. He was enthralled by the image of three generations of Rose men sharing this moment for posterity.

After hanging up his spikes at age forty-five, he stayed on as manager of the Reds. The world was his oyster and he could have enjoyed perpetual awe, admiration, and super-celebrity status as a model for striving for and attaining greatness in America. He could have become a living legend of his generation. The accomplishments of his twenty-four seasons spoke for themselves. Instead, he became a pariah and an embarrassment to the national pastime. Unlike other baseball icons like Sandy Koufax and Joe DiMaggio, who cherished their privacy and cultivated and protected their postretirement image, Pete Rose needed action. Like a supreme narcissist, he seemed to develop a belief system that he could do whatever he wanted without regard for the consequences of his actions. Rose's addictive potion was gambling. When he was a kid, his father, whom he idolized, introduced him to the world of horseracing, and Pete soon became a regular at the track. But when you are a baseball legend, betting on the ponies is different than betting on sports.

During his stewardship as manager of the Reds, rumors began circulating that Rose was a heavy gambler on all of the major sports. Actually, suspicions had been floating around since the late 1970s, but nothing substantial came of them. He would have been a shoo-in to be elected to the Hall of Fame in his first year of eligibility, and he seemed oblivious to the implications of being exposed as a gambler. How could he have been so arrogant, above it all, and so self-destructive? The answer is unbridled hubris.

In Greek mythology, the famous tale of Daedalus and his son Icarus highlights the role of grandiosity, hubris, and the denial of reality in self-destructive personalities. The father and son had been living in exile in Crete for many years, and Daedalus devised a plan for them to return to their native land of Athens. He fashioned a pair of wings for himself and Icarus made out of bird feathers and wax. He fitted them to their bodies, and they practiced flying up into the sky. When they were ready to depart, Icarus was told to fly a middle course between the sea and the sun. Daedalus cautioned him that flying too low could pull his wings into the sea, and flying too high could result in his wings melting from the heat of the sun. Icarus followed his father into the sky and, imbued with the exuberance of flying, he dared to soar to higher zones in the sky. Disregarding the limitations of reality, Icarus flew too close to the sun, whereupon the wax that held his feathers together melted, and he plunged to his death in the sea below.

Pete Rose is a modern-day Icarus, who acquired the distorted belief that he could walk on water or fly too close to the sun; he was determined to do the world according to Pete, while flying in the face of the obstacles of reality. When you march exclusively to the beat of your own drummer, reality is blurred and always comes in second place. It is a risky course of action, because sooner or later, a clash with the forces of reality will occur. Like Icarus, Rose's urge to violate the margin of safety, his poor judgment, and his disregard for consequences combined to set the stage for his self-destruction.

Since the dark days of the Black Sox scandal, when eight Chicago White Sox players were banished from the game for conspiring to throw the 1919 World Series, MLB has been committed to policing its own house. Gambling activity, with its implications of tarnishing the integrity of the game, has been viewed as the sport's most egregious violation. Alcoholics, drug abusers, sexual offenders, wife beaters, and even convicted rapists have been forgiven and even welcomed back to the baseball family; but those believed to be involved in gambling, or with ties to shady characters who were affiliated with the underworld, have been treated more harshly. In 1943, William Cox, owner of the Philadelphia Phillies, was banned for life and ordered to sell the team, by Commissioner Kenesaw Mountain Landis, after admitting that he had made fifteen to twenty bets on Phillies games. In 1947, Leo Durocher, the popular feisty manager of the Brooklyn Dodgers, was suspended for one year, because of "conduct detrimental to baseball." His association with gamblers was the final straw in a series of incidents in which Durocher snubbed his nose at the moral standards of that era. And in 1970, Dennis McLain, the Detroit Tigers sensation, who was the last pitcher to win thirty games in a season, was suspended for bookmaking activity and association with gamblers.

Accordingly, Rose had to know about these precedents, but his need for action and his narcissistic approach to the world made him undeterred. Rose believed that he was a national treasure, and he had good reason to think so. Our culture, hungry for record-breaking athletic performance that people could embrace, placed him on a lofty pedestal, which endured beyond his playing days.

In 1989, as rumors about Rose's betting on games intensified, Commissioner Bart Giamatti launched an investigation headed by respected attorney John Dowd. After a six-month probe, a lengthy treatise, which came to be known as the Dowd report, concluded that Rose had definitively bet on sports games, including baseball, while he was the manager of the Reds. Giamatti was compelled to honor the findings of the Dowd report, but he did not want to alienate the fan base of one of baseball's all-time favorite sons. Moreover, many of the informants were sleazy associates of Rose, who were facing different criminal investigations of their own; they could be suspected of ratting on Rose to improve their legal positions. Thus, the evidence against Rose, while substantial, was less than airtight.

Commissioner Giamatti believed that he had the goods on Rose. Nevertheless, he agonized over the situation. The commissioner could have summoned Rose to a hearing and presented the evidence, but Giamatti believed that Rose would never admit to betting on baseball. Instead, he determined that it was in the best interests of the game to propose a deal. On August 24, 1989, an agreement was reached in which Pete Rose would accept the findings of the Dowd report that he had bet on baseball, and he would be banned from the game in any and all capacities. It was agreed that MLB would couch the terms of the suspension in a somewhat vague and ambiguous way—that is, it would not disclose that Rose had bet on baseball, only on other sports, and he could apply for reinstatement in one year, although no guarantees would be offered. Under the circumstances, these conditions were palatable to Rose, and he signed the written agreement in good faith. He assumed that the baseball officials would treat him benevolently, and that after enforcing a limited suspension, they would be willing to move on with him in their good graces. After all, he must have thought, he had not broken any laws, he had not harmed anyone, and, in his mind, he had not done anything that terrible. His distorted self-image, brimming with entitlement, would not enable him to fathom the long-term consequences.

Once again, Rose had miscalculated. Arrogance, the very personality characteristic that had fueled his success, was at play in his misconception that he was too big to be punished with a permanent suspension from baseball. But in the mind of the commissioner, a lifetime banishment of Rose would serve as the best deterrent to gambling by future players. MLB held all the cards and had no intention of reinstating him any time soon. Ironically, Commissioner Giamatti suffered a fatal heart attack eight days after the agreement was signed, and many insiders believed that his death was hastened by the prolonged stress from the Rose debacle.

Fay Vincent became the next commissioner, and he was even less sympathetic to Rose's situation than his predecessor. Rose made matters worse by portraying himself as an innocent and proclaiming repeatedly that he had not bet on baseball, only on other sports. In effect he was campaigning for public support, and portraying the commissioner as the villain who was maligning him. If MLB had any intention of reinstating Rose, which is questionable, it was soon abandoned when Rose began shooting his mouth off, instead of maintaining a low profile.

In view of the agreement, his public statements disclaiming his involvement in baseball betting were a profoundly self-destructive act, and demonstrated that he was not taking matters seriously enough. Rose was acting like he could still call the shots. Rose's public persona antagonized baseball's power structure, which then tightened its grip on the position that he was exhibiting conduct detrimental to the game. As a result, his attempts at reinstatement have been consistently rebuffed.

The self-destructive side of his personality has resulted in prison time. Although it is not against the law to bet on baseball games, it is a legal violation to fail to report income. In 1990, Rose pled guilty to tax evasion. He was sentenced to five months in prison, and in his book *My Prison Without Bars*,[1] he roundly protested the unfairness of the sentence.

Baseball stonewalled, and it was not until 2002, thirteen long years later, that Bud Selig, the commissioner who succeeded Fay Vincent, agreed to meet with Rose and to hear him out. In part, Selig was responding to fan pressure to do so, because whenever he and Rose appeared at the same public event, Rose was wildly cheered and Selig was derisively booed. Rose's boyish charm and down-to-earth style resonates with the average fan who seems ready to forgive and to anoint him as a hero. Selig, in contrast, comes across as formal, stilted, and lawyerly, which frequently triggers a reaction of disdain toward his autocratic authority. Rose's popularity around this time may have filled him with a false sense of confidence that it would put pressure on the MLB to welcome him back to the game, but he misread the mood of the commissioner.

Baseball insider Mike Schmidt maintains that Rose, in his face-to-face meeting with Selig, admitted candidly that while he was manager of the Reds he not only had bet on other sports, as he previously had acknowledged, but also had bet on baseball games, specifically, those involving the Reds.[2] Rose left the meeting with a feeling of optimism about his reinstatement. In his mind, he had served thirteen long years in baseball exile, much longer than he felt was warranted for his not-so-terrible misdeeds. Now that he had been forthright and come clean, Rose thought he would be forgiven. But this was not to be. Selig continued to withhold an official ruling, which meant the ban on Rose remained in effect.

The most likely explanation guiding Selig's inaction is that Rose's confession, while counteracting his previous public denials, lacked genuine remorse. Rose the supreme narcissist, who in his playing days was accustomed to the world bowing down to him, could not handle the humiliation that would accompany the exposure of his lies. A display of remorse would feel too humbling and weak, and he could not present himself that way. In essence, in the psyche of Rose, it was a major concession for him to issue a confession, but his sense of entitlement could not allow him to experience, let alone express, remorse. Contrition was simply foreign to him, and, more to the point, he was more invested in his aggrieved position. While his story changed, and he eventually revealed the full scope of his betting activity, Rose consistently minimized the seriousness of his infraction and highlighted the unfairness of his punishment.

Bud Selig had the power to determine Rose's fate within baseball, and Rose refused to plead or squirm. His grandiose self-image could not allow him to repent. His ongoing narcissism resulted in a false expectation that the court of baseball would be beneficent at this juncture. The reality is that, in his confrontation with Selig, Rose was between a rock and a hard place. A decision for reinstatement was contingent on a confession plus a presentation that required groveling and eating a large portion of humble pie. His inflated self-image could not bring him to do so. Selig may have been influenced by his predecessor, Fay Vincent, who warned that, "Any Commissioner who reinstates Rose has to accept the responsibility for lessening the deterrent to gambling that has been almost totally successful."[3]

Selig exploited the Rose gambling scandal to bolster an image of MLB taking the high moral ground in policing its constituents. While turning a blind eye to the developing crisis of ballplayers using performance-enhancing drugs, which to an even greater extent threatened the integrity of the game, Selig maintained a hard-line stance on Rose and kept him locked out. In response to having lost a lot of ground in popularity to the NFL and the NBA (National Basketball Association), MLB was attempting to reposition itself as the most ethical bound of all the sports leagues. Selig presumed that his anti-Rose crusade was protecting the public from a tainted superstar, and thereby promoting fan loyalty to a clean game. But many fans did not feel the need for that protection; their love of the game endured, and they were more enraptured by Rose's accomplishments as a player than soured by his gambling demise while manager of the Reds. Ironically, Pete Rose would probably not get elected to the Hall of Fame, even if he was eligible to be on the ballot, because his demeanor has created too much ill will among the writers and the insiders.

Was Bud Selig disingenuous in offering this meeting with Rose? Did he set Rose up, knowing that the all-time hits leader would need to present some face-saving compromise—that is, a confession short of remorse? While Selig kept the Rose issue on hold, Rose authored a bestselling book, *My Prison Without Bars,* in which he acknowledged publicly, for the first time, that he had often bet on the Reds to win, and never on them to lose, during his managerial tenure. It was presented with a slant that suggested that this was almost an acceptable thing to do. The timing of the book release, and excerpts printed in *Sports Illustrated* (January 2004), unfortunately, knocked the current baseball news concerning the 2004 Hall of Fame inductees off the sports pages. This was all the excuse that Commissioner Selig needed to perpetuate the ban.

Selig, with support from the Hall of Fame, could afford to adopt a holier-than-though stance and stall making a decision about Rose's status within a reasonable time frame. Empowered by the office of the commissioner, and perhaps unduly influenced and identified with the righteousness of baseball's first czar, Commissioner Kenesaw Mountain Landis, Selig functioned as judge and jury, but did so without arriving at a conclusive verdict. Even in a court of law, a jury renders a verdict (and the judge a sentence if the verdict is guilty) within a reasonable period of time. At the very least, Rose deserved a response. A part of Selig might have sadistically enjoyed his power in symbolically making Rose squirm and thwarting the expectations of MLB's all-time base hits leader.

For someone like Rose, a man who thrives on action and has been conditioned to have his needs responded to in a quick fashion, endless waiting for MLB to welcome him back into the family is a living nightmare. He was left to stew in the juices of impotent rage, while others determined his professional future, over which he had zero control. His mantra embraced a rallying cry that "in America everyone gets a second chance," which was a thinly veiled plea for reinstatement as a bridge to getting his name on the Hall of Fame ballot. It is true that in the judicial system sports heroes usually have been treated more leniently than the general population. When Barry Bonds went to court seeking reduced family support payments, the judge, an ardent baseball fan, ruled in favor of his request, and quickly approached Bonds for his autograph. Fortunately, this decision was later overruled. In another high-profile case Marcus Moore, a pitcher with the Colorado Rockies, was acquitted of rape charges. One of the jurors later stated that the group of jurors all thought he was guilty, but because of his status as a baseball player, they decided to set him free. And volumes have been written about how O. J. Simpson got away with a double murder.

In *My Prison Without Bars* and the television interviews to publicize his book, Rose came across as short on contrition, instead lobbying for compassion for all that *he* had endured in his persecution by MLB over the preceding fourteen years. His presentation is skewed toward portraying himself as the victim, and he doesn't fully get it that he violated the most sacred unofficial sports law, the one that most threatens the integrity of the game and that the leagues take most seriously.

He trivializes the immorality of his actions by proclaiming that, yes, he bet on baseball, but only on his team to win and never to lose. He attempted to discredit the findings of the Dowd investigation by externalizing the problem—that is, casting the blame for exposing him to shady associates who were merely interested in cutting better deals in their own criminal proceedings. Rose feels that he has been unfairly treated and is the victim of a witch-hunt, but in the current culture of coming down hard on corruption and cover-ups, celebrities need to be mindful that such misbehavior will be judged harshly and penalties will be severe. In a way, Pete Rose has been used by MLB as a poster boy for corruption, especially gambling activities within its family, and its severe punishment.

Rose has had a legion of supporters from within the baseball fraternity. Jim Bouton actually argued that by not providing counseling programs, nor "guidance to help players cope with life's collisions," MLB has been a complicit enabler to Rose's gambling addiction.[4] Hall of Famer Mike Schmidt proposes that Rose, his former teammate, should be reinstated, placed on the Hall of Fame ballot for consideration by the Veteran's Committee, and "be used to counsel current players on the dangers of gambling."[5] This biased suggestion comes from someone who is too close to Rose and therefore cannot maintain an objective stance. The idea of Rose counseling current players seems absurd, because without genuine contrition, which he seems unable to generate, who would believe him? How convincing could he be? In all of those intervening years, he seems never to have made an attempt to get sustained professional help. It would be a gamble for the national pastime to take a chance on Rose. It is too risky to expose youth, who cherish their sports heroes, to further disillusionment.

In March 2007 in an interview on ESPN radio, stimulated by the Reds opening a new exhibit at their stadium on his career, Rose further indicated that his betting on the Reds was more extensive than previously acknowledged. In his 2002 meeting with Selig, Rose had downplayed his involvement in confessing that he bet on his team four or five times a week. Now he admitted the full extent of his addiction in stating, "I bet on my team to win every night because I loved my team; I believed in my team. I did everything in my power every night to win that game." Still yearning for reinstatement, he arrogantly stated, "I believe I'm the best ambassador baseball has."[6]

His confession about "betting on the Reds every night" confirms that his breaking the rules of baseball was not an impulsive lapse in judgment, but rather a long-term pattern of playing by his own rules. This alone should be sufficient to disqualify him from ever being an ambassador for the game.

One week after his radio interview, he appeared on the *Jay Leno Show* and conveyed an attitude that suggested he did not feel like he did anything wrong, with the rationalization that his betting did not hurt his team. When confronted by Leno about the new revelations in the ESPN radio interview, Rose dismissed this as old news that "was documented twenty-seven years ago." In appealing for sympathy because his betting activity was predicated on his faith and love for his team, he further stated, "It was like my sons playing for me . . . I bet on them every night. . . . It was wrong, but it's kind of human when you think about it." He then waffled on admitting that he had a gambling addiction, and spun off the following elaborate rationalization to justify his behavior: "I almost reached older type status in baseball, and, all of a sudden, it gets taken away from me as a player. No one wants to get old and you can't play, and that was my addiction—to be part of the game by gambling on my team." In conclusion he reiterated, "it was wrong, but it's kind of human when you think about it."[7]

In most families, the sons either repeat or learn something about how to be different than their fathers. One of Pete Rose's fondest dreams was to see Pete Rose Jr. become a major leaguer. Rose Jr. aspired to follow in his father's footsteps, but he was not talented enough to make the grade.

For several years, he shuffled around on minor league rosters, and in 2005 he was charged with distributing GBL, a steroid alternative, to his team-mates. He pleaded guilty and was sentenced to one month in prison and five months of home detention. Given the ordeal that he had seen his father go through for "breaking the rules," one would think that Rose Jr. would have been supercautious about stepping over the line. Instead, he found his own pathway to self-destructive off-the-field behavior.

ART SCHLICHTER: OUT-OF-CONTROL ADDICT OR SOCIOPATH?

Art Schlichter ranks high on the all-time list of self-destructive sports heroes. He morphed from a high school and college football poster boy to a pariah in the throes of an out-of-control gambling addiction that ruined his career and his life. In contrast to Denny McLain, discussed later in this chapter, he was not driven by a need to repeat a pattern involving humili-ation and punishment; instead, humiliation and punishment became the by-products of his irrational behavior designed to prove his invincibility and provided a misguided way to soothe himself and counteract rejection in times of stress.

His attraction to gambling and a need for action started at a young age, and during his high school years, he played the horses on a regular basis. Later, while at Ohio State University, he spent more time at the track than attending to academic requirements. Nonetheless, he was a gifted athlete and gained all-state honors in high school in football and basket-ball. As a freshman at Ohio State, he beat out the established quarterback for the starting position. The next season, he led his team to the Rose Bowl and finished fourth in the coveted Heisman Trophy balloting. This was unprecedented recognition for a college sophomore, and he flourished as the national football golden boy. In 1982, he was drafted by the Balti-more Colts and heralded as the incipient savior of their floundering fran-chise. He received a $350,000 signing bonus as part of a three-year, $830,000 package, an exorbitant contract for that era. His performance in training camp did not measure up to the hype, and he lost the starting quarterback position to Mike Pagel, another rookie. Unaccustomed to being shot down, he turned increasingly to betting on college football and basketball games to repair the loss of his exalted self-image. In such situa-tions, the typical fantasy is that by demonstrating his skills to pick win-ners, he would cushion the blow to his ego. He deluded himself into thinking that since he was betting only on college games, he was not jeop-ardizing his position in the NFL. Soon, however, he lapsed into betting on professional football games as well. His judgment was poor, and he spiraled out of control, betting on as many as ten basketball games a night; and within two months, he had lost his entire signing bonus plus his $140,000 salary.

During this period, he ran afoul of his bookies, who threatened him with exposure and physical harm if he did not pay $159,000 in gambling losses. Schlichter responded by participating in an FBI sting that entrapped the bookmakers, and he confided to the NFL authorities about what was going on. He rationalized that because he had not thrown any games in which he played and had not placed bets on games involving the Colts, he would be treated leniently for his infractions. This was an exercise in wishful thinking, and Commissioner Pete Rozelle suspended him for the entire 1983 season. This assumption, more than any of his actions, reflects Schlichter's irrational state of mind. He not only was gambling on sports, but also extending this out-of-control self-destructive behavior to betting on NFL games. Most anyone would know that this behavior would be viewed as an egregious offense to the image of the game; NFL stars have been suspended in the past for such gambling behavior. But Art Schlichter was hoping for leniency or a pass, because this is what he had been conditioned to expect. At Ohio State, for example, he had received multiple speeding tickets that repeatedly were dismissed by a friendly judge. Such accommodation reinforced his inner belief that he was free to act irresponsibly without facing repercussions.

Gambling or associating with gamblers has always been treated harshly by the presiding commissioners of the major sports leagues. Players associated with the Black Sox scandal (MLB), Leo Durocher (MLB), Jack Molinas (NBA), Denny McLain (MLB), Paul Hornung (NFL), Alex Karras (NFL), and Merle Hapes (NFL) had been suspended from their respective leagues in the years before the Schlichter affair. It was predictable that Rozelle would rule with an iron hand, because more than any other offense, gambling was viewed as the primary threat to the integrity of the game. A chief source of concern in a situation like this is that a player who is prone to gambling could progress to betting on games involving his own team, or, more outrageously, that he could be susceptible to fixing a game to square his debt to his bookies. Schlichter did play in future NFL games and could have been targeted as an easy mark, but there is no evidence, nor even a suggestion, that he ever was approached to fix a game.

Schlichter, accustomed to people bailing him out of trouble, could not squirm out of this one. He was given a second chance, however, and after being reinstated at the end of his suspension, he played two seasons with the Colts; however, amid rumors about his ongoing gambling activities, he was dropped by the team and permanently banned from the NFL. The power of his addiction outstripped his ability to meet the challenge of maintaining an untarnished image, and he quickly became a tragic sports figure.

Like many star athletes, Art Schlichter's talents were recognized and groomed from early childhood. His self-image was shaped by admiration and coronation from a legion of admiring fans, and he was hoisted on the pedestal as "King Arthur." In a form of induced narcissism, he acquired the belief that he could do whatever he wanted, and that any transgressions would be overlooked or taken care of by others. As the all-American hero, he was universally sought after and idolized. At one point, he had to leave his college dorm, because girls who were total strangers were pursuing him at all hours of the night. He was determined to write his own ticket while living out the role of King Arthur. Undisciplined as a student, he spent considerable time during college at the track and never graduated. But who needs a college degree when you are America's darling?

Art was the youngest of three siblings and his parents were indulgent, overly permissive, and lax in setting appropriate limits. His father introduced him to the track when he was a boy and also took him to Las Vegas; he seemed to provide little supervision or intervention when Art was gambling during high school. By ignoring the early signs of Art's incipient gambling addiction, his parents may have assumed the role of enablers. By the time he got to college, he was a regular gambler at the track and betting with bookies, but his self-destructive pathway was masked by his charm and denial when he was confronted by his football coach.

A close friend and Ohio State booster later highlighted the origins of Schlichter's gambling disorder:

> Art was never told no. Every time he got in any kind of trouble, somebody was pulling him out of it. He has uncanny control over people. And he has unbelievable balls. Art Schlichter could walk in a damn office, sit down, prop his feet up on the desk and say, "You know, I could use a hundred grand."[8]

Another friend and teammate, Bill Hanners, recalled,

> He sent me one time to one of the banks where he knew my face would be recognized, with three checks. He sent me down there to cash them, and I walked out with $25,000, and he flat out did not have the money in the bank. He had called the president of the bank, who had watched us grow up, and he said he would transfer the funds in. I couldn't believe it. I walked out with $25,000.[9]

The bank got ripped off as Schlichter used the funds to finance his gambling activities.

These stories illustrate that Art Schlichter was also a consummate con man. His early experiences with getting away with things propelled him to act with disregard for the rules and regulations of society. By the time he was in college, he was functioning both as an addict and as a sociopath.

As his debts mounted, his sociopathic solutions increased, and many people were hurt by him along the way. His judgment was poor and he frequently chased losing bets, only to further accelerate his indebtedness. Inside the mind of a sociopath is the belief that he will find his way out of a jam, by hook or by crook, and Schlichter was extremely skillful at hooking people and concocting crooked schemes. As he spiraled out of control, he became increasingly desperate and he pursued numerous illegal operations. These acts included cashing bad checks, stealing checks from his wife's sister and trying to cash them, and bilking people, including his parents and anyone else he could connive, to support his habit. These actions fit the profile of a sociopathic personality. In sum, he lost more than $1 million betting on basketball and NFL games. Gambling became central to his identity; the power of his gambling addiction outstripped his ability to honor his pledge to repay his father for the bailout from an insurance fund related to his mother's cancer. His lack of conscience about ripping people off is another hallmark sign of his sociopathic tendencies. Although he sought help from the founder of the Center for Compulsive Gambling, after he was banned from the NFL in 1987, it was all downhill for Art Schlichter. He became a pathetic figure, on a self-destructive treadmill, a shadow of the former sports hero who at a time had the world on a string.

In interviews with sports publications, he talked a good game about cleaning up his act, but in reality, he continued to be locked in to the pull of his addiction and sociopathic solutions. Never one to learn from negative experiences, he landed in jail an incredible seventeen times between 1994 and 2000 for repeated infractions of money laundering, bank fraud, forgery and theft, and violating parole.

At the moment of placing bets, the idea that he was making a risky choice in doing so was anathema and foreign to him. The possibility of damaging consequences was a distant realization in the background of conscious awareness, while the foreground was dominated by his expectation that a winning wager would restore and confirm his special talent. As a compulsive gambler, the part of him that recognizes the dangers and consequences to self and family are overruled by the part of him that is addictively driven time and again to bet on games.

In 2002, Max Schlichter, Art's father, committed suicide. We can only speculate that his father's grief over his son's life of crime, his guilt over perceived parenting failures, like being an enabler, along with the financial drain and family humiliation related to Art's pathology, may have played a part in driving him tragically to kill himself. Art was not at the funeral, because he was serving a five-year sentence in jail for credit card fraud and money laundering. This was one of his many stays in more than forty prisons. He seemed to be an incorrigible criminal who would invariably cook up a new scam each time he was released. Two years after his father's suicide he was back in jail after being convicted of a ticket-selling scam that garnered $500,000 from twenty-two victims.

It is tempting to vilify Schlichter for his pathological choices that led to his demise. Certainly, he developed and pursued his schemes and scams to deliberately defraud many innocent people who were taken in by his con-man persona. These were conscious sociopathic decisions on his part. At the same time, current medical research suggests that a defective circuitry in the brain plays a major role in addictions. Dr. Nora Volkow, who specializes in the study of addictions, states:

> Addiction has a specific definition: You are unable to stop when you want to, despite being aware of the adverse consequences. It permeates your life; you spend more and more time satisfying your craving. . . . In the brains of addicts, there is reduced activity in the prefrontal cortex, where rational thought can override impulsive behavior.[10]

Gambling addiction is a very serious affliction, and two million American adults are pathological gamblers. Schlichter's track record meets the primary criteria for the diagnosis of pathological gambling. For Schlichter, the appeal of gambling, when it reached pathological proportions, was a route to compensate for his loss of status and to avoid the pain of depression. Cognitive distortions, such as magical thinking and the overestimation of his betting skills, undoubtedly played a part in his pursuits. While the sources of the addictive features in Art Schlichter's personality might generate a modicum of understanding and compassion, the sociopathic solutions that he enacted vigorously are unforgivable.

Can Schlichter, now a broken man in his late forties, who has spent ten of the last twelve years in prisons, with one relapse after another, be saved from himself and the powerful grip of addiction? Sometimes, in middle age the flame that energizes the need for action burns out, and this process—along with a lifetime commitment to Gamblers Anonymous combined with long-term psychotherapy—offers the best hope for recovery. In reality, his record of habitual reform and relapse suggests that such a bet would be a long shot.

JACK MOLINAS: CORRUPT WITHOUT CONSCIENCE

The name Jack Molinas is synonymous with scandals in college and professional basketball. In the 1950s and 1960s, he was at the center of major gambling episodes.

Molinas had been an outstanding high school and college player and was drafted by the Fort Wayne Pistons, predecessors to the Detroit Pistons, in 1954. During his rookie season, he quickly got into trouble for betting on games in which he played. Initially, when questioned by the police,

Molinas, who had a genius intelligence quotient of 175 and felt that he could outsmart everyone, openly admitted that he had bet on his team to win and dismissed its significance. He brazenly stated: "I am not and never have been involved with point shaving. I've done nothing wrong here. Hey, I bet a few times, that's all. I never dumped games or shaved points."[11] Despite his flagrant violation of the no gambling clause in his NBA contract, Molinas's position was that he had not done anything morally wrong, and he had not done anything to harm his team. For Molinas, it must have seemed ludicrous to be apprehended for only betting on his team to win in eight to ten games, a much less serious infraction than point shaving, which he was rumored to have done frequently in college with impunity.

Molinas had not committed a crime, but clearly this was scandalous activity within the early years of the NBA. When he was summoned to meet with Commissioner Maurice Podoloff, Molinas was strangely indignant about his integrity. He again maintained, "It's true that I bet on some of our games, less than a dozen, but I always bet on us to win. I've never done anything dishonest in my life."[12]

Upon being confronted by Podoloff, Molinas was not hoping for leniency like Denny McLain and Art Schlichter, when they were questioned. The concept of leniency was not on Molinas' radar screen. In his distorted belief system, he actually believed he had done nothing wrong, because he had not broken any laws and had not attempted to fix any games. He was so ensconced in this rationalization that he convinced himself that he was innocent and should not be subjected to any kind of punishment. Apparently, he did not take the investigation seriously, and he was stunned, outraged, and aggrieved when Podoloff suspended him from the league. It turned out to be a lifetime expulsion.

In spite of his high level of intelligence, Molinas's judgment was poor, and his grandiose sense of invulnerability did him in. How could someone so smart present himself so stupidly? In effect, Molinas was acting out against the constraints of authority. He had grown up with an overbearing father who often exhibited a violent temper and was a harsh disciplinarian. At a very early age Molinas experienced an excessive emphasis on obedience; he was given no wiggle room to be mischievous or break the rules. He was given no opportunity to question his father's authority or dominance, and any sign of rebelliousness was met with cruel punishment. In this oppressive environment, Jack learned early on to fear the wrath of his father in response to any disobedience, but this level of censorship also programmed him to test out, rebel against, and defeat authority and rules and regulations in the outside world. In contrast to his tyrannical, heavy-handed, and unaffectionate father, his mother provided an emotional refuge and modeled how to maneuver around the dictatorial patriarch. It became a challenge for him to get what he wanted through devious methods, and he used his genius-level intelligence toward achieving his goals.

In this type of punitive parental environment, the squashed child may evolve in either of two ways. One route is for the child to become a docile, passive, and obedient adult, and to repeat interpersonal patterns in which they are subservient, solicitous, and fearful of disapproval. An alternative psychological profile occurs when the rebellious, antagonistic, and hostility toward authority side emerges along with a persistent need to challenge, provoke, and defy authority and the system. Molinas's personality development followed the latter route. Moreover, he was showered with so much attention and acclamation from the outside world for his athletic talent—along with his tall, dark, and handsome good looks and his charm and intelligence—that he acquired a self-image wrapped in specialness and entitlement.

When he was banned from the NBA, Molinas protested loud and often about how he was unfairly treated and used as a scapegoat to clean up the league's image. It was widely rumored that other star players, including several prominent Pistons players, were actually dumping games, a much more serious offense. Nonetheless, these other players were treated as beyond reproach and the NBA officials looked the other way, because widespread exposure would have threatened the continued existence of the fledgling professional league. Being designated as the fall guy for a widespread problem infuriated Molinas, who experienced his expulsion as overkill, reminiscent of the cruel punishments levied by his father when he was a child. He assumed an attitude that conveyed, in effect, if I'm going to be nailed and unfairly targeted and expelled from the NBA for a comparatively minor infraction, then I might as well engage in truly deviant behavior. Four years later he applied for and was denied reinstatement to the NBA. This denial reinforced his angry and bitter reaction and made him indifferent to taking advantage of others just as he had been.

Molinas decided to take on the NBA through the judicial system. After he was expelled from the league, he became a lawyer. In 1960, when his request for reinstatement was turned down by Podoloff, he filed a lawsuit against the league for restraint of trade, asking for $3 million. Still hoping that the powerful authorities would recognize that he was treated unfairly and succumb to his request, he pointed out that "the punishment given me is more than commensurate with the acts performed."[13] This effort to gain restitution and reinstatement was thrown out of court.

Agitated, humiliated, and vengeful about being mistreated, he revealed his personality's dark and villainous side by masterminding college basketball fixes. This rocked the sports world as the point-shaving scandal of 1961, in which fifty players from twenty-five schools participated in fixing at least forty-four games. The magnitude of this corrupt operation dwarfed the earlier scandal of 1951, which permanently dethroned the New York schools as the mecca of college basketball. Molinas refined an expertise in corrupting college athletes who were vulnerable to greed and the supply of sexual favors. He concocted an organized system in which susceptible players were targeted and approached by intermediaries who arranged to dump games and passed the information along to Molinas. Molinas then "sold" the games to serious gamblers and, through his cohorts, placed large bets for himself on the designated games.

The operation imploded when one of the players under scrutiny wore a wire and recorded Molinas urging him to lie to the investigators about being paid to fix three games. Molinas was arrested on charges of bribery, attempting to suborn a witness, and conspiracy to fix twenty games involving twenty-two players at twelve colleges. Prior to his trial in 1963, Molinas was offered a deal by the district attorney's office. It was proposed that in exchange for admitting his role in several point-shaving games, and submitting to the revocation of his license to practice law, he would receive only a six-month prison sentence. Confident in his ability to win, Molinas was reluctant to negotiate a plea bargain. He was prepared to gamble on a better outcome in a trial, and he arrogantly turned down the deal. He lost his bet and was convicted and sentenced to serve ten to fifteen years. Always portraying himself as the aggrieved figure, Molinas once again cried foul and maintained that "my so-called crimes hadn't hurt anybody except some bettors and some bookies."[14] Molinas displayed an absence of guilt and lack of remorse for his criminal activity. How easily he overlooked the impact he had on all of the young players he had corrupted, whose careers and lives now were permanently stained by the scandal. An empathy chip was clearly missing in the psyche of Jack Molinas. In drawing attention to Molinas's calculating, manipulative, mean-spirited dark side, the judge who ruled in the case vehemently proclaimed, "In my opinion you are a completely immoral person. You are the prime mover of the conspiracy. . . . You callously used your prestige as a former All-American basketball player to corrupt college basketball players and defraud the public."[15] Through a series of appeals, the sentence was later determined by the court to be excessive, and his prison term was reduced to serving six to nine-and-a-half years. He was released from Attica prison in 1968 after serving five years.

Upon his release, his career in crime really took off. As noted by Charley Rosen, his definitive biographer,

> In his time, Jack Molinas was a world class athlete, a lawyer and a master of the stock market, but he was also a big time gambler and fixer in league with the Mafia, a double and triple crosser, a jailbird, a pornographer, a loan shark, and quite probably a murderer.[16]

Once he was out of prison, Molinas escalated his involvement in illegal schemes. He got connected to organized crime in Los Angeles and carved out a stake in transporting pornographic films and loan sharking, and he built up considerable debt to the wrong groups of people. It is likely that his overarching hubris made him oblivious to the consequences of alienating powerful figures who could do him harm. Molinas had serious lacunae when it came to understanding the consequences of his actions. He tried to construct the world according to Molinas, which at times led him to function in a cocoon. By playing hardball with mobsters, he was flirting with disaster. Ultimately, in what was widely believed to be Mafia orchestrated, Molinas was murdered, gangland style, at his home on August 4, 1975. Because of his sleazy reputation in the community, the police were glad to be rid of him and made little effort to solve his murder. Three years later, the hit man, Eugene Conner, a thirty-one-year-old truck thief, was convicted and given a life sentence. Conner had been turned in by his vindictive brother, who allegedly discovered that Eugene was sleeping with his wife.

DENNY MCLAIN: HUMILIATION SEEKER

Denny McLain stands out as the quintessentially tragic sports hero—one who achieved magnificent success on the ballfield and plummeted to the depths of corruption in his off-the-field activities. In 1968, at age twenty-four, he ruled the baseball world. He became a thirty-one-game winner while playing for the Detroit Tigers. In the twenty-first century, when pitchers are coddled and stringently held to a limited pitch count, it is unlikely that anyone will ever approach this exalted feat again. He easily won the MVP award for that year and the Cy Young Award in 1968 and 1969, and he was anointed as the premier hurler of his time.

To understand McLain's downfall, several psychological questions need to be understood: How could someone so supremely talented and successful throw it all away? What were the inner demons that orchestrated McLain's transition from hero to bum? What motivated him to participate in illegal schemes that culminated in not one but two lengthy prison terms?

Things began to unravel for McLain in 1970, when a *Sports Illustrated* article revealed that he had had connections with bookmakers during the 1967 season. He was summoned to a meeting with baseball Commissioner Bowie Kuhn, in which he acknowledged his involvement in a bookmaking operation and associating with mobsters. Under pressure to protect the integrity of the game, Kuhn responded by invoking the seldom-used personal conduct clause and suspending McLain for half of the 1970 season due to

Admissions related to his involvement in purported bookmaking activities in 1967, and his associations (i.e., mobsters) at that time. . . . McLain's association with gamblers was contrary to his obligation as a professional baseball player to conform to the standards of personal conduct, and it is my judgment that his conduct was not in the best interests of baseball.[17]

Kuhn was a newly appointed commissioner, and he seized the opportunity to establish his authority in safeguarding the integrity of the game and creating his legacy as a tough commissioner who could stand up and make unpopular but necessary decisions. If McLain needed to engage a new edition of his disciplinarian father, he found his match. To Kuhn's credit, he cracked the whip while McLain was at the pinnacle of his career. In contrast to the controversial suspensions of Leo Durocher and Pete Rose, who were in managerial positions by the time they were sanctioned, Kuhn took action against the best pitcher in baseball at that time. By suspending McLain for only half a season (in contrast to the harsher punishments levied against Durocher and Rose), however, Kuhn's edict was somewhat of a cop out. He mollified the hard-liners who believed that a sterner penalty needed to be enforced, and appeased the apologists who promoted a more lenient and forgiving reaction.

Early in his major league career, Denny McLain acquired a distorted self-image, fueled by fan adulation and pumped up by the media, and characterized by arrogance, grandiosity, and a powerful sense of entitlement. This syndrome is prevalent among sports heroes and often propels them toward self-destructive off-the-field lapses in judgment and serious consequences. McLain retrospectively mused,

> I learned long ago that when you have a highly sought talent, you can write your own ticket. I was a damned good pitcher, and I knew it. Unless I became intolerable, teams weren't going to discipline me much for breaking a few rules. . . . I blame sports writers in part for giving me the big head. Ever since I was a teenager newspapers have run stories about how great a pitcher I was. That was nice, but the problem was that I started to believe what I read. And the more they wrote, the more I believed it. My ego grew to a proportion that was out of whack with reality.[18]

With his "do you know who I am" and "I can write my own ticket" attitude, McLain ignored the fact that any perceived involvement in gambling was then and always has been the bete noir in professional sports. He admitted that, in 1967, as a participant in a bookmaking ring, he did call-in bets from the press lounge of the Tigers training camp within hearing range of sports writers (these bets were later recounted to the Tigers management and the press). This was self-destructive arrogance at its finest.

True to form, McLain felt unfairly treated and betrayed by the commissioner's ruling. Kuhn had invited him in to discuss the rumors and allegations that were circulating; Denny trusted him and disclosed his transgressions candidly; and then Kuhn used these admissions to suspend him. McLain could not believe that he would be brought down from the pedestal. After all, he stated, "Gambling is part of the baseball culture. We gambled at cards every day on the road. It just doesn't add up to suspend me for half a season."[19]

McLain was unable to see his part in the provocation. He could only focus on the injustice of it all. Essentially he was repeating a central pattern of his early background in which he was in the familiar position of feeling that his father was irrationally overreacting with a harsh punishment to a perceived offense by his son. From a psychological perspective, it is likely that in admitting his guilt to Kuhn, McLain's underlying and unconscious wish was to be treated with leniency by a forgiving and benevolent father figure.

The outstanding dynamic in McLain's early family constellation was his relationship with an abusive, impulsive, and unpredictable father. He never knew when to expect an explosive tirade or a beating at the hands of his alcoholic father. Tom McLain was a 6'3" 250-pound authority figure with a penchant for drinking. When he was drunk, as was often the case, he would erupt violently, and verbally and physically abuse his sons for minor or misperceived transgressions. McLain's early memories revolve around the terrifying presence and rage of his father, and "the more he had to drink, the worse the beating would be."[20] Given an atmosphere in which he could get whipped at a moment's notice, McLain was never able to internalize a feeling of a safe environment. His sense of danger and vulnerability was compounded by the role of his mother, who was unprotective and even an instigator in stirring up her husband's wrath and brutal outbursts toward McLain. In healthy two-parent families, when one parent irrationally steps over the line, the other parent often softens the impact by trying to protect the child from excessive abuse and humiliation. McLain experienced his mother as indifferent and neglectful, and as "incapable of consoling me or even giving me a hug on a bad day."[21] As a result, he harbored a life-long animosity and resentment toward her. Without appropriate models available, McLain was limited in his ability to develop relationships in which he could be aware of the needs and feelings of others. Instead, his early family experiences programmed him for one-sided involvements; and this put him at risk for repeating the abusive patterns he experienced with his dad.

McLain never had the opportunity to effectively rebel against his father and to separate himself from the overarching authoritarian yoke of dictatorial rules and regulations. This might have occurred as a developmental milestone during a stormy adolescence, but Tom McLain died suddenly when Denny was fifteen. Under these abrupt circumstances, the pendulum swung ferociously to the other extreme. As noted by McLain, "Without Tom McLain to fear, I stopped worrying about consequences."[22] Thus, with no one to control him and make him accountable for his actions, he could freely exhale and do whatever he wanted to do; but a part of him remained attracted to seeking out situations in which he could provoke harsh punishments for his transgressions. In this way, he could preserve and recapture the essence of his attachment to his father. In effect, his later pattern of acting out, and breaking the rules of society in a repeated fashion, was a reaction to his abusive father, who did not tolerate the breaking of his dictatorial rules. McLain needed to flirt with testing the limits to see what rules could be violated and what he could get away with. By getting caught and given punishments, he inadvertently was recreating the early relationship he had with his powerful father.

During his glory years with the Tigers, McLain's teammate Mickey Lolich observed, "Denny never wanted to go along with the program. He always seemed to be challenging management, flaunting it, seeing what he could get away with."[23] Lolich's depiction suggests that, by extension, McLain was enacting what he would have wanted to do with his tyrannical father. He was deprived of this right of passage, however, by his father's death during his early adolescence. He later went from having to buckle under the pressure of too many restrictions, to forming an inflated self-image bent on a disregard for society's standards. This disregard was reinforced by fan adulation and other privileges that accompanied his success on the ballfield.

In addition to his suspension for his admitted involvement in a bookmaking operation, McLain was suspended twice more in 1970: once for dousing a reporter with a bucket of water and once for allegedly carrying a gun on a plane. In classic form in which he disowned his provocative and rebellious behavior, he never acknowledged his part in bringing about these suspensions, and essentially, he felt victimized and persecuted. These punishments would turn out to be small potatoes compared with his later infractions.

Following his reinstatement for the second half of the 1970 season, McLain was an ineffective shadow of the dominating pitcher he had been; and by 1972, he was out of baseball at the age of twenty-eight.

After leaving baseball, he floundered and was susceptible to the pull of the self-destructive and grandiose components of his personality. He got involved with marginal underworld characters and mobsters who specialized in a series of shady illegal operations. He was flirting with disaster and, in 1985, the roof caved in on McLain when he was convicted of racketeering (the illegal collection of money from bookmaking), loan sharking, extortion, and cocaine possession with the intent to distribute. In portraying himself as an innocent, and a victim of the legal system, he denied all charges except bookmaking. He was given a harsh sentence of twenty-three years in prison, but he served only two and a half years because his legal appeal based on procedural misdeeds at the trial were upheld. A retrial was ordered, and he subsequently walked away with a suspended sentence of twelve years.

At this juncture, McLain could have counted his blessings and taken this as a valuable learning experience, but he instead turned down the volume on reality and continued to put himself at risk by engaging in criminal activity. Having spent two and a half years in jail was an insufficient deterrent for him to steer clear of further illegal transgressions. It seems likely that he was unconsciously seeking a repetition of the humiliating treatment he received at the hands of his overbearing father.

McLain found a way to become a co-owner of a meat-packing company, a business that he knew nothing about. This was a failing company, and under the sway of his grandiose self-image, he viewed it as a challenge to turn this company around and create a bonanza. As a testimony to his pervasive need to distort reality in accordance with a misguided belief system, he later noted that, "I'd gone to jail (previously) by conveniently ignoring the obvious but this was a level of truth avoidance new even to me. I was still convinced I was going to make the impossible work."[24] Not surprising, for someone destined to court disaster and punishment, this investment became yet another episode in self-destructiveness.

In 1994, after taking over the Peet Packing company with a partner, McLain assumed a trustee role over a $14 million pension plan, and summarily allowed more than $3 million to be illegally borrowed from the assets of the plan. When this scheme was exposed, he portrayed himself as the innocent and naïve victim of unscrupulous confederates. Once again he assumed the identity of "poor me"; he did not own or acknowledge his role or participation in what evolved as a criminal action. With the law breathing down his neck, he was in the familiar territory of disavowing culpability in bringing about the ensuing punishment. The defense mechanisms of externalization, projection, avoidance, and disavowal became his weapons. Years later, he was able to acknowledge, "I'd grown up taking the attitude that nothing was my fault and I was always the one falsely accused."[25] In 1996, McLain was convicted and sentenced to eight years in prison for embezzlement.

As a two-time convict, McLain had succeeded in ruining his marriage and his life, and fulfilling his unconscious need to be severely punished and humiliated by unsympathetic authority figures. Fortunately, while he was in prison, he sought out professional help and gradually was able to grasp the overdetermined nature of his desire to cross the boundaries of society's rules and regulations. With retrospective insight, McLain noted the dynamics of the repetitive pattern of his acting out and being punished:

> When you get punished repeatedly as a youngster, you get used to it, expect it, and in a masochistic way, create it. My Dad had been dead for 10 years, but I kept on symbolically getting the belt even though it was no longer Tom McLain wielding it . . . my father, mother, and the nuns at school had convinced me that I deserved to be punished, and it looked like I'd lived my life to affirm their assessment. In my house, every error or mistake in judgment

drew harsh punishment. Now, even as an adult, I was constantly putting myself at risk and then wondering why everybody wanted to beat me.[26]

This insight shows how deeply embedded such a pattern from early childhood familial relationships can become and be perpetuated throughout the life cycle. A major part of McLain identified with the physical and psychological abuse he received in childhood, and he was drawn like a moth to a flame, to repeat these interactive patterns in his adult life. Another part of him was driven to push the envelope in the hope of obtaining a more benevolent response, and thereby symbolically converting his dad to a more loving and accepting figure.

Many of our sports heroes whose abusive behavior toward others—for example, domestic violence or sexual abuse—gets them into trouble are playing out such inherent patterns toward others or finding ways to be mistreated. These are deeply embedded relational interactions that can continue for generations, unless therapeutic intervention can uncover, understand, and change these behaviors. The value of psychotherapy is that with the self-awareness and insight that comes with treatment, an individual can acquire a greater degree of choice over their behavioral pathways, rather than automatically yielding to the repetition of self-defeating ways of being.

In contrast to Pete Rose, Denny McLain, in his autobiography, *I Told You I Wasn't Perfect*, does convey a degree of contrition for his corrupt activities and the impact it had on those around him.

ROSCOE TANNER: THE WORLD ACCORDING TO ROSCOE

The postcareer meltdown of tennis star Roscoe Tanner is one of the most enigmatic downfalls of a sports hero. Tanner was not a hedonistic athlete whose privileged background and early fame produced a personality that was driven by a heavy dimension of self-centeredness. In this way, he was different from the multitude of athletes who are catered to from a young age and given the world on a string by throngs of hero-worshipers. Throughout his career, he stayed clear of trouble; only later did he pursue a path characterized by the world according to Roscoe, in which narcissism prevailed, and he functioned in a bubble of magical thinking and an attitude that ignored reality. It is the pathological magnitude of his readiness to ignore, override, and run away from reality that pushes Tanner over the border from mental health to mental illness.

In many situations, a star athlete becomes self-destructive or destructive toward others after his career in sports has ended, but Tanner carries the transition from golden boy to rogue to an extreme. When you no longer have stardom to rely upon, with agents and handlers monitoring your access to the mainstream public and reminding you about protecting your image, it can become easier to lapse into immoral behavior, and account-ability becomes a blurred requirement.

Roscoe Tanner is best known as the tennis player with the cannonball serve, which was once clocked at 153 miles per hour, who during a fifteen-year professional career won eleven singles titles, and achieved some noto-riety as a Wimbledon finalist against Bjorn Borg in 1979. Reaching that level of athletic prominence does not come only from natural talent. It requires a serious work ethic, constant training without shortcuts, and a willingness to sacrifice the irresponsible joys of youth for the fantasy of a successful future as a sports figure. Tanner accepted the trade-off and devoted himself to his career. For more than a decade, the handsome and personable Roscoe Tanner was a darling of the tennis world.

On the surface, Tanner's childhood was essentially normal and nontrau-matic. He was the youngest of three children in a traditional Southern well-to-do but emotionally distant family. His father, a successful Tennes-see attorney, related to Roscoe as an extension of himself and planned a life for his son to follow in the footsteps of his own social climbing, coun-try club membership, and flourishing law practice. Tanner's teenage memo-ries are of a father who was critical and dissected his tennis matches ad nauseam, but he never openly rebelled during his adolescent years. It is striking that his later misadventures were like a belated adolescent acting out—behavior in which Tanner viewed himself as invulnerable and invin-cible and lived in his own self-centered world, thinking only about his own needs and satisfactions.

This provides a classic example of how fame infused Tanner with a distorted view of himself and an outrageous sense of self-importance. After he retired from the pro tour in 1984, Tanner's downward spiral began. Together with his second wife, he embraced a cocaine-reliant lifestyle, which clouded his judgment and led him to be irresponsible in his business enterprises. He sought solace in female companionship and engaged in scores of one-night stands, a pattern that began during his heyday on the pro tour. As a result of one such tryst, Tanner got a woman from an escort service pregnant, and in turn the woman tried to extort $500,000 from him. Tanner stonewalled, did not show up in court when she filed a judg-ment against him, and later gambled that a DNA test would exonerate him. That move backfired when the results came back with a 99.4 percent certainty that he was the father. When his calculated gamble failed, Tanner had no choice but to agree to the $500,000 settlement, but he failed to make good on the payment. Against all logic, he was operating on the fantasy that if he did not want the results of the paternity test to be true, then it would not be. Tanner was relying on magical thinking, a primitive defense mechanism, which along with denial and avoidance became his mainstays.

In keeping with his out-of-touch approach to reality (if I do not deal with it, it will go away), Tanner not only neglected to make the agreed-upon child support payments, but also ignored court summonses to appear in Somerset, New Jersey. Roscoe had to know that failing to appear in court in a child support allegation is a serious evasion, but, like a child in denial, he simply ignored reality. Predictably, a warrant for his arrest was issued, and he was picked up in the midst of a senior tennis tournament. His only out was to declare personal bankruptcy, and a lien was placed on his house, which was sold in foreclosure, and $119,000 was awarded to the child's mother.

Tanner learned little from this episode. He continued to live in a bubble of unreality. In his next debacle, Tanner purchased a yacht with a $35,000 check that bounced, on the wishful-thinking expectation that a $50,000 consulting fee from developers would be forthcoming for lending his name to a Roscoe Tanner tennis villages project. Apparently, Tanner did not take seriously the risks associated with child support or reneging on the boat purchase payment. When the boat broker hounded him for payments, Tanner kept stalling and hoping that a deal would materialize and get him out of trouble.

He dissociated from reality, and relying on denial and avoidance, he continued to live in the fantasy world that somehow the problem would disappear. He clung to the antiquated belief that he was special, the world was his oyster, and everything would work out. He was unprepared to face the music for his illegal activities, and, using poor judgment, he dealt with the conflict by running away to live in Germany.

By 2003, his trail of antisocial behavior included grand theft, passing bad checks, forgery, and failure to pay child support. Unable to face the implications of the legal jams he had crafted, he could cope only by going on the lamb to a foreign country. He was tracked down by the German authorities, who responded to an international warrant for his arrest and incarcerated him in prison for six weeks as an interim step toward extradition to the United States. Once again, magical thinking led him to believe that he could escape from his legal problems without consequences and start a new leaf. When he was sent to jail in Germany, he lamented,

I thought I could run away from my problems, but I could not hide . . . if only I had faced up to my problems before Margaret [his wife] and I left Florida. But I had ignored the creditor's demands and court injunctions against me, hoping my financial difficulties would go away. Instead they multiplied and built to a critical mass. The long arm of the law collared me in Europe.[27]

These statements reveal an absurd degree of naivete and absence of emotional intelligence, and reflect the magnitude of how far out of touch with reality Roscoe had traveled.

He was extradited to Florida where he spent several months in jail until his court date in 2004. At that time, he acted as his own attorney in the grand theft allegation, and he persuaded the judge to extend a lenient ruling in which he was sentenced only to ten years probation and an agreement to a restitution plan to pay $102,000 to his debtors.

At this stage of his life, Tanner had transitioned from former golden boy and revered tennis star to a disingenuous scoundrel who talked the talk but did not walk the walk. He indulged his dark side in unscrupulous behavior that was destructive to himself and others, and he bent reality and utilized primitive defense mechanisms to cushion himself from facing his criminal actions.

It would be logical to think that someone subjected to the daily humiliations of prison life, as described poignantly by Tanner in his autobiography, would be determined, upon his release, never to allow this to happen again. But Tanner was not one to learn from experience. He failed to make the restitution payments required, and, as a result, in 2006, he was sentenced to two years in a Florida prison for violating probation.

One wonders why Roscoe was not given financial assistance by his wealthy father or other relatives and prominent friends. It is noteworthy that although his father was a well-to-do attorney, Roscoe was represented by public defenders in his legal proceedings in jails in Germany and New Jersey. It seems that Tanner Sr. distanced himself from his disappointing and disgraced son. Roscoe, on his part, appeased his guilt for sullying the Tanner name and attempted to retain some semblance of pride by not asking for help to pay his debts. This would have kept him out of the horrors of prison life. On some emotional level, it is likely that Roscoe resented his father for not becoming his advocate.

It could be speculated that, for Tanner, failing in life and destroying himself and others became a pathological way of expressing his repressed rage at his father's terms of conditional love, and signaled a way of conducting his life on his terms despite the enormous cost.

Mental health experts would debate whether Tanner's repeated self-defeating actions were driven by his masochism or his narcissism. Were these episodes generated by a need to suffer and be humiliated, or by an unrealistic picture of himself in negotiating his world? It seems most likely that his core problem was the inability to forge an adequate postretirement adjustment in which the reality was that he could no longer live the world according to Tanner.

He operated with a mask of charisma and charm, but his underlying feelings of vulnerability and disaster emerge in a dream he reveals in his autobiography. "I dreamt about [daughters] Tamara and Anne. They were taking a bath when they called for me. I rushed in, and they were on the bottom of the bathtub, looking as though they were holding their breath. I tried to get them to surface, but I couldn't."[28]

This is a classic anxiety dream that reflects his impotence in saving his daughters from disaster. Because characters and actions in dreams generally are about the dreamer, it might be inferred that he is projecting his desperate plight, a struggle for survival, onto his daughters, and he unconsciously identifies with the need to be rescued by a family member. All indications suggest that he is disconnected completely from these feelings on a conscious level.

THE ROLE OF INDUCED NARCISSISM

When players cross the line into self-destructive misconduct in their off-the-field activities, we often assume that it is simply the dark side of their personality that drives them in that direction. In many situations, however, a more complex set of factors are operating, and we sometimes fail to recognize the systemic effect that influences athletes to believe that they can operate in the world on their own terms without consideration for the acceptable standards of society.

The plunge of Rose, Schlichter, Molinas, McLain, and Tanner from the heights of superheroism to the depths of disgraced star occurred as a result of the interaction of their dispositional tendencies to cross the line, along with a cultural system that conditions them from an early age to believe that they can do whatever they want without regard for the consequences. This acquired and distorted self-image, in which they function as if they are larger than life, becomes so deeply embedded that when their transgressions are exposed, they react as though they have been unfairly victimized.

Thus, athletes and other celebrities are programmed to become narcissistic as a result of the enormous adulation and special treatment that they receive. A central characteristic in the definition of narcissism is an inflated sense of self, which in the athlete is systematically induced. If you are consistently treated as someone special, you begin to think of yourself in those terms. Pete Rose referred to himself as the best ambassador that baseball has (a national treasure); Art Schlichter was viewed as King Arthur; and Jayson Williams, a professional basketball hero who was accused of murder, described himself as "the king of New Jersey." Thus, the system in which famous athletes are celebrated is pivotal in proliferating sports stars who are narcissistic.

Pete Rose, Art Schlichter, Jack Molinas, Denny McLain, and Roscoe Tanner, the disgraced athletes depicted in this chapter, were all victims of induced narcissism, which fed their inclination toward crossing the line into off-the-field corrupt behavior. They thought they were larger than life and tuned out any concern about accountability and penalties that might come their way for their transgressions. Another perception common to this group is that they all felt that they were mistreated, or too harshly punished for their misdeeds. They tended to downplay the seriousness of their corrupt behavior, and they externalized responsibility for the decisions that led them to cross the line. Each of these athletes suffered the ultimate comeuppance of having to serve time in prison. The central similarity among these athletes is their inflated sense of self—that is, induced narcissism, which triggered them to violate the rules and standards of society or their sports leagues. Each of these sports stars was responsible, in different ways, for damaging or inflicting wounds on other people, as well as being self-destructive.

CHAPTER THREE

Recent Gambling Scandals

Historically, sports gambling scandals primarily involved players who were induced to fix games by professional gamblers or their organizational associates. The lawmakers pursued the fixers as targets of interest, and the players who succumbed were generally treated lightly by the legal system. In the infamous Black Sox scandal in which eight players on the Chicago White Sox were implicated in throwing the 1919 World Series, the athletes were exonerated in a trial, but the baseball commissioner, charting a new hands-on approach, nevertheless imposed a lifetime expulsion against the players. Since that time, it has been the province of each sport to police itself when gambling problems emerge.

The college basketball scandals of 1951 and 1961 highlighted the prevalence of game fixing in that era, and exposed scores of young athletes who accepted bribes to shave points. Most of these players were enticed by the easy money offered to them by corrupt gamblers, and they were responsive to the group contagion effect, which influenced them to cross a line that they suspected many of their peers already were crossing. The budding careers of these talented sports stars were derailed in the process, and the shame of being exposed and humiliated in these scandals would ruin their promising future lives.

The landscape has changed significantly in recent times, with respect to athletes and gambling scandals. The exorbitant salaries garnered by professional athletes in the major sports leagues in itself serves as a huge deterrent for active players to risk enmeshment in gambling activities. Therefore, in the early twenty-first century, it is no longer predominantly the players—except in sports like tennis and golf, for which there are no contracts and income is directly related to performance (that is, victories) in a succession of tournaments—who are at the center of sports gambling scandals. Nevertheless, the sports world continues to be besieged by new episodes, but not only from active players. Instead, these scandals focus on retired players, coaches, and referees. Such gambling scandals, with their vicarious turn-on for the public, always attract the biggest headlines. Of late, the major sports gambling scandals have occurred in hockey, tennis, and professional basketball.

THE NBA REFEREE GAMBLING SCANDAL

The world of professional basketball was rocked in July 2007 when an explosive breaking news story indicated that Tim Donaghy, a tenured and high-tier referee, was under federal investigation for betting on NBA games in which he refereed during the 2005–2006 and 2006–2007 seasons, and for making officiating calls that altered the point spread in numerous games. After betting on games for two years, which was in flagrant violation of the NBA's code of conduct, he allegedly ramped up his involvement by colluding with organized crime figures by using inside information to predict winners and losers. According to the FBI affidavit, Donaghy received $2,000 to $5,000 for making correct picks, which netted him at least $30,000.

Ever since Jack Molinas's betting scandal in the early days of the league a half century ago, the NBA has been on guard about the danger of corrupt influences. Before each season, it disseminates a booklet to all players and league personnel called "Bad Bets: Understanding the NBA's Anti-Gambling Rules," which delineates the prohibition against any gambling activity by referees other than off-season visits to the racetrack.

Although he earned more than $200,000 per year as an NBA referee, Donaghy, allegedly under the sway of gambling indebtedness, envisioned greener pastures and chose the path of corruption. Several earlier signs indicated that Donaghy was capable of breaking rules, crossing boundaries, and marching to the beat of his own drummer, which conflicts with the circumspect image sports officials are expected to demonstrate.

In 2005, the NBA had pursued an investigation of Donaghy amid accusations about his gambling at an Atlantic City casino, a violation of the league rules governing referees' behavior; however, it was unable to substantiate these allegations. Rather than serving as a warning signal and deterrent from other infractions, the toothless probe apparently made Donaghy more brazen and emboldened.

Earlier hints that Donaghy might operate as a loose cannon occurred in 2000 when he engaged in an altercation with his postal carrier and was charged with disorderly conduct and harassment. In 2005, he was embroiled in a lawsuit with his neighbors who accused him of stalking, and more seriously aggressive actions of setting fire to their lawn mower and driving their golf cart into a ravine. Although Donaghy contested that he was the victim of his neighbors' harassment, these incidents portray a man who has a short fuse, is ready to fight fire with fire, and is not level-headed and may not use good judgment in dealing with conflict or following rules. Within the game, Donaghy has had more than his share of altercations. As a referee, three other incidents reflected his aggressive and impulsive character. There were reports about a bloody fistfight in a hotel involving Donaghy and Joey Crawford, another referee. This incident, coupled with the Atlantic City casino investigation, should have suggested to the league's executives that Donaghy might be contentious, but the NBA turned a blind eye to these events and seemed to go out of its way to keep Donaghy employed in the refereeing business.

Donaghy had a serious run-in with Rasheed Wallace, the Portland Trailblazers star, who physically threatened the referee after a game in 2003. Wallace, known as one of the NBA's bad boys, was perceived to be the culprit in that incident, and the league suspended him for seven games and supported Donaghy. In 2005, Doc Rivers, the Boston Celtics coach, filed a complaint with the league that Donaghy's officiating was biased against him, but the matter was not taken seriously. As a veteran referee, Donaghy was in a position of authority and was accountable to the league, but he never seemed to get a direct message that his behavior was questionable. Instead, he was consistently backed when embroiled in controversy and was foolishly provided with a false sense of security. The NBA was remiss in not pursuing a thorough investigation into Donaghy's pattern of involvement in controversial episodes and confronting him more directly with warnings or the threat of probation.

This was a scandal that the NBA could ill afford to endure in the midst of its preexisting image problems. Of all the major professional sports, basketball is the most readily susceptible to corruption. If a referee is inclined to do business with organized crime figures, several approaches are available that could violate the integrity of the game. One favorite method, which appealed to Donaghy, was to pass along to his gambling associates confidential information about players' injuries and general health. He also disclosed the referee assignments for various games and revealed the implications of personal likes and dislikes toward certain players or coaches, which could influence the direction of how the referees controlled the game. This level of information could be invaluable to gamblers who then adjust their betting patterns accordingly. An even more lethal method for tainting a game is for a referee to increase the number of fouls called during a game, even if this is done to both teams equally, to affect the total points scored. Informed gamblers then benefit by placing large bets on the over/under line, counting on the probability that game scores would exceed the over mark. In fact, during the last two seasons of Donaghy's reign, his games went above the over/under line 57 percent of the time. This statistic casts considerable suspicion on Donaghy, especially because his record indicated that in the period between 2003 and 2005 his games went over the line in total points only 44 percent of the time.

In August 2007, in the face of the evidences amassed in the probe, Donaghy pleaded guilty to two felonies for betting on games that he refereed and for providing inside information to gamblers. In legal terms, he admitted his guilt in conspiring to engage in wire fraud and transmitting wagering information across state lines. The government's case did not accuse him of point shaving or game fixing, a sports bribery charge, because it would have been more difficult to prove that his actions changed the outcome of a game. Nevertheless, he faced up to twenty-five years in prison and up to $500,000 in fines for the charges to which he pleaded guilty.

In an effort to reduce his sentence, Donaghy disclosed to the court that his misdeeds were driven by a gambling addiction for which he was now being treated, and in a pitch for sympathy, he acknowledged that he was currently taking antianxiety and antidepressant medications. According to ESPN, he offered to cooperate with the authorities by naming twenty other officials who had violated the NBA prohibitions on gambling. The league rules prohibiting referees from indulging in any form of gambling, except visits to the racetrack during the off season, is a small sacrifice to make for those who earn upward of $200,000 in their coveted positions.

In light of Donaghy's claim that he was only one of many referees who gambled, the NBA conducted an internal review that revealed that more than 50 percent of the league's referees had committed gambling transgressions, such as playing blackjack at casinos and betting in golf games. Although none of these officials were purported to have gambled on sports events, these findings suggest that the antigambling rules were not taken seriously and were treated by the referees as optional. This further tarnished the image of the NBA.

Reluctant to intensify a new layer of scandal by disciplining a majority of the officials, Commissioner David Stern conceded that the existing rules were excessively harsh and unrealistic; he stated a plan to draft new policies that gave referees more latitude in their off-season gambling activities. This was a colossal capitulation and sellout by Stern, who previously labeled Tim Donaghy "a rogue, isolated criminal,"[1] and described the scandal as "the most serious situation and worst situation that I have ever experienced . . . as a commissioner of the NBA."[2] By pandering to the referees instead of solidifying appropriate and necessary antigambling prohibitions, Stern was risking that at some future time other referees could incur substantial gambling indebtedness and thereby become vulnerable to game-fixing involvements at the behest of organized crime figures. In a transparent public relations gesture, Stern pledged to institute more extensive background checks on the NBA cohort of referees. Why this had not been in place as standard procedure all along is inexplicable and makes the commissioner look ineffective.

Before Donaghy's sentencing, the NBA filed a claim seeking $1.4 million in restitution for the cost of its internal probe into the gambling activities of their roster of referees, for their review of games that Tim Donaghy refereed, and for a portion of his salary. At about the same time, Donaghy's lawyer petitioned the court for leniency based on a plea of compassion for his pathological gambling addiction, over which he supposedly had no control. It was unlikely that this request would be given much weight, because the judicial system generally does not excuse criminal acts because of psychological problems (except in certain murder cases in which the accused has been diagnosed as psychotic and unable to properly defend himself at trial).

The sentencing guidelines for Tim Donaghy were in the range of twenty-seven to thirty-three months, and his lawyer argued for a reduced sentence based on his cooperation, which led to the convictions of two co-defendants, and on the additional information he provided about the prevalence of misconduct by the league officials and referees. The government, however, maintained that many of Donaghy's allegations were unsubstantiated. The guilty pleas of Donaghy's co-defendants, James Battista and Thomas Martino, were processed first, and they received prison sentences of fifteen months and twelve months, respectively. They had not cooperated in providing information to the authorities, and their terms were at the high end of the federal guidelines. On July 20, 2008, Tim Donaghy was sentenced to fifteen months, which was on the lenient side of the guidelines, with Judge Carol Amon indicating that he should benefit from having provided substantial cooperation in the government's investigation.

One unfortunate message to be drawn from the outcome in this scandal is that if you engage in illegal activities and are caught, you can lighten your penalty by implicating other offenders.

After the Donaghy case was concluded, the NBA announced that it was further pursuing its in-house investigation and would be examining the league's antigambling policies and officiating program. They asked for Donaghy's participation in the probe, but Donaghy predictably declined the invitation. Given how Commissioner Stern had eviscerated Donaghy as a traitorous rogue referee when the bombshell erupted a year earlier, and considering the league's demand for $1.4 million in restitution, it would be ludicrous to expect that Donaghy would now cooperate with an investigation of other referees' wrongdoings. More likely, the invitation was a ploy on the part of the NBA to shift the focus in the court of public opinion away from issues related to referee misconduct, and instead shine the spotlight on Donaghy as an uncooperative villain. The NBA internal investigation concluded that despite Donaghy's efforts to implicate other officials, he was the only referee involved in gambling misconduct, including betting on games, providing inside information on players' injuries to gamblers, attempting to manipulate or alter the outcome of games, and being paid to predict winners.

In an interesting sidenote, FoxNews.com cast the shadow of suspicion on NBA referee Scott Foster, who was a close friend of Donaghy's. It reported that Foster had received 134 cell phone calls from Donaghy during the period encompassing his illegal violations, and the implication was that he was somehow in on the scheme. This report triggered an inquiry by the NBA as well as the FBI, and both agencies cleared Foster of any wrongdoing. In a postmortem interview with the media, Foster highlighted the role of selective journalism in this matter. He pointed out that when the story broke, his name and face were posted next to Donaghy's on ESPN and all over the Internet, and, in contrast, when he was cleared, the story received merely one line of coverage. In commenting on the Tim Donaghy scandal, former MLB commissioner Fay Vincent warned Stern and other commissioners about the urgency to strengthen the deterrents against gambling in their sports. Vincent argued, "It's naïve not to recognize the threat to corrupt sports through gambling and naïve not to think gamblers aren't looking for an advantage. They're there, they have a lot of money, and in the right circumstances, they use it on vulnerable people."[3]

It is generally believed that the Tim Donaghy scandal was the first of its kind in professional basketball. It is seldom remembered that in 1951, during the fledgling era of the NBA, referee Sol Levy was apprehended for conspiring with organized crime figures to fix six games. Levy's role was to ensure that certain designated players would foul out early in the games, for which he received $400 to $500 per game.

THE NATIONAL HOCKEY LEAGUE GAMBLING SCANDAL

Rick Tocchet

In February 2006, while the National Hockey League (NHL) was slowly recovering from a season-long labor strike in the previous year, a gambling scandal erupted. Rick Tocchet, assistant coach of the Phoenix Coyotes, under Wayne Gretzky, was the central figure in this scandal. After a four-month investigation, the New Jersey police accused Tocchet and two associates of running a highly organized sports betting system for the past five years. The police labeled their probe "Operation Slapshot" and revealed that, in a forty-day period culminating in wagers placed on the 2006 Super Bowl, the group had handled one thousand wagers amounting to more than $1.7 million on professional and collegiate sporting events. It was alleged that this highly lucrative operation had ties to the Bruno-Scarfo crime family. The assertion that up to a dozen present and past NHL players were betting clients sent alarm ripples throughout the league's administration. Tocchet, and his primary co-conspirator, James Harney, were charged with promoting money laundering, gambling, and conspiracy.

When the New Jersey state police announced the findings of its under-cover investigation, the media, especially in Canada, where hockey is regarded as the national pastime, played it up as a major sports gambling scandal, which threatened the integrity and survival of the NHL. The fact that Tocchet was a highly respected figure in the world of hockey masked the dark side of his personality, which was receptive to corrupt activity. After an outstanding eighteen-year All-Star career as a player, Tocchet moved into the coaching ranks as an assistant to his long-time friend Wayne Gretzky. As managing partner and coach of the Coyotes, the leg-endary Gretzky, affectionately known as The Great One, was grooming Tocchet as his head coach replacement. As a forty-one-year-old retired athlete, Rick Tocchet did not struggle with the transition issues as much as many other sports heroes. He could remain in the game he loved with a rosy future ahead of him; to be the handpicked coaching heir to The Great One was indeed a privilege. So what prompted him to put himself at risk legally and professionally, as the alleged financier for this illegal betting ring, in which, according to the investigation, he accepted a large volume of sports wagers and funneled the winnings and losings to his co-conspirator, Harney, from Arizona to New Jersey. It appears that Tocchet, like many star athletes who are corrupted by fame and whose psyches are dominated by the belief that that they would not be held accountable for transgres-sions, had the capacity to convince himself that his central involvement in an illegal gambling operation was not a significant crime. Relying on the defense mechanisms of denial, rationalization, and compartmentaliza-tion, Tocchet defended his actions by proclaiming that there was no gam-bling on hockey games under his umbrella and that it was purely "a football thing," as if this made it okay.

It did not seem to cross his mind that his lucrative sideline could create a public relations disaster for the NHL. Concern over the public's percep-tion that his involvement in a gambling scandal could damage the reputa-tion of hockey as a sport with integrity was not on Tocchet's radar screen. His hubris and greed seriously interfered with his judgment and allowed him to become a major player in the gambling enterprise. Somehow, he rationalized that as long as he was just trafficking bets in other sports, but not hockey, his participation was harmless. The denial and compartmen-talization dimensions in his personality also made it possible for him to ignore the immoral behavior of Harney, who took bets on his cell phone while patrolling the New Jersey Turnpike.

Other NHL Gambling Scandals

Of the four major sports leagues, the NHL has been the least tainted by scandal. Sports historians must go back sixty years to discover that in 1948, two players, Dan Gallinger of the Boston Bruins and Billy Taylor of the New York Rangers, were given life suspensions for betting $50 on games. As a token gesture of forgiveness, they were both reinstated by the league in 1970, long after their athletic skills had waned.

More recently, Jaromir Jagr, a five-time NHL scoring champion, ran up a $500,000 debt to an Internet gambling company dating back to 1998. In 2003, when Jagr ignored owning up to his agreed-upon payments, the site's owner went public with the story. In an attempt to squelch additional negative publicity, Jagr quickly ponied up 20 percent of his balance, which was accepted as a final payment. Jagr had gambled primarily on football, and because the NHL did not prohibit betting on other sports, he was not disciplined by the league. In their shortsightedness, by not instituting stringent antigambling policies in the NHL, its administrators are indirectly inviting additional scandals.

Steve Budin, who accepted a lot of Jagr's betting action, authored a book in which he alleged that the star player was consumed by his gambling involvement. He wrote,

> Jagr was sometimes late taking the ice [for the New York Rangers] because he was busy placing $40,000 U.S. bets in the dressing room. . . . Jagr, who sometimes would win or lose as much as $250,000 a week, was a poor bettor who never made money over the course of a week.[4]

Budin estimates that between twenty and twenty-five current hockey players bet on sports. He notes that "they all had the kind of built-in competitive nature that led them into always doubling down in an attempt to get even, which is a bad betting strategy."[5]

Jeremy Roenick, an outstanding forward with the Philadelphia Flyers, paid more than $100,000 in 2004 to a sports consultant company that made millions by providing betting tips to its clients. Roenick's propensity for gambling was discovered in the course of an FBI probe of the company. The investigators found no evidence that he had placed bets on hockey. In a curious absence of oversight, in addition to allowing players to bet on sports, the NHL does not even forbid them from associating with gamblers. With such a laissez-faire attitude on the part of the league, Roenick brazenly admitted that he was a client of the sports consultant firm and that he had been betting on sports for many years. Roenick claimed that he stopped gambling when the Flyers reprimanded him with a stern warning after the 2004 revelations, but his name was one of the first to surface in the current Tocchet scandal. Roenick and Tocchet were teammates when they played with the Coyotes, and Roenick was believed to have placed $100,000 in bets with the gambling ring.

It was alleged in the New Jersey police investigation that from six to twelve current and former players had done business with Tocchet and Harney's ring, but the only other active player named by the authorities was Travis Green of the Boston Bruins.

When news of the Tocchet scandal broke, the Canadian media circle shifted into high gear with rumors and speculations about a wider domino effect that could target many other top names in the world of hockey. Their suspicions were fueled by the observations of gambling counselors who have worked with professional athletes. Athletes are purportedly prone to gamble on sports because of certain aspects of their personality, including "high levels of energy, unreasonable expectation, very competitive, [and] distorted optimism."[6] This media thirst was rewarded when the authorities identified Mike Barnett, the general manager of the Coyotes, as having placed a bet on the Super Bowl with the gambling ring. In response to the intense media hype, the NHL was obliged to conduct an internal investigation about gambling activity. It was determined that no players or other NHL personnel had bet on hockey games.

Wayne Gretzky

International interest in the scandal accelerated when Janet Jones, the actress and wife of the legendary hero Wayne Gretzky, was implicated as one of the clients of the gambling ring. Apparently, Jones had placed bets amounting to $500,000, including a $75,000 wager on the Super Bowl. Gretzky, affectionately known as The Great One, was universally perceived as the king of hockey, and any transgressions by those close to him threatened to smear his reputation as well as the image of the league. Janet Jones vehemently denied that she had placed any bets on her husband's behalf, and under intense media questioning, Gretzky portrayed himself as squeaky clean. In protecting her husband from involvement in this case, Jones claimed that Wayne only bet on an occasional horse race. Gretzky maintained that he only gambled in Las Vegas and never on sports teams, and he stated, "If I had made one bet, I would have quit the Coyotes. I would never embarrass the team, or the organization."[7] The Great One also claimed that he was unaware that his wife had placed bets with Tocchet's gambling ring. This assertion requires a significant suspension of belief, and it aroused considerable skepticism within the media. This view was succinctly put forth by Adrian Wojnarowski of *The Record*, who wrote,

> Reasonable people have a hard time believing that this could've gone on between Gretzky's wife and his most trusted assistant without his knowledge. He didn't have to be gambling in this ring to be an enabler of it. . . . As long as he's the managing partner of a franchise, a coach, he needs to explain why his wife was allegedly betting through his assistant coach.[8]

Gretzky's image was tarnished further when police wiretaps caught him in phone conversations with Tocchet in which they speculated that they need not worry. Because the gambling ring involved a state trooper, James

Harney, investigators would be reluctant to prosecute. They also speculated on ways Gretzky's wife could evade prosecution. Ultimately, no charges were filed against Janet Jones.

The Aftermath

After lengthy legal wrangling, Rick Tocchet pleaded guilty to charges of conspiracy to promote gambling. Although he could have received up to five years in prison, first-time offenders on these charges generally do not get jail time. Tocchet got off easy and was sentenced to only two years of probation for his role in the conspiracy network. In contrast, his co-conspirator, Harney, received a five-year prison sentence. When his probation period ended, Tocchet returned to his position with the Coyotes, and in a move that let bygones be bygones, he was selected as the interim coach of the Tampa Bay Lightning in 2008.

Rick Tocchet might have restored some degree of dignity had he had the courage and desire to make a statement along the following lines:

> I fully realize that what I did was wrong. In saying that my involvement in the gambling ring "was not hockey-related" and "was a football thing," I was foolishly trying to justify my actions and obfuscate the truth, which was that my greed and arrogance prompted me to participate in this illegal activity. I am also guilty of having betrayed my family, my friends, the Phoenix Coyotes and all other hockey players, and I am irreparably humbled by tarnishing the image of the National Hockey League and having caused a storm of negative publicity for the sport. I would like to volunteer my services to the league in being a part of their educational program so that other players could benefit from my unfortunate and misguided actions. My commitment is to alert other players to the perils of corruption that can attract sports celebrities.

The rumors and speculations surrounding the illegal betting ring created a media frenzy in which alleged gambling links to current and former players, game fixing, and mob ties were highlighted as chapters in what was presented as a salacious scandal. Ultimately, the investigation conducted by the police and the NHL revealed that there was no betting on hockey, there were no charges levied against Janet Jones or any players who placed bets with the ring, and there was no direct stain on the game. The allegations about mob ties and concerns about game fixing never materialized. The expectation that where there is smoke there will be fire did not evolve, and Operation Slapshot was put on ice. Nevertheless, it was a wake-up call for the NHL to repair its overly lax position on non-hockey-related gambling. Players who amass large betting debts are potential targets for arranging game-fixing activity. To protect the integrity of the league, it needs to institute antigambling regulations for its players and other personnel.

CORRUPTION IN TENNIS

Nikolay Davydenko

Sports gambling scandals, which touched basketball, football, and hockey in recent times, extended into the world of tennis in 2007. The bubble burst around a relatively obscure tournament match in Sopot, Poland, between Nikolay Davydenko, ranked fourth in the world, versus Martin Vassallo Arguello, ranked eighty-seventh. Betfair, a British online betting organization, revealed that it had received approximately $7 million worth of bets on the match, which was ten times the usual amount for a secondary tournament.

A large portion of the sum had been wagered on Arguello before the match. After Davydenko easily won the first set, an even larger amount came in for Arguello to pull an upset victory. Arguello won the second set, and then Davydenko abruptly retired in the third set, claiming that a sore toe forced him to withdraw. Because of the irregular pattern of the betting, Betfair assessed that something fishy was going on, and they promptly voided all bets on the match and notified the Association of Tennis Professionals (ATP) about their suspicions.

The ATP was caught off guard, and officials initiated an investigation into the matter. Speculation floated that Davydenko had collaborated with gamblers to fix the match. The ATP, looking for possible connections to organized crime, sought to review Davydenko's telephone records, but the Russian star and his defense team were uncooperative with this request. The always-outspoken John McEnroe demanded that the ATP get to the bottom of the situation and declared that it would be "insane" for Davydenko, ranked fourth in the world, to have risked fame and fortune to participate in such a scheme.

McEnroe's point is logical, so to make meaningful sense out of this episode, one can conclude that either Davydenko was not corrupted or, conversely, that he was persuaded to tank the match by threats of bodily harm to his family or himself. A less sinister popular theory is that inside information regarding Davydenko's injury and his questionable ability to endure more than one set of tournament play was passed along to the gamblers.

Davydenko's personality is somewhat enigmatic. If he was totally innocent of any wrongdoing in the Arguello match, as he proclaimed, we would expect that he would be motivated to go out of his way to play at his very best in subsequent matches. Instead, only two months later, in a St. Petersburg tournament, he was fined $2,000 for not giving his best effort against little-known Marin Cilic. In an eerily familiar scenario, Davydenko won the first set in twenty-seven minutes and then proceeded to lose the match with an explanation that his legs had collapsed. However, no unusual betting patterns were logged by the gambling companies.

Ultimately, Davydenko was cleared of allegations that he had bet on tennis matches, but many followers of the scandal remained unconvinced.

Other Suspicious Betting Patterns

Previous investigations of professional tennis matches with irregular betting patterns did not yield any suspicious findings, and no player had ever been formally sanctioned. In 2003, betting was suspended before a minor tournament match in Lyon, France, between Yevgeny Kafelnikov and Fernando Vicente when a large wager was placed on Vicente, who had lost twelve consecutive matches. Surprisingly, Vicente defeated Kafelnikov in straight sets, but nothing illicit was uncovered.

In the 2006 Wimbledon event, a first-round match between Richard Bloomfield, a wild card, and Carlos Berlocq, who was ranked 170 places higher, drew attention when the bulk of the wagers were on Bloomfield, who proceeded to win in straight sets. The International Tennis Federation (ITF), which oversees Wimbledon, stepped in but found no wrongdoing.

Match Fixing Attempts

The Davydenko episode prompted other players to speak out. Within several weeks, a cluster of revelations emerged. Tim Henman, a leading British star, told the BBC that he heard of players being approached to fix matches. His account was quite vague but full of insinuation. Bob Bryan, a top doubles player, told the *L.A. Times* that he knew of players who had received anonymous phone calls asking them to influence the results of their matches; but all of the players in question turned down the offers. Paul Goldstein went a step further in acknowledging that he had been directly approached to fix a match within the last two years and had dismissed the request, and Arnaud Clement weighed in and admitted that he too had turned down money to tank a match. Gilles Elseneer disclosed that he was offered and refused a bribe in excess of $100,000 to lose a first-round Wimbledon 2005 match versus Potito Starace. Two Czech players, Tomas Berdych and Jan Hernych, told reporters that they had been approached or knew of offers made to other players at tournaments in Moscow and St. Petersburg.

Andy Murray, a highly ranked player, was quoted by the BBC as indicating that it is widely known in the tennis world that match fixing takes place. These comments prompted the ATP to summon Murray to a conference, but before the meeting took place, Murray backtracked, claimed he had been misquoted, and only meant to imply that tennis matches attract a lot of betting.

Curiously, all of these revelations that emerged after the Davydenko fiasco in Poland were made to the media, rather than directly to the tennis authorities. In a peculiar breaking of the code of silence, players wanted the truth to be known, but they did not want to be called in by the tennis authorities who might press them for more specific information about other comrades on the tour. The stigma of a professional athlete being perceived as a tattler is profound, and potential informants struggle with the conflict between reporting information that preserves the integrity of the sport versus ratting on fellow players in a familial environment.

This was an embarrassment for the officials of the four governing bodies, the ATP, the ITF, the WTA (World Tennis Association), and the Tennis Grand Slam, who responded by uniting to establish an Integrity Unit designed to bolster the clean image of the game and to crack down on any corruption. As in other professional sports, it was already forbidden for players to bet on tennis matches, but the primary provision of the new guidelines was that players are required to report to the authorities within forty-eight hours about any approach to influence the outcome of a match. Failure to do so would be a sanctionable offense. Previously, the authorities had been fearful of attracting negative publicity and were delinquent in pursuing players suspected of withholding relevant information about potential corruption, and players had been indifferent about accountability. The reality is that this gentlemen's sport has been sullied, and it behooved the governing bodies to spell out guidelines and to put teeth into the Integrity Unit's regulations.

In spite of the preexisting zero tolerance policy for players betting on tennis, and the antigambling education program provided by the ATP as part of an anticorruption program instituted in 2003, players have not always taken the restriction seriously. Robin Haase, a first-round loser in the 2007 U.S. Open, claimed ignorance about this policy and expressed his belief that it was no big deal if players bet small amounts on matches.

As the controversy continued to swirl, Patrick McEnroe, the well-respected captain of the U.S. Davis Cup team, acknowledged the likelihood of some fixed matches. McEnroe observed, "Tennis is a very easy game to manipulate. I can throw a match and you'd never know. . . . I don't think it's going on at the top level, but it wouldn't shock me that it might happen on the lower levels."[9]

Highlighting Integrity in Tennis

Two issues need to be addressed to restore and preserve the integrity of the game. The first is to monitor and crack down on players who violate the antibetting provision in tennis policy. Under siege from the recent corruption headlines and determined to show that it meant business, the ATP sanctioned Alessio di Mauro, the 124th-ranked player, in November 2007 for gambling on tennis. An investigation disclosed that di Mauro had made 120 bets with an online gambling company from November

2006 to June 2007. In his defense, di Mauro claimed that he was unaware of the ban on wagering in tennis, that he never bet on his own matches, and that he bet very small amounts, as little as $15 at a time. In the current climate of scrutiny in all sports, di Mauro's behavior was supremely self-destructive. His naivete or grandiosity made him a sacrificial target for the governing powers. Although match results were not in the least affected by di Mauro's actions, the ATP, claiming that ignorance of the law is no excuse for breaking it, seized the opportunity to discipline a nominally corrupt player; and they levied a nine-month suspension and a $60,000 fine against him. In view of the fact that other players had been suspended for six months for drug violations, the penalty against di Mauro seemed like overkill on the part of the ATP, which was out to resurrect a stronger policing image for itself. Two other less prominent Italian men's players, Daniele Bracciali and Potito Starace, also were fined and given limited suspensions for betting on matches other than their own; and French player Mathieu Montcourt was suspended in 2008 for two months and fined $12,000 for betting on other players' matches in 2005.

The second, and more serious, issue involves the danger of match fixing. In his controversial statement, Andy Murray pointed out that the opportunity to make extra money by throwing a match can be too tempting for some players to turn down, especially the lower-ranked players whose tournament earnings as a first-round loser would be quite negligible. Furthermore, the structure of the ranking system could make a player susceptible to a bribe. When playing in a minor tournament, a player could afford to lose early and suffer no negative impact on his ranking, because only the top eighteen tournament results each year are counted. Another source of temptation is that players could receive payoffs for sharing inside information with outside gamblers about the health and injuries of other players or themselves. These pathways to corruption could prove more difficult to pin down and require vigilant oversight by the Integrity Unit.

In October 2007, Martina Hingis, a former women's champion, under the threat of allegations about cocaine use, chose to retire rather than fight against what she claimed were horrendously erroneous charges. The ATP president, Etienne De Villiers, used the occasion to emphasize his crusade against gambling activity.

In the shadow of the Hingis cocaine charges, De Villiers took the position that players caught doping should be punished and then allowed to come back to the game. In contrast, he stated, there should be no second chance for any player involved in match fixing; they should be barred permanently from the game. The distinction is based on the view that doping is forgivable because it is self-destructive, but throwing a match is destructive to the sport and, therefore, unpardonable.

The tennis world encountered another assault to its credibility one week later, when allegations surfaced that Tommy Haas, who had withdrawn from

Germany's Davis Cup match against Russia with a severe stomach virus, really had been poisoned by Russian crime figures. The ITF was forced to launch yet another investigation. At this point, professional tennis was under siege and seemed to be subjected to the cockroach theory—that is, finding one in the kitchen means there are others in the wall.

OTHER RECENT GAMBLING SCANDALS

College Game Fixing

In a throwback to the point-shaving corruption affecting college basketball and football of earlier eras, a new scandal emerged in 2007 involving the University of Toledo. Harvey (Scooter) McDougle Jr., a running back on the football varsity team, was charged in an FBI criminal complaint with participating in a bribery plot to influence sporting events. More specifically, McDougle was accused as serving as a liaison for Ghazi Manni, a professional gambler, to teammates on the football squad as well as other players on the basketball team to conspire to rig games, that is, to arrange that their teams would fall short of or beat the point spread in selected games from 2003 to 2006. McDougle and the players he recruited allegedly were rewarded for their efforts with cash, gifts, groceries, and as much as $10,000 to sit out of a game while hiding behind a fake injury.

McDougle tried to lessen the shadow of corruption cast upon him by insisting that although he received perks, including a car and a telephone from Manni, he never played in a way that altered the outcome of games, as if the rest of the charges against him were inconsequential. Such a self-deceptive rationalization was unlikely to carry much weight with the authorities, and for his role as a frontman, if convicted, McDougle faced penalties of up to five years in prison and a $250,000 fine.

When the U.S. attorney's office dropped the charges in April 2007, McDougle asserted that he had been used by the authorities in their quest to pursue Manni, and he frantically demanded that he be reinstated to the Toledo football team. Prosecutors clarified that the dropped charges were merely a procedural move to buy them more time to gather information and that federal investigators were continuing to press the case. The NCAA announced that it was conducting its own separate probe into the McDougle situation. In May 2009, McDougle was indicted on federal charges of conspiracy to commit sports bribery.

Two categories of gambling issues involve elite athletes. The first focuses on those sports stars who are corruptible and indulge their dark side in the direction of participating in attempting to influence the outcome of games. These offenses are directly harmful to the integrity and image of the sport, and assault the public's trust and belief in the honesty of sports and the integrity of their heroes.

Basketball, because of the structure of the game, is the sport that most readily lends itself to tampering. A referee can call an excessive number of fouls. A player can produce big numbers offensively and slack off just a little on defense. A player can be bribed to keep his team under the point spread and still win the game. And in contrast to the other major sports, there is a higher probability that one player on a five-man team can influence the point spread.

Since the 1950s college basketball has had a game-fixing scandal in every decade, but it seems likely that point-shaving episodes occur with even greater frequency than we have realized. Obviously, not all attempts to rig games have been exposed, and a recent NCAA poll indicated that 1.5 percent of players acknowledged either accepting a bribe to play poorly or knowing of a teammate who had done so.[10] In addition, a large study conducted by a University of Pennsylvania economist, Justin Wolfers, revealed that heavy favorites barely miss covering the point spread to a greater degree than can be attributed to chance. Based on his research covering more than forty-four thousand college games over a sixteen-year span, Wolfers concluded that point shaving is going on in about 6 percent of all games with large point spreads.[11] These findings are routinely minimized by the universities, which rely on the public's faith in the sport to keep the turnstiles clicking and television revenues flowing.

The second cluster revolves around sports stars whose propensity for gambling can have serious personal consequences. Athletes may be especially predisposed to engage in gambling. Although NCAA rules prohibit any sports gambling by players, another study of collegiate athletes indicated that 45 percent of male athletes gambled on sports. Moreover, 5 percent admitted that they had wagered on games in which they played or had been given payoffs for subpar play.[12] And Keith Whyte, executive director of the National Council on Problem Gambling, explains that the high incidence of problem gambling among athletes is quite predictable because "they believe that they can make their own luck and have the skills to succeed where others don't."[13] In other words, their on-the-field athletic skills that enable them to succeed at a superior level may generalize to an illusory belief that they have the skill to pick winners.

Michael Jordan

In his heyday as the premier player in the NBA, Michael Jordan developed a serious gambling problem, primarily centering around betting in casinos and on golf games. There were widespread rumors that he had acquired huge losses and that he was not making good on certain payments. It was even speculated that his retirement from the game in 1993 at the young age of thirty was predicated on a deal with the NBA to hush up his gambling problem. Sadly, when his father, James Jordan, was murdered later that year by two young men out to rob tourists, several unprincipled journalists sought to sensationalize a connection between Michael's unpaid gambling debts and the murder.

ADDICTION

An addiction is a repetitive behavior in the face of negative consequences and the desire to continue something that you know is bad for you. According to this definition, many athletes suffer from gambling addictions whether they own up to it or not. For athletes who are conditioned to view themselves as having special talents, the lines of reality are already blurred, and it becomes that much harder to resist the desire to engage in high-risk gambling adventures that are sanctionable and can get them in trouble. To make further sense out of these boundary-crossing activities, we must recognize the maladaptive defense mechanisms such as denial, dissociation, and distanciation, which are used to mute reality and are designed to protect the players from dealing with the potential dangers of their gambling compulsions.

In recent times, several high-profile sports stars, most notably John Daly and Charles Barkley, have come forward in revealing what they describe as their "gambling problems." Daly, who is notorious for his across-the-board difficulty in moderating his appetites (he has struggled with alcohol addiction and food addiction), freely admitted to twelve years of heavy gambling, which resulted in losses of $50 to $60 million.

Considering his relatively modest total earnings on the golf tour, this figure is undoubtedly highly exaggerated and driven by a self-deprecating need to sensationalize his problems. In one example of his out-of-control gambling indulgence, after losing in a playoff round to Tiger Woods in the American Express Championship in San Francisco, he impulsively drove to Las Vegas and lost $1.65 million in five hours of playing the slot machines. As with many gambling addicts, dealing with frustration and despair is not Daly's strong suit. Unlike Barkley, Daly at least acknowledges the seriousness of his gambling addiction, and asserts, "If I don't get control of my gambling it's going to flat out ruin me."[14] But much of this seems to be lip service, since he is infamous for making pledges to regulate his excessive behavior only to slip back at the first opportunity. This is a central characteristic of a true addict—that is, in spite of the recognition of the self-destructive side of his gambling activities, he continues to indulge his impulsive desire.

Charles Barkley, who often comes across as outrageously arrogant and condescending, estimates that he has lost about $10 million in gambling. He minimizes the magnitude of the issue in stating, "Yeah, I do have a gambling problem. But I don't consider it a problem because I can afford to gamble."[15] In a moment of partial insight, Barkley emphasizes that the thrill of competition plays a big role in his attraction to gambling, but after acknowledging that he is hooked, he relegates it simply to a bad habit that he expects to continue. He views it as "a stupid bad habit, a waste of money, but I love it,"[16] and his plan is to scale down his blackjack involvement from $20,000 a hand to a meager $1,000; but this would probably not provide him with the requisite thrill of a very high-stakes game. It seems likely that Barkley is fooling himself into thinking he can effectively regulate and control what appears to be a compulsive gambling addiction.

Barkley, who is indifferent and even disdainful about the role model influence that sports stars have on kids, seems entirely too comfortable with his gambling addiction. His reflections also suggest that he is placing himself in a special category of gambling addicts, because his financial status allows him to sustain millions in losses in contrast to the plight of more ordinary people who are compulsive gamblers.

Charles Barkley is an intelligent and articulate individual. Instead of waxing eloquently about his love of gambling, he would do well to abandon his quest for moderation, make a commitment to more fully clean up his act, and provide a service to society by becoming an antigambling spokesperson.

It is sad that both John Daly and Charles Barkley seem to have opened up about their gambling issues not so much in the spirit of dealing with their addictions in a hands-on fashion and to face the difficult path of reform, but rather in the hopes of generating publicity. Their disingenuous admissions represent salacious confessionals that may be crafted to promote their book sales.

CHAPTER FOUR

Athletes Who Flirt with Disaster

Many athletes have a talent that propels them to succeed and a corresponding knack for courting personal failure. It is striking to see how frequently sports stars, who are heralded with financial rewards and glorified status, disregard the rules of society and indulge their dark side, with little consideration for the consequences to their careers or their lives. It seems like they just do not understand the consequences and treat legal charges as simple nuisances. Although their athletic accomplishments bring them enormous wealth and other advantages that come with celebrity, they continue to function as rebellious adolescents who become embroiled in antisocial and sometimes dangerous off-the-field activities.

NFL SUSPENSIONS

During 2006, nine players on the Cincinnati Bengals were arrested for off-the-field misbehavior. Most of the arrests were for relatively minor legal infractions like possession of marijuana or driving under the influence (DUI) charges, but the repeated offenses by some of the players speaks to their ongoing defiance and a readiness to cross legal boundaries. This group of Bengals is noted for their character defects and self-sabotaging behavior. Fortunately for the plight of the team, most of those involved were peripheral players.

Chris Henry

The highest profile case of the Bengals nine was Chris Henry who was arrested four times since his 2005 entry into the NFL. The multiple charges against Henry include marijuana possession, carrying a concealed weapon, and speeding. Henry was also given a three-month prison sentence for providing alcohol to minors, but he was only required to serve two days. He was suspended by the NFL for the first eight games of the

2007 season. He was permitted to return on the condition that he attend counseling and avoid any further legal trouble. Henry's track record of misconduct conveys a profile of poor judgment and indifference to the mores of society. His four arrests within fourteen months suggest that he is either out of control, defiantly testing the limits of what he can get away with, or begging through his actions to be shut down or punished. The NFL needs to enforce a zero-tolerance policy with players like Chris Henry to ensure that he understands that, his football prowess notwithstanding, he is at risk for sabotaging his career. Chris Henry was unable to take seriously the conditions of his reinstatement. In April 2008, the Bengals cut ties with him after he was arrested again, this time for allegedly punching an eighteen-year-old man in the face and breaking a window in the man's car with a beer bottle. Many will wonder about what part of zero tolerance Henry did not understand. Yet, it is common for some athletes to resort to familiar destructive patterns in dealing with conflict, regardless of the potential consequences for their career.

Pacman Jones

Adam (Pacman) Jones is another NFL player who repeatedly thumbs his nose at authority and seems committed to testing limits and breaking the rules of society without thinking about the consequences. He does not appear to understand that, as a professional football player, he is jeopardizing his career by his repeated involvement in off-the-field incidents. When he is penalized for his misconduct, he reacts as though he is being victimized.

Since being drafted by the Tennessee Titans in 2005, Jones has been arrested five times and questioned by the police in ten separate incidents. Thanks to smart legal maneuvering, he has never been convicted of a crime, but he is an expert in putting himself in harm's way. Jones's specialty is altercations in nightclubs and strip joints. In October 2005, during his first NFL season, he was cited for violating the terms of probation regarding a suspended sentence for a barroom brawl when he was in college. Like many arrogant sports stars who act as if they are above the law, Jones did not take the conditions of his probation very seriously and treated them like an interfering annoyance in his life.

The most serious incident was his involvement in a Las Vegas strip club fracas in February 2007 that left one person paralyzed from the waist down, and two others injured, after they were shot by a member of Jones's entourage. Pacman faced felony charges for his role in the melee in which he allegedly threatened to kill employees of the club and bit a bar bouncer on the ankle. The police characterized Jones as the instigator in the altercation. After extensive legal wrangling, Jones accepted a plea deal of one-year probation in exchange for his cooperation in testifying against the gunman.

A most formative issue in Adam (Pacman) Jones's early development is the fact that his father was shot and killed when he was ten years old. When a child is traumatized by such an event, he is prone to internalize a belief that violence is a standard response to conflict. For Jones, frustration leads directly to aggression, and several nightclub incidents—including one in which he allegedly spit in the face of women during arguments, and another in which he supposedly grabbed a dancer by the hair and slammed her head on the stage (in the Las Vegas episode)—suggest that his rage is easily triggered when he feels thwarted. Jones is substantially deficient in skills that relate to resolving interpersonal conflict. His wrathful aggressiveness may be an effective tool on the football field where he can pulverize opponents, but it does not work in life.

As a consequence of his repeated arrests and off-the-field incidents, Roger Goodell, eager to promote his law-and-order image as a new commissioner, suspended Jones for the entire 2007 season under the aegis of the NFL's personal conduct policy. The player's union raised an appeal on Jones's behalf citing that he had never been convicted of a crime, and that his penalty was excessive when compared to three hundred other cases of NFL players who had been arrested or charged with off-the-field misconduct. The case was reviewed ten games into the season, and Goodell stood firm in denying the appeal and ruled that Jones must sit out the whole season.

Jones was traded to the Dallas Cowboys during the off-season and geared up for his return to the NFL in 2008. However, after six games (only forty-one days since his reinstatement), his pattern of self-destructiveness reemerged when he courted trouble again by getting into a brawl with his personal bodyguard. Jones and the bodyguard played down the incident, but Goodell was not amused at this apparent lapse into violence, and sensitive to the tarnished image of the league's players, he cracked down on Jones with another suspension.

Tank Johnson

The third player to be suspended in Goodell's crackdown on off-the-field non-drug-testing offenses was Terry (Tank) Johnson. Johnson entered the NFL in 2005, and during his first season with the Chicago Bears, he was arrested at a nightclub for possession of a handgun and was sentenced to eighteen months probation. Like Pacman Jones, he ignored the conditions of his probation and, in December 2006, the police searched his home and found six firearms, including two assault rifles. For violating his probation and possession of unlicensed weapons, he was sentenced to four months in jail. Two days after his arrest, he frequented a nightclub with William Posey, his bodyguard, and Posey was shot and killed during a fight at the club. Johnson, while present, was not part of the violent altercation.

Commissioner Goodell suspended Johnson for the first eight games of the 2007 season, and the Bears initiated a zero-tolerance parameter for him. When he was arrested in June 2007 for suspicion of driving under the influence, the team, fed up with Johnson's repeated legal entanglements, released him. Ironically, subsequent test results revealed that his blood-alcohol level was under the legal limit, and the charges were dropped. But the Bears, claiming that he "compromised the credibility"[1] of the team and that he was an embarrassment, were glad to be rid of him.

After serving his jail time and NFL suspension, he was given a contract by the Dallas Cowboys.

Chris Henry, Pacman Jones, and Tank Johnson are linked together as NFL players who repeatedly have crossed boundaries in off-the-field misconduct and metaphorically have shot themselves in the foot by jeopardizing their careers. They are defiant, acting out personalities who happen to be talented football players. Henry, Jones, and Johnson share a common chronic disregard for society's rules and regulations, and a malignant defiance toward authority. As high-profile sports celebrities, they are indifferent to the bull's eye they wear on their back, and they place themselves in situations that can become explosive. Time and again, they engage in creating a situation in which they or others wind up in harm's way. They frequent nightclubs where trouble embraces them, and they readily get involved in confrontations that escalate into violence. Their readiness to engage in a rumble when they are challenged or thwarted conveys a mind-set in which their need to react belligerently outdistances using good judgment, and it blinds them to the costs that accompany their brawling activities. Previous brushes with law enforcement that resulted in probationary terms are taken lightly and are routinely violated. It is a mentality characterized by high-risk behavior and an obliviousness to consequences.

The multi-million-dollar contracts that athletes receive convey the message that they are indispensable. Under these circumstances, they often lose their perspective and lose track of appropriate boundaries. Many athletes, because of their celebrity, lose sight of the fact that there are limits and that they have to be respectful toward authority. A major erosion of respect toward authority is evident in sports, which parallels what is happening in our culture. This trend is reflected in the way many of our political figures are being questioned about their moral and ethical behavior.

In earlier eras in the major sports leagues, coaches and managers were paid more than the players, and, because of their status, the players looked up to them. The general understanding was that the coaches were in charge and the players had to toe the line and adhere to the standards of the coach. In the twenty-first century, all that has changed, and respect for the coach has lost some luster and regard on the part of the players. Some superstars even feel that they can demand that a coach be fired as a condition for their continuing to play for their team. Many sports stars acquire a distorted view of themselves in relation to the world and come to think of themselves as living by a special set of rules. When they operate from that kind of privileged position, as a special person who does not need to comply with society's rules, they put themselves at risk for going over the line and for behaving in ways that are not acceptable and not exerting appropriate control over their feelings. Chris Henry, Pacman Jones, and Tank Johnson are NFL stars who seem to fall into this category.

OTHER OFF-THE-FIELD TRANSGRESSIONS

Michael Phelps

The 2008 white knight in American sports was Michael Phelps, who, as a twenty-three-year-old swimmer, enchanted the nation by winning eight gold medals at the Beijing Olympics. He became the darling of young fans who thrived on relating to his competitive spirit and successful achievements, and he was anointed by the Associated Press as the male athlete of the year. He was sought after for endorsements by major companies, including Visa, A&T, Kellogg's, and Subway, and he was in a position to earn more than $100 million from these long-term sponsors. The world was his oyster, but Phelps was not sufficiently mindful of protecting his superstar image as the clean-cut All-American Hero. Instead, he indulged in youthful indiscretions that knocked him off the hero pedestal.

In February 2009, a British newspaper, *News of the World*, printed a photo of Michael Phelps inhaling marijuana from a bong while attending a party at the University of South Carolina. Recognizing the incipient damage to his career that would follow, Phelps's management team attempted to make a deal with the newspaper to cover up the story. In rejecting the cover-up deal, the newspaper revealed that, in exchange for quashing the story, Phelps would have agreed to become a columnist for the publication, host events, and even get his sponsors to advertise with them. Michael quickly apologized for his lapse, and he acknowledged that his behavior had been an inappropriate expression of his youthfulness, and he resolved to be more mindful of his image and his influence as a role model.

The fallout, however, was predictable. The U.S. Olympic Committee suspended Phelps from competing for three months, and it issued a statement excoriating him for not living up to the standards of responsibility and accountability that comes with the status of being a major role model for young kids. His portfolio of lucrative endorsement deals was placed in jeopardy as Kellogg's, one of his leading sponsors, revoked its contract with him. Phelps did not face any criminal charges related to this event, but the incident was self-destructive in terms of the damage to his career. There is a price to be paid for celebrity status, which is that even relatively minor transgressions will be picked up by the media and used to call into question your character and integrity. This episode highlighted the dissonance between Michael Phelps the poster boy swimming star, and Michael Phelps the carefree youth. Flirting with scandal was a familiar pathway for Phelps. He had been arrested in 2004 for drunken driving and was placed on parole for eighteen months.

Marcus Vick

Marcus Vick, a standout quarterback at Virginia Tech, wanted to play in the NFL like his brother Michael; but he was on an unstoppable path of self-destruction. During his college years, he was convicted of providing alcohol to three underage girls and for marijuana possession. His defiant behavior toward authority was reflected in nine traffic arrests, while he was enrolled. He was suspended from the university for the 2004 season, and after he was reinstated in 2005, he was charged with additional legal infractions and was dismissed from the university. Three days later, he was in an altercation in which he allegedly pulled a gun on three teenagers and was charged with three counts of brandishing a firearm. In a plea bargain, Vick received a six-month suspended jail sentence. He brazenly shrugged it off, expecting to be chosen in the NFL draft, but no team selected him. Ultimately, he was signed by the Miami Dolphins, and he played with them for a brief time in 2006 before being dropped. His promising professional football career ended in its infancy.

Jamaal Tinsley

Professional athletes who parade flamboyantly in their personal lives invite trouble. Too many players are indifferent, defiant, or oblivious to the reality that their celebrity status makes them more susceptible to danger in their off-the-field activities. When you have a professional sports contract that brings wealth and all the toys that money can buy, it is important to recognize that some people will admire you, some will envy you, and some will resent you. To be flashy about your cars, jewelry, or cash in bars or nightclubs is to court conflict. In being flamboyant, these high-profile athletes indirectly provoke and generate confrontations between the haves and the have-nots. Envy and resentment can spark extreme and sometimes violent reactions.

Jamaal Tinsley, the Indiana Pacers star, is a case in point. In December 2007, Tinsley and his entourage became victims of a shooting spree after a confrontation at an Indianapolis nightclub. The violence was triggered when Tinsley and his group left the club in a Rolls Royce and a Mercedes. People gathered around the fancy Rolls Royce and taunted Tinsley about his cars and earnings. The player and his friends were followed and an exchange of gunfire took place. Tinsley was not injured in the violence, but one person in his group suffered wounds in both elbows.

What is striking about this episode is that for Tinsley it was the third such incident in bars or clubs within the past fourteen months, suggesting that he had learned little from his previous experiences about the advisability of keeping a low profile when frequenting late-night spots. Thankful that he was not seriously hurt in this latest incident, he sheepishly admitted, "I made a stupid mistake, again."[2] He pledged to make changes in his lifestyle, and his coach, Jim O'Brien, convinced him to hire a bodyguard to accompany him everywhere. O'Brien also prevailed upon Tinsley to absorb the reality that "it's a very dangerous society. It seems to be somewhat more dangerous for professional athletes because of their wealth."[3] Only time will tell if Tinsley truly understands his coach's message.

In addition to engaging a bodyguard to travel with them, players like Tinsley could benefit from having a mentor whom they would consult on a regular basis. In fact, it would be prudent for the NBA to institute a mentorship program that would be required for players after one off-the-field incident.

ATHLETES USING GUNS

Plaxico Burress

After making the game-winning touchdown catch for the New York Giants in the 2007 Super Bowl, Plaxico Burress was rewarded with a $35 million five-year contract. In the following season, the full magnitude of his self-sabotaging personality emerged, when he was fined and suspended for on-the-field misbehavior and defiantly missing a team meeting. His self-destructiveness accelerated on the night of November 28, 2008, when he accidentally shot himself in the thigh while partying in a Manhattan nightclub.

Fortunately, he was not seriously wounded, and after a brief hospital stay, he retreated to his home. The gun discharged while he was holding a drink, and Burress faced serious felony charges for possession of a loaded unlicensed weapon. The story created tabloid headlines for a week, and much was made about the cover-up actions related to this incident (see chapter 7 for a full discussion of this aspect).

Plaxico Burress is one of an increasing breed of NFL players whose fame and history of transgressions with minimal consequences prompts them to ignore reality and to use poor judgment in their off-the-field actions. They pride themselves on being able to march to the beat of their own drummer. In Burress's case, he seemed to be disconnected from previous reprimands, as he escalated his defiant behavior toward authority. During his professional football career, he was involved in numerous controversial episodes including minor infractions, such as failing to participate in the

Giants' tickertape parade after their Super Bowl victory, not showing up for the team's off-season mini-camp, and receiving a suspension for failing to keep an appointment for medical treatment. Additionally, he has been involved in more serious issues, such as twice being slapped with restraining orders after domestic disturbances, a reckless driving charge for which he ignored the court date and was given only a thirty-day suspended sentence, and arrests for public intoxication. These series of slap-on–the-wrist penalties must have felt like a mere nuisance to Plaxico Burress.

Ultimately, in the illegal weapons possession charge, Burress was suspended for the remainder of the season by the Giants for conduct detrimental to the team. He faced even greater legal consequences of a minimal prison term of three and a half years, if he was found guilty of illegally carrying a loaded firearm. While the case was slowly winding its way through the legal system, the Giants, fed up with Burress's history of defiant behavior that frequently distracted other players, put team harmony above a talented receiver and released Burress. This resulted in his losing the nearly $27 million remaining on his contract. Furthermore, no other team was willing to sign him until his legal case was resolved. Ultimately, in August 2009 he pleaded guilty to attempted gun possession and agreed to serve two years in prison.

A general perception exists that high-profile athletes are treated more leniently by the judicial system than other people. The Plaxico Burress case highlights the other end of the spectrum. The belief is that, when they get into trouble, they hire high-priced lawyers who are successful in getting them off easy. In an effort to crack down on offenders of illegal weapons possession, New York State in 2006 passed a new gun law that mandates at least three and a half years in prison time for those found guilty, with no exceptions based on a judge's discretion. Within the complicated maze of the state's judicial system, however, less than 10 percent of those accused of this offense in New York City have been convicted, and many received a conviction of a lesser charge. Former teammates of Burress have suggested that the prosecuter's insistence on pursuing jail time was driven by the need to use this high-profile case to set an example of the serious consequences attached to illegal gun possession.

It is a challenging task to grasp the psyche of Plaxico Burress. His level of disconnection to previous transgressions and indifference to financial penalties attached to his suspensions are difficult to fathom, but we cannot impose our value system in assessing how he functions. What seems to be of central significance in his psychological makeup is that it is vitally important for him to do things his way, even if it violates the usual standards of behavior in our society. Moreover, learning from negative experiences is not one of his strong suits.

In an uncharacteristic self-reflective moment, Plaxico acknowledged, "I'm my own worst enemy. The things that have happened to me, I have no one to blame but myself. That's what makes Plaxico Burress Plaxico Burress."[4] The last part of his statement suggests that he takes pride in his behavior and wears it like a badge of honor, rather than considering the need to change his maladaptive approach to the world. A glimmer of hope was revealed when Burress's lawyer claimed that he was devastated and felt humiliated by the ridicule directed toward him by the press and radio and television talk shows. This reaction suggests that, beneath his façade, he is not totally impervious to other people's reactions to his misbehavior.[5]

The illegal gun possession incident was not to be taken lightly. Actually, Burress was fortunate that he only suffered a superficial thigh wound, because more lethal circumstances could have occurred. By carrying a loaded gun in an alcohol-laced nightclub environment, he potentially put himself and others in a danger zone. This realization needs to be embedded in the mind-set of prominent athlete-celebrities and must replace the common rationalization that such action is a necessary precaution to protect themselves from the world of would-be celebrity assaulters. Burress's Giants teammates Mathias Kiwanuka and Steve Smith, who was robbed outside his home by a gun-wielding thief, have spoken out about the necessity for players to be aware of the potential for trouble when they pursue night-life activities. The players are forewarned about these dangers in preseason lectures, but for many of them, it apparently does not serve as a sufficient deterrent. It would be difficult to enforce, but some form of supervision or a list of restricted venues might go a long way toward reducing the number of violent incidents in nightclubs involving athletes.

It is interesting to note that following his self-inflicted wound misadventure, Plaxico Burress apologized to his teammates for "letting them down," but expressed no remorse about the impact on children who idolized him. One of the major problems when star players are involved in such incidents is the effect it produces in the legion of admiring kids. This is but one of the reasons why athletes need to be held to a higher standard than the general public. The power of the identification process in which children will emulate their heroes is profound. This issue far outweighs any sympathy we may have for Burress's lapse of judgment. A judge who applies the appropriate full penalty should be applauded, as doing so can send a message of deterrence about handgun possession to thousands of young fans.

Maurice Clarett

Maurice Clarett is the quintessential troubled college football athlete who was programmed to be an NFL marquee player, but, instead, he was derailed by his off-the-field misconduct. In 2002, Clarett was a phenom freshman at Ohio State University and led his team to victory in the national championship game. His star shone brightly and future notoriety awaited him, but before the next season, he filed a falsified police report in which he claimed that more than $10,000 in cash and personal property was stolen from his car. As a result of this misdemeanor, he was suspended by the university for the entire 2003 season. Clarett dropped out of Ohio State and, eager to launch his professional career, challenged the NFL restriction against turning professional until a player is three years beyond high school. His case was reviewed all the way up to the U.S. Supreme Court, which ruled against him. He was eventually drafted in 2005 by the Denver Broncos but was cut from the squad in training camp.

Clarett also created controversy at Ohio State by shedding light on the duplicitous practices employed by many college athletic programs to attract and keep talented athletes. He claimed that coaches and boosters had manipulated the system to get him passing grades, cars, and thousands in cash, but he declined to be interviewed by the NCAA about these allegations, and they remain unsubstantiated.

In 2006, any semblance of good judgment collapsed for Clarett, and within eight months, he was apprehended twice in gun-wielding incidents. On January 1, 2006, he bizarrely held up two people at gunpoint in an alley behind a bar, but only took their cell phone. He was identified and charged with aggravated robbery. Then, in August 2006, he was arrested after a high-speed chase with police, who seized four loaded guns in his car. He pleaded guilty to the felony charges involving gun possession in both cases and was sentenced to seven and a half years in jail. He was required to serve a minimum of three and a half years. After the first incident, he should have attempted to present himself as an exemplary citizen while waiting for a ruling from the court. Instead, he put himself at further risk and compounded his punishment by carrying loaded guns in his car. It seems like Maurice Clarett was on a mission of self-destruction, and by age twenty-two, his up-and-coming football future was in shambles.

Stephen Jackson

In an all-too-familiar scenario, NBA star Stephen Jackson was flagged in July 2007 for firing a gun in an altercation outside an Indianapolis strip club. Jackson and three Indiana Pacers teammates got involved in an argument at the club. During the fracas, Jackson was punched in the face and hit by a car. Jackson fired several pistol shots at his assailants, but the police report did not clarify which action came first. He pleaded guilty to a felony count of criminal recklessness and was fined $5,000. The NBA, trying to neutralize the growing thug-ridden image of the league, suspended him for seven games.

Jackson should have known better than to put himself in a compromising position by going to strip clubs where fights are waiting to happen. At the time of this incident, his image was still in need of repair from his participation in the infamous 2004 brawl with fans during a game against the Detroit Pistons, which had garnered him a thirty-game suspension.

Sebastian Telfair

The trend of athletes disregarding the law, as well as league policies regarding handguns, continued in 2007 with the arrest of Sebastian Telfair, a Boston Celtics guard. On April 25, 2007, Telfair was stopped for speeding and a loaded handgun was discovered in his car. He was arrested and charged with felonious possession of a weapon. As with many athletes who cross legal boundaries, this was not Telfair's first incident involving gun possession. Fourteen months earlier, while playing with the Portland Trailblazers, he was caught with a loaded handgun aboard the team plane. No charges were filed in this incident, which reinforced the belief that he was immune from the rules of society. The Trailblazers levied a small fine and a two-day suspension, in what amounted to a symbolic slap on the wrist, which, apparently, Telfair did not take very seriously. He also was attracted to nightclubs where trouble ran afoul. In October 2006, Telfair reported that a $50,000 chain was snatched off his neck at a club, where coincidentally a rapper, Fabolous, was shot on the same night. When violent night clubs are your favorite milieu, dangerous things can happen.

In the wake of the 2007 incident, the Celtics cut Telfair from the team. The management had set forth behavioral guidelines in which they warned their players about consequences for legal transgressions and specifically cited its antihandgun restriction. In essence, it was a zero-tolerance policy, but Telfair chose to ignore it. The team viewed Telfair's behavior as irresponsible and as directly violating their standards of behavior. The Celtics went on to have one of the best seasons in NBA history in 2007–2008, and if Telfair had not blown his opportunity because of handgun possession, he could have been part of that glorious journey.

By dropping Telfair, the Celtics took a step in the right direction in communicating the message to sports stars that they must be mindful of their image and how they function in society. Off-the-field misconduct will be scrutinized and subject to consequences. Telfair's penchant for carrying loaded, unregistered handguns, and driving without a valid license, is tantamount to disregarding the rules and laws of society and is outrageously defiant and arrogant. The Celtics organization should be applauded for cracking down and not tolerating these actions.

Of course, it is easy to dismiss a fringe player like Sebastian Telfair, who had been a high draft pick but underperformed in his first season with the Celtics. The true test will come when a more productive member of the team crosses the line with off-the-field violent or illegal activity. Up to now, professional teams have been too protective of their stars and have failed to respond adequately to law-breaking infractions.

THE PREMIER SPORTS SCANDAL OF THE 2000s: MICHAEL VICK

The premier sports scandal of 2006 centered around the Michael Vick dog-fighting operation. Vick was once the highest paid NFL superstar, who electrified fans with his multiple skills as a quarterback. When the Atlanta Falcons played on the road, people came to watch him rather than the Falcons as a team. Vick had it all, but he had a penchant for dog fighting, a sideline that eventually disgraced him, doomed him to a prison term, and truncated his illustrious and lucrative professional football career.

Vick's downfall represents a classic example of a sports hero who reached the highest pinnacle of success and then self-destructed. As is the case with many fallen sports idols, his self-image, colored by a grandiose "I can do whatever I want, without regard for the rules and regulations of society," did him in. Michael Vick is the epitome of the professional athlete who is not sufficiently mindful of the necessity to protect his image and who blithely proceeds through his behavior to test moral and legal boundaries.

At the time of his dog-fighting indictment Vick had endured no previous arrests, but there had been earlier incidents. In 2005, a woman filed a civil suit against him for infecting her with genital herpes, citing that he had not informed her about his disease. An out-of-court settlement was reached in this matter. The easy financial solution to this problem probably reinforced Vick's misguided belief that any transgressions could readily slip through the system. Then, in January 2007, while passing through security at a Miami airport, Vick's water bottle was seized amid allegations that it contained marijuana. The media jumped on this report and sensationalized it, but the subsequent lab tests on the bottle found no evidence of drugs, and no criminal charges were filed. The media, which had treated the allegations as a headline story and had excoriated Vick in a rush to judgment, underreported the outcome when there was no further scandal to be pursued.

In an eighteen-page indictment, federal felony charges were levied against Vick in July 2007. The authorities alleged that for six years (since 2001), he was the central figure in a dog-fighting scheme in which he had authorized and participated in acts of cruelty toward animals on his property, and that he had gambled on dog-fighting events. Some of the allegations were graphic in their goriness and depicted the hanging, strangling, electrocuting, drowning, shooting, and slamming into the ground of dogs that had performed poorly in testing situations. Other dogs had been starved to make them more aggressive in competition. Three co-defendants were named as participants in the scheme, and it was alleged that Vick had directly authorized the killing of eight dogs that had under-performed. The investigators asserted that they found a rape stand used for mating purposes and, in another charge, that the gambling monies used by the ring, known as the Bad Newz Kennels, were financed almost exclusively by Vick.

Vick initially disclaimed any wrongdoing and pleaded not guilty; and he received an outpouring of support from many famous sports stars. Football greats Deion Sanders and Emmitt Smith expressed the view that "Vick is being persecuted because of his fame while the ringleaders in the dog fighting business go unpursued."[6] And, in a similar vein, NBA star Allen Iverson, who has had his own conflicts with the media, opined that Vick "is being pursued by authorities because there is always a 'bull's-eye' on prominent athletes."[7] This is a familiar refrain often offered by sports stars, which in this case overlooks the despicable actions and activities that Vick participated in while conducting the dog-fighting operation.

To some extent, the situation is compounded by the reality that in certain cases in which athletes have been accused of criminal behavior, there has been a propensity on the part of zealous prosecutors to go after a high-profile star to enhance their reputation. But this observation makes it all the more urgent for athletes who are in the limelight to be ultra mindful of their image. Therefore, it is essential for these sports figures to be selective about the company they keep, the places that they frequent, and not to display the proverbial "bull's-eye" on their back. Many people will wonder what Vick was thinking. Unfortunately, all too often in the grip of arrogance and hubris, the Michael Vicks of the sports world tune out or ignore the reality of needing to protect their image, and do not consider the consequences of their actions.

In response to Vick's initial not guilty plea, the federal prosecutors prepared an additional set of indictments against him, including charges of gambling and associating with gamblers in relation to the dog-fighting events, which could increase his potential sentence. A link to gambling, of course, was in violation of the NFL personal conduct policy and could result in a lifetime expulsion from the league. Vick's loyalists proclaimed that by pressuring him to plead guilty, under the threat of more charges, the feds were further victimizing him. At about this time, one of the co-defendants, Tony Taylor, pleaded guilty and agreed to cooperate with the government's case against Vick. Taylor indicated that the gambling monies used by the ring were financed primarily by Vick. The remaining two co-defendants followed Taylor in agreeing to a guilty plea deal, and on August 28, 2007, Vick capitulated and entered a guilty plea to one count of conspiracy. In a carefully scripted apology he stated,

> I made a mistake in using bad judgment and making bad decisions. . . . I'm totally responsible. . . . I want to apologize to all the young kids out there for my immature acts and, you know, what I did was very immature, so that means I need to grow up.[8]

In acknowledging that when he was first confronted by the allegations, he had lied to investigators, Vick said, "And I was not honest and forthright in our discussions, and, you know, I was ashamed and totally disappointed in myself, to say the least."[9]

Chris Berman, the host of ESPN's *Sports Center* described the Michael Vick scandal as "one of the most tragic falls in sports,"[10] and Hank Aaron, who had befriended Vick, lamented, "I've never seen someone with so much ability, who has fallen so far."[11] In considering the case, federal prosecutor Chuck Rosenberg indicated that first-time offenders like Vick generally would be spared a prison term under the sentencing guidelines. However, the government viewed the actions of Vick and two co-defendants as "heinous, cruel, and inhumane," and therefore, they would seek jail time.[12] Once Vick admitted in court that he not only was directly involved in the brutal killings of pit bulls, but also that he had financed the dog-fighting wagers, the NFL stepped in and levied a suspension of indefinite duration, citing that his role in gambling was a violation of the personal conduct policy. Commissioner Roger Goodell admonished the one-time All-Universe football hero as follows:

> Even if you personally did not place bets, as you contend, your actions in funding the betting and your association with illegal gambling both violate the terms of your NFL player contract and expose you to corrupting influences in derogation of one of the most fundamental responsibilities of an NFL player.[13]

What Vick needed to do at this juncture, while awaiting his sentencing, was to mount an all-out public relations campaign in which his prominent and well-respected friends might portray him to the prosecutors, to the judge, and to the media as a generous, community-minded player who advocates for underprivileged youths, visits kids in hospitals, and makes significant contributions to charitable organizations. Instead, he further self-destructed by failing a mandated drug test. Under the terms of his being free on bail, he was required to be tested, and less than one month after his plea deal, he tested positive for marijuana. When you are waiting to be sentenced on federal felony charges, this action is supremely self-sabotaging. Vick further compounded the offense by giving conflicting accounts about when he had used the drug. It could appear to the court that Vick did not take his predicament sufficiently seriously, and he was to pay the price.

Vick's co-defendants, Purnell Peace and Quanis Phillips, were sentenced to eighteen months and twenty-two months, respectively, but the government upped the sentencing recommendations for Vick from twelve to eighteen months to eighteen to twenty-four months, because he had not been forthright in his debriefs. Letters of support poured into the court from famous sports celebrities like Hank Aaron and George Foreman, and Vick wrote a humble, emotional letter asking for leniency. He apologized for his marijuana lapse and attributed it to the fact that he was broken-hearted after his father had condemned him in the media for his dog-fighting involvement. Vick felt betrayed by his father's negative public statements and hoped that Judge Henry Hudson would treat him in a more benign fashion, but this was not to be.

Vick opted to begin his prison term before his sentencing, and he requested that he be allowed to appear in court in a dress suit, a request that is often granted, rather than his prison uniform. Hudson's wish to humiliate Vick was apparent in his denial of this request, and the writing was on the wall about how he would be treating Vick. Hudson was unimpressed by the letters of support for Vick as well as Vick's own letter. He expressed skepticism about Vick's "acceptance of responsibility" and sentenced him to twenty-three months in prison, which was near the upper margin of what the prosecutors had recommended.

Vick is fortunate that he did not receive a stiffer penalty, because he was facing a judge who thrives on and takes pride in his hard-line, nonempathic approach to criminals. Hudson was not obligated to abide by the recommended guidelines and had full power to impose a sentence of up to five years. When he was a prosecutor, Hudson had pursued a borderline re-tarded man for a brutal rape and murder. Despite flimsy evidence, Hudson and the detectives in the case used extreme hardball tactics to induce a confession. Hudson threatened to prosecute for the death penalty, which the accused man circumvented by pleading guilty and accepting a thirty-year prison term. Five years later, it was discovered that a serial killer had committed this crime, but Hudson offered no apology, and in his memoir, he refers to his work on this prosecution as a "career-defining" case.

After disposing of Vick, Judge Hudson imposed a two months' sentence on Tony Taylor, the remaining co-defendant in this case. The prosecution, which was satisfied with Taylor's part in testifying against the others and thereby building their case, had recommended that Taylor should receive only a term of probation; however, true to form, Hudson opted for a stiffer penalty. Although Taylor would have to serve only a short stint, Hudson, at least symbolically, required him to face his punishment. After eighteen months in a federal penitentiary Vick was released and soon was reinstated in the NFL. In August 2009 he was picked up by the Philadelphia Eagles.

Vick's signing added controversy to the 2009 season because he was considered to be damaged goods by some of the Eagles' fans. The images of dogs being drowned, electrocuted, and hanged will not be easily eradi-cated. In reflecting on the dog-fighting episode, Vick proclaimed, "For the life of me, I can't understand why I was involved in such pointless activity. Why did I risk so much at the pinnacle of my career?"[14]

RECKLESSNESS

Ben Roethlisberger

Ben Roethlisberger became the darling of Pittsburgh Steelers fans in 2004 when he won the first thirteen games in which he was the starting quarterback. He followed up this achievement the next year as the youngest quarterback to lead his team to a Super Bowl championship. Roethlisberger was the epitome of the high-flying adored sports hero who fulfilled the dreams and fantasies of thousands of admirers who thrived on affiliating with a winner and the imagined connection to greatness—and he did so in a city whose other sports franchises were performing woefully. Many diehard sports fans rise and fall with the performance of their heroes, and when a hero is successful, it allows these fans to feel special by walking in the shadow of the admired athlete. In extreme form, this type of attachment symbolically becomes a satellite relationship, in which one feels powerful and secure by personally identifying with a star. Conversely, when the admired hero falters, such fans can feel deflated.

Roethlisberger was fond of driving around town on his motorcycle, and the Steelers organization was concerned that he might get injured. A cluster of athletes have been involved in motorcycle accidents, including football's Kellen Winslow Jr. and Jerome Mathis; basketball's Robertas Javtokas and Jay Williams; baseball's Ron Gant, Robin Yount, and Jeff Kent; and ski champion Hermann Maier. In the wake of the Kellen Winslow Jr. accident—in which the Cleveland Brown's star player sustained internal injuries and torn knee ligaments and missed the entire 2005 season—the Steelers' coach, Bill Cowher, paternalistically cautioned Roethlisberger about the dangers inherent in riding a motorcycle. Cowher was particularly alarmed because his young quarterback was riding without a helmet. Pittsburgh legend Terry Bradshaw also warned Roethlisberger about safety issues and urged him to "ride when you retire."[15]

These avuncular admonitions fell on deaf ears. Roethlisberger, like an adolescent imbued with his sense of invincibility, expressed his self-confidence in his "safe approach" and voiced his reluctance to wearing a helmet. He was sitting on top of the world as the Prince of Pittsburgh and felt that he was invulnerable. The illusion of safety and invulnerability came crashing down on the morning of June 12, 2006, when Roethlisberger's Suzuki Hayabusa, known as the fastest street-legal motorcycle, collided with a car at a busy intersection in downtown Pittsburgh. Big Ben was on his way home after taping a radio interview, and he was not drunk, on drugs, or speeding; however, the impact of the collision threw him over the handlebars of his bike, and he landed on the sedan, shattering the windshield with his head. As was his custom, he was riding without a helmet and he suffered a concussion, fractures to his jaw and nose, multiple head lacerations, and two lost teeth. Paramedics on the scene told him that he had ruptured a major blood vessel in his mouth and was minutes away from dying. He required seven hours of surgery to repair his wounds. His injuries might have been less serious if he had been wearing a helmet, but true to form, he had chosen not to do so. To make matters worse, Roethlisberger had been riding without a motorcycle license. He had had a learner's permit that had expired three months earlier, and he neglected to take the written and driving tests necessary to obtain his license.

The Pittsburgh fans rooted for his quick recovery, much as they would for a beloved family member, but many of them were also disappointed, hurt, and angry. They excoriated Roethlisberger for his poor judgment in arrogantly deciding to ride without a helmet. He was widely viewed as reckless for blithely putting himself in a vulnerable position. As the team's anointed franchise player, Roethlisberger had an obligation to manage his celebrity in a responsible way. It is important for sports stars to recognize that their admiring fans invest heavily in their connection to their heroes, and they feel tremendously let down and disillusioned when these heroes behave self-destructively through misguided or risky off-the-field actions.

Notably, Roethlisberger's mother died in a vehicular accident when he was eight years old. One has to wonder about a possible psychological connection between these two accidents, and whether Roethlisberger's insistence on not wearing a helmet was related to a need to deny the potential for bodily harm in the absence of proper protection on a vehicle. On the surface, this incident simply looks reckless, but it may have other implications. For that matter, these meanings may be beyond Roethlisberger's awareness as well. We can speculate that the sudden loss of his mother at a young age was understandably quite traumatic for Roethlisberger. By putting himself in jeopardy as a way of demonstrating his fearlessness, he masked an underlying fear of succumbing to the same fate as his mother. In this paradigm, the thing most feared almost came to pass.

ALCOHOL AND SUBSTANCE ABUSE CASUALTIES

The sports world has become increasingly alarmed about the health hazards related to steroids, but many players ignore these warnings and are willing to take risks concerning their future health. These athletes see this as a trade-off for gaining the perceived performance edge that will facilitate their getting on a professional team roster, or that will enable them to sustain or accelerate their productivity once they have reached stardom.

There, indeed, may be serious long-term effects to ballplayers who rely on steroids, but, in contrast, when it comes to alcohol and substance abuse, the short-term effects can be even more disastrous. Sports establishments naively maintain an expectation that players will police themselves, but the truth is that drug overdoses and vehicular accidents while under the influence frequently have lethal consequences.

The coverage of sports stars who put themselves or others in harm's way because of their alcohol or substance abuse problems is somewhat tilted. The media are vastly more attentive to the allegations and denials about Barry Bonds's and Roger Clemens's steroids involvement than they are to these stories.

Steve Howe

In the era before performance-enhancing drugs, cocaine was the drug of choice for some ballplayers. Steve Howe stands out as a tragic figure of this era, a cocaine addict who was suspended seven times during his baseball career, and had the distinction, in 1992, of being the first player who was issued a lifetime ban for substance abuse. The ruling was subsequently reversed by an arbitrator, and Howe continued his major league career until 1996. His talent was so great that he was still able to perform at a high level in spite of the physical erosion caused by his recurrent cocaine relapses. His on-the-field success while struggling with a self-destructive vice is reminiscent of earlier heroes like Babe Ruth and Grover Cleveland Alexander, who were glorified for their excellence on the baseball diamond even when they played drunk.

After leaving the game, Steve Howe sadly became an accident waiting to happen. In 2006, in a self-destructive finale, he was killed when his pickup truck drifted and crashed on a desert highway in California. He was not wearing a seat belt, and the pathology report indicated that he had methamphetamine in his system.

Ken Caminiti

Ken Caminiti, who blew the whistle on steroids in baseball and attributed his MVP 1996 season to performance-enhancing drugs, died eight years later from an overdose of cocaine and opiates.

Rod Beck

When Rod Beck, a former star relief pitcher, died in 2007, large quantities of powder, crack, and rock cocaine were found in his home. According to his personal assistant, Beck used cocaine on a daily basis, and his ex-wife claimed that his addiction killed him.

Sidney Ponson

Sidney Ponson, a Baltimore Orioles pitcher, has had multiple drunken driving arrests for incidents that have endangered his life and the lives of others.

Dwight Gooden, Darryl Strawberry, Mickey Mantle

Dwight Gooden and Darryl Strawberry, heroes on the New York Mets of the 1980s, had their careers truncated and spent time in jail because of their alcohol and drug problems. Mickey Mantle's death from liver cancer was believed to have resulted from years of heavy drinking.

Rob Ramage

Hockey star Rob Ramage was driving with a blood-alcohol level that was over the legal limit in a crash that killed another former NHL player, Keith Magnuson, on a Toronto highway in 2003. Magnuson, who was a standout defenseman for the Chicago Blackhawks for eleven seasons and later coached the team, was a passenger in Ramage's car. Ramage was convicted on five impaired and reckless driving charges, and was given a four-year prison sentence for the fatal crash.

Reggie Lewis, Len Bias, and Don Rogers

When Reggie Lewis, a Boston Celtics superstar, died suddenly from cardiomyopathy in 1993, two pathologists reported that their autopsy findings were consistent with a cocaine-damaged heart. Another basketball star, Len Bias, was selected by the Celtics in the 1986 draft and within forty-eight hours he died of cardiac arrest, which purportedly was related to cocaine intoxication. Only ten days after the Bias tragedy, Don Rogers, a Cleveland Browns standout player, died of cocaine-induced cardiac arrest. These examples represent only a small sample of athletes whose lives have been wrecked or lost as a result of alcohol and drug abuse.

STEROIDS USE VERSUS SUBSTANCE ABUSE

One of the main caveats against steroids in sports is that athletes who use them set a poor example and serve as a poor role model for college students, high school students, and even younger youth. The media zealots who focus on steroids sometimes lose perspective and give unbalanced and reduced coverage to athletes like Rod Beck, Steve Howe, and Ken Caminiti who self-destruct through drugs, which is an even more serious near-term issue.

On the day that Rod Beck died, the sports pages highlighted Bonds's hitting career home run number 749 and Tank Johnson's DUI charges, and they gave scant attention to the Beck story. When Ken Caminiti overdosed and died, the focus of the *New York Times* sports section was on Mariano Rivera's absence from the Yankees, because he went to Panama for the funerals of two family members, just before the start of the

American League Championship Series (ALCS) playoffs. And when Steve Howe died, the *New York Times* dwelled on Pedro Martinez being knocked out early in a game in his return to Fenway Park with the Mets. The readers would have been better served if the self-destructive consequences for these substance-abusing players had been highlighted.

Josh Hancock

St. Louis Cardinals pitcher Josh Hancock was killed on April 29, 2007, when his sport utility vehicle rammed into a flat-bed truck that had stopped on the highway to help a driver involved in a prior accident. Hancock was dead within seconds from head injuries sustained in the crash. It was a devastating loss for his family as well as for the entire Cardinals organization. Unfortunately, the tragedy became more complicated when it was later determined that the thirty-year-old Hancock was intoxicated (his blood-alcohol level was almost twice the legal limit), talking on his cell phone, not wearing a seat belt, and speeding in a fifty-five-mile-per-hour zone at the time of his collision. Moreover, a bag of marijuana and a glass smoking pipe were found in his vehicle. When these details emerged in the aftermath, reactions of grief, sympathy, and compassion toward those connected to Hancock became mixed with reactions of anger about his self-destructiveness.

Three days earlier, Hancock had been involved in another car accident and had walked away without any injury. On the same day, he caused a stir of apprehension among his teammates, when he failed to show up on time for a day game. Hancock claimed that he had overslept and thought it was a later starting time, but there was speculation that he was hung over. It was no secret to the ballclub that Hancock was a heavy drinker, and Manager Tony LaRussa broached the subject in a heart-to-heart talk with him just two days before his fatal crash. LaRussa himself was awaiting a trial on a drunken driving charge (police found him asleep at the wheel at a traffic light), so it represented a "do as I say, not as I do" lecture. Undoubtedly, Hancock did not take LaRussa very seriously.

On the night of his fatal accident, Hancock had been drinking for three and a half hours at a restaurant owned by Cardinals broadcaster Mike Shannon. Hancock's father, in his grief, bitterly claimed that the bartenders irresponsibly plied Hancock with drink after drink, and in an eerie postscript, he filed a lawsuit against the restaurant management. The tow truck company, the driver of the tow truck, and the driver of the stalled car who was being assisted also were named as defendants. A quick investigation by the Missouri authorities found no wrongdoing by Shannon's restaurant in Hancock's death, and the lawsuit was dropped. After Hancock's untimely death, in recognition that some players could not police themselves properly, several major league teams banned alcohol from their home clubhouses.

The notion that professional athletes are adults who need to behave responsibly is valid, but the truth is that many of them continue to be immature youths in talented grownup bodies who make poor decisions in their off-the-field lives. It would be a big step forward in curbing self-destructive behavior if players designated as high risk, because of their personal history or prior incidents, were monitored on a regular basis by team psychologists.

CHAPTER FIVE

Women Involved in Sports Scandals

Male athletes accused of breaking performance records with the aid of steroids have received the bulk of the sports headlines, but they are not the only offenders.

MARION JONES

Marion Jones, who was once regarded as the best female athlete in generations, pleaded guilty in October 2007 to lying to federal officials in two separate government investigations: the Bay Area Laboratory Co-Operative (BALCO) case and a check fraud case. In her 2003 interrogation in the BALCO case, Jones denied recognizing that the substance provided to her by her coach, Trevor Graham, was THG, a steroid known as "the clear," and denied that she had used it. In a concoction eerily reminiscent of Barry Bonds's statements about steroids use, Jones maintained that Graham had told her that the substance was flaxseed oil. In her confession, she admitted that she had used "the clear" for two years beginning in 1999, but that she did not realize it was a steroid until 2003, when she stopped taking it. Trevor Graham himself has been convicted of lying to federal agents in the BALCO investigation.

Jones's outstanding performance in the 2000 Olympics resulted in five medals, including three gold medals, and she was the first woman in history to win five track-and-field medals at the same Olympics. After her guilty plea, the International Olympic Committee quickly moved to strip her of these medals and wiped her wins from the record book. The prosecutors were eager to use her as an example demonstrating that athlete-celebrities are not above the law and that they will be punished for actions that impede the efficiency of government investigations.

Jones appealed to the court for a sentence limited to probation, because she had already endured substantial punishment and suffering based on the humiliation and national disgrace thrust upon her. The prosecutors seemed flexible in suggesting a range between no time and six months in jail, but the presiding judge, Kenneth Karas, conveyed that he was not bound by sentencing guidelines; and in flexing his muscles, he pointed out that it was within his jurisdiction to impose a lengthier sentence.

In the final analysis, the judge levied a six-month prison sentence and indicated that he found her to be disingenuous in claiming in her guilty plea that she had not realized, until 2003, after she had disassociated from Coach Graham, that she had been taking the steroid. Karas declared, "Athletes in society have an elevated status. They entertain, they inspire, and perhaps most importantly, they serve as role models for kids around the world. When there is this widespread level of cheating, it sends all the wrong messages, to those who follow these athletes' every move."[1]

In sentencing her to jail time, Karas was motivated by the wish to send a message to other athletes—that is, that there are consequences for lying to government officials. At the time of her guilty plea, Marion made a statement of apology that was tearful and carefully scripted. She lamented,

> It is with a great amount of shame that I stand before you and tell you that I have betrayed your trust. You have the right to be angry with me. I have let them [my family] down. I have let my country down and I have let myself down.[2]

She may have spoken these words with heartfelt sincerity, but she might have had greater impact and received more compassion if she had emphasized something like the following:

> Most of all I am remorseful about my complete failure as a role model for young females. I had the opportunity to make a difference, and to demonstrate that with the right values and dedication to hard work, a woman athlete can achieve excellence. I had the opportunity to be a true torch bearer for women to strive for success in our society. That should have been more important to me than cheating to win those five Olympic medals, but my overarching ambition, hubris, greed, and quest for personal fame blinded me to the true purpose of my mission. After I serve my sentence, I will devote myself to working with young female athletes, teaching them to learn from my mistakes and helping them to stay on course.

Amid speculation that a presidential pardon might be granted, Doug Logan, the newly appointed chief executive of USA Track and Field, issued a strongly worded letter to President Bush, recommending that he resist such consideration for the beleaguered Jones.[3] Logan argued that sports stars who cheat too often have been treated leniently by the judicial system and that, in our hero-worshipping culture, the misdeeds of our sports heroes need to be more fully reckoned. In echoing the statements made at sentencing by Judge Karas, he maintained that it would be a serious mistake to reduce Jones's sentence or pardon her, because it would send a message to youth that you can cheat with minimal consequences.

The point is well taken, and in essence, it may be necessary to hold athletes to a higher standard than others, because of their role model status in our society. Marion Jones projects a likeable image, and it is easy to sympathize with her, but sending a message of deterrence about cheating in sports is of paramount importance.

Logan's cautionary letter notwithstanding, it was unlikely that George Bush, as a law and order president, would grant a pardon or commuted sentence, especially because in his 2004 State of the Union address he had called for the professional sports leagues to crack down on athletes who pursue shortcuts to performance accomplishments. In July 2008, as commander in chief, Bush approved the first execution of a U.S. military soldier since 1961, in a case in which a private was convicted of murder and rape. In effect, Logan's letter to President Bush was tantamount to preaching to the choir.

Celebrity sports stars are catered to and made to feel special, a process that begins when their athletic talent first emerges in childhood. They are conditioned by their admiring followers to expect instant gratification in satisfying their needs and desires. As a result, their adult relationships are generally one sided, with their needs constantly in the foreground, and their partners serving as satellites who become well versed in deferent and compliant attitudes and behavior. In addition, many partners of athletes are mistreated in criminal fashion. Because aggression is so well rewarded in male sports, it is thus the case that women turn up quite often as the victims in contemporary sports scandals.

DOMESTIC VIOLENCE

Poor frustration tolerance characterized by an inability to delay or postpone the satisfaction of their needs is often a predisposing factor in sports stars who are prone to domestic violence. A second predisposing factor is that many athletes come from a background is which the primary solution to conflict is achieved through violence. Many athletes have attested to the fact that seeing men abuse women and seeing their mothers being beaten were standard fare in their early environment. These templates of what goes on in relationships, and how conflict is handled, become internalized and embedded in future sports stars and often are repeated in their adult relationships. It is interesting to see how some sports stars who are at the top of their game can be dysfunctional in their personal relationships. Their aggression and ability to assert their supremacy on the ballfield become liabilities when carried over into the realm of personal relationships.

The athlete who feels entitled to have his every whim met may over-react to situations in which he feels he is not being given his proper due. This type of mental state in which an abuser has the need to control and dominate another person is frequently an underlying factor in domestic violence. The capacity to anticipate consequences, both legally and in the world of sports, is often underdeveloped in players who lash out in this way.

Seattle Mariners pitcher Julio Mateo was not thinking about the impli-cations for his career when he assaulted his wife in 2007 in their hotel room following a game with the New York Yankees. His wife required five stitches to treat a wound in her mouth inflicted by the 220-pound pitcher. As a result, Mateo was arrested and charged with third-degree assault.

Major league sports teams historically have been delinquent in consider-ing penalties for athletes' assaults against women, as compared with their readiness to impose suspensions for offenses involving gambling and drugs. Fortunately, the trend is increasing toward treating offenses toward women with parity to other transgressions. After the Mateo incident, the Seattle organization wasted little time in reassigning him to a minor league team. In a similar situation, the Houston Astros released Julio Lugo in 2003 after he was arrested and charged with assaulting his wife, Mabel Lugo.

In professional football, the New England Patriots owner, Robert Kraft, drafted Christian Peter in 1996 and then swiftly cut him from the team when he learned about Peter's history of arrests for violence against women during his college years at the University of Nebraska. These owners are to be commended for sending out the message that players who engage in violent actions toward women will be treated harshly within their sport.

Lugo and Peter were able to resurrect their careers, and they signed on with different teams. To their credit, they seemed to internalize the mes-sage that violent behavior toward women would not be tolerated, and they stayed clear of further incidents.

Repeat Offenders

Some high-profile sports stars do not learn from their mistakes and lapse into repetitive entanglements with domestic violence.

Dwayne Carswell of the Denver Broncos was arrested in 2003 for assaulting his girlfriend. It was a familiar scenario for Carswell, who had received a one-year probation for grabbing a former girlfriend by the neck in a 1998 incident, and was arrested in 2002 for grabbing another woman by the arms and hair. The charges were dismissed in the latter incident after he agreed to pay restitution and do community service.

Dale Ellis of the Seattle Supersonics stands out as another repeat offender. When Ellis pleaded guilty to domestic violence against his wife in 2002, it was revealed that he had been convicted of assaulting his wife and resisting arrest some thirteen years earlier. Responding to conflict with violence can become embedded as the standard modus operandi in players like Carswell and Ellis, especially if they have been exposed to these types of solutions to relational problems in their backgrounds.

Lawrence Phillips's episodes involving violence toward women are legendary. In what had become a repetitive pattern, Phillips was convicted in August 2009 for twice choking his girlfriend in violent encounters in 2005. At the time of his recent conviction he was already serving a ten-year prison term for hitting three teenagers with his car. Phillips was once one of the most promising college football players, but he wrecked his future through a series of violent attacks on women. He was a first-round draft pick by the St. Louis Rams in 1996, and his brief NFL career was punctuated by his off-the-field misconduct involving repeated abusive behavior toward women. The most serious incident occurred in a 1995 brutal attack on a former girlfriend, who filed charges against him and claimed that, in a rage, Phillips had kicked her, beaten her, choked her, and slammed her head into a wall. She also contended that during the course of their two-year violent relationship, he had raped her and threatened her life. Phillips was sentenced to one-year probation after pleading no contest to these charges. His athletic ability was outstripped by his off-the-field misconduct, and his NFL career (with St. Louis, Miami, and San Francisco) was cut short by probation violation and several more arrests on charges of assaulting other women. Lawrence Phillips stands out as the prototype of the talented athlete whose unmanageable off-the-field aggression was destructive toward others and ruined his professional football career.

Ron Artest

Ron Artest is a classic example of a talented athlete whose violent reactions repeatedly trump good judgment. His NBA profile is checkered with a history of violent action while on the court. He is well known for committing a preponderance of flagrant fouls that led to multiple suspensions, and for the November 11, 2004, incident in which he ignited a brawl by running into the stands to attack a fan who had thrown a cup of beer at him, during the waning seconds of a Pacers-Pistons game. Artest was charged with assault and battery, pleaded no contest, was given a one-year probation, and was required to do anger management counseling. Instead of expressing remorse for violating a cardinal prohibition in professional sports against a player engaging in a physical altercation with a fan, Artest's spin was that he was betrayed by Commissioner David Stern for not supporting him, because the man who doused him was a convicted felon on parole.

Artest's violent side has also emerged in his personal relationships. In 2002, he was sent for anger management counseling after a domestic violence incident involving the mother of two of his children, who later became his wife. There were numerous calls to 911 with complaints of domestic violence, and in 2007, Artest was arrested on felony charges of assault and using force to restrict his wife from reporting a crime. Under upgraded guidelines that give the league leverage to suspend and even to void the contract of a player convicted of a felony, Artest was placed under indefinite suspension by the Sacramento Kings during the course of the investigation. He subsequently served a seven-game suspension. Artest pleaded no contest and was sentenced to one hundred hours of community service and ordered to get extensive counseling, including a one-year violence treatment program.

Fan Dissent

When fans rise up against teams that support players who engage in moral or legal transgressions, it can have considerable impact. After all, it is the loyal fans who ultimately pay the salaries of high-priced athletes. In a unique situation, after several Trail Blazers players were arrested, a group of basketball fans in Portland advocated for the boycotting of Trail Blazers games. The biggest offender was Ruben Patterson, who has had multiple domestic violence arrests in addition to jail time for sexually assaulting his children's nanny. Two other Trail Blazers players, Rasheed Wallace and Damon Stoudamire, were arrested on marijuana possession charges. In a commendable expression of disgust and protest, one fan posted a billboard in downtown that said, "Boycott Blazers! We need a team that can beat L.A., not women and the justice system."

ATHLETES WHO ARE ASSAULTED BY THEIR WIVES

There is usually a power imbalance in violent relationships, in which the man, who is bigger and stronger, is the physically aggressive partner. Sometimes, however, especially in the frenzy of an escalating argument, the man becomes the bigger victim. In recent years, several established sports stars have been in this position.

Nick Harper

Daniell Harper, the wife of Indianapolis Colts prominent cornerback Nick Harper, was arrested on felony charges of battery with a deadly weapon and criminal recklessness after stabbing her husband. The incident occurred in January 2002 on the eve of an NFL playoff game between the Colts and the Steelers.

Apparently, during an argument, Daniell approached Nick with two knives and slashed his knee in what could have been a career-threatening injury. The wound was substantial, but miraculously Harper played in the game, which the heavily favored Colts lost. Amazingly, he made an outstanding run return late in the game, after recovering a fumble, and was stopped by Steelers quarterback Roethlisberger, the slowest man in his path, in what would have been a game-winning touchdown. Many fans speculated that a fully healthy Harper would have led the Colts to victory.

In a violent episode between the couple seven months earlier, Nick Harper had been arrested on a domestic battery charge of hitting his wife in the face. It is conceivable that Daniell was harboring rage and deep resentment over the previous incident, and that her attack on Nick before his big game represented some payback.

Chuck Finley

Only three months later, in April 2002, Chuck Finley, a veteran Cleveland Indians pitcher, was attacked by his wife in the course of a dispute. Tawny Kitaen, a glamorous actress, who had appeared with Finley in a *Sports Illustrated* swimsuit issue, allegedly assaulted her husband while he was driving, creating a highly dangerous scenario. Kitaen was charged with spousal abuse and battery, and she faced up to a year in jail if convicted. The incident derailed Finley's first start of the season. In recognition of the dangerous nature of her actions, a judge issued a restraining order against Kitaen, and also indicated that she was in jeopardy of losing custody of their two young daughters.

Such incidents, which are all too common in our society, make headlines when they involve prominent sports figures. In the same year, 2002, there were two other high-profile cases of women's violence toward male athletes. Jeff Stone, a former MLB player, was hospitalized after being stabbed several times in his upper torso by his wife. Linda Stone was charged with first-degree assault. Anthony Davis, a star running back at the University of Wisconsin, was almost killed when he was stabbed close to a major artery in his thigh, by his girlfriend, who was charged with second-degree recklessly endangering safety.

Stabbings seem to be the assault method of choice by women who have assaulted male athletes. The NFL star Irving Fryar was attacked with a knife by his wife shortly before his 1986 Super Bowl game, and Houston Astros baseball hero Jimmy Wynn was stabbed in the abdomen by his wife during a domestic dispute in 1970.

The most serious violent incident in this category involved Fred Lane, a Colts running back, who was killed by shotgun blasts from his estranged wife, Deidra, in 2000. It was alleged by prosecutors that it was a premeditated murder motivated by Deidra Lane's design to collect Lane's $5 million insurance policy.

SEXUAL ASSAULTS

Sports heroes are conditioned to expect a quick fix when it comes to their sexual needs. The availability of accommodating women is generally abundant, but in circumstances in which such accommodations are absent, some athletes turn to rape and other misguided channels for satisfaction. There are many talented athletes whose careers have been significantly shortened as a result of their off-the-field misconduct, and their inability to internalize a constructive message from their brushes with the legal system.

A. J. Nicholson

One such player who stands out in this group is A. J. Nicholson. On the field, Nicholson was a ferocious linebacker at Florida State who led his team to a berth in the 2005 Orange Bowl. As a senior with a team-high 100 tackles, he was destined to be selected in the upcoming NFL draft.

A few days before the Orange Bowl game, Nicholson was suspended from the team after he was accused of raping a nineteen-year-old woman in his hotel room. He was spared possible incarceration when the woman later recanted on filing charges against him. This outcome seemingly reinforced his misguided belief that he would not be held accountable for his misbehavior. In what was to become a larger pattern, in that same year, Nicholson had already had two incidents involving the police: a DUI charge to which he pleaded no contest, and an unrelated charge of resisting arrest, which was dropped.

When athletes walk away unscathed from these encounters, they either learn from the experience of a close call and clean up their act, or they become increasingly emboldened in crossing boundaries and violating the standards of society. Nicholson was not one to learn from experience.

Although he was prohibited by his coach from playing in the Orange Bowl game, he was selected in the 2006 draft by the Cincinnati Bengals. His next episode in living on the edge occurred when he broke into the apartment of a former Florida State teammate. For this transgression, he served a sixty-day sentence in a work camp and was given two years' probation, with the stipulation that he not get arrested. This amounted to a zero-tolerance condition, which Nicholson could not fulfill. He was charged with assaulting his live-in girlfriend and mother of their two-year-old in May 2007. Once again, a woman recanted her story, on Nicholson's behalf, but he was deemed to have violated the terms of his probation by the Florida authorities. The Cincinnati Bengals, who had endured considerable negative publicity surrounding nine players who had been arrested during a nine-month span, responded by cutting Nicholson from the team.

David Meggett

The culture of celebrity sports stars who are unmindful about crossing sexual boundaries is epitomized by the off-the-field misbehavior of Dave Meggett, who has faced repeated charges of sexual assault. During his ten-year tenure with the Giants, Patriots, and Jets (1989–1998), Meggett enjoyed a highly successful NFL career as the all-time leader in punt returns.

While he was with the Giants, he was charged with lewdness, after allegedly soliciting sex from an undercover Baltimore police officer. After moving to the Patriots, he engaged in a bizarre sexual liaison in a Toronto hotel with a former Patriot player and a prostitute. During group sex, the players' condoms broke, and the woman refused to continue with sexual intercourse. She filed a complaint indicating that Meggett then beat her and forced her to pay back the money she had been given. Meggett and his buddy were charged with sexual assault and robbery in the episode, but the charges were dismissed after a jury was unable to reach a unanimous verdict.

Meggett protested that he had been set up in the Toronto incident, but instead of counting his blessings for getting off easy, he continued to act criminally. In 2001, he was arrested and charged with criminal sexual conduct in South Carolina, after he allegedly forced a woman he met in a bar into his car and compelled her to have sex with him. When it was determined that the woman was drunk, which under state law prohibited the authorities from charging him with rape, this case against Meggett also was dropped.

Meggett's profile of sexual misadventures and absence of consequences is in harmony with a USA Today report that athletes generally avoid legal penalties in sexual assault cases.[4]

While many athletes who get into trouble for off-the-field misbehavior are able to clean up their act and redirect their trajectory, Meggett may be the proverbial leopard who does not change his spots; he seems driven by inner forces to repeat the same inappropriate actions over and over again. In September 2006, at age forty, he was once again apprehended for second-degree rape. The woman, a former girlfriend, claimed that Meggett, with whom she had had a tumultuous relationship that ended a year earlier, broke into her home and raped her. Although he has eluded convictions and jail time for sexual assaults, the cumulative incidents cited here suggest that Meggett may be representative of the cadre of sports stars who have been conditioned to expect that their needs will be readily gratified by others.

Mel Hall

To prey on the vulnerability and innocence of underage victims to gratify your sexual needs is one of the most egregious acts of misconduct. Some sports stars, fueled by their distorted view of self, which prompts them to override and disrespect the rights of others, have been involved in such allegations.

After completing a successful thirteen-year MLB career in 1996, Mel Hall transitioned into coaching a select girls' basketball team. In 2007, he was arrested on charges of sexually assaulting two of the girls he had coached in 1998 and 1999. The girls were only twelve and fourteen years old at the time of the alleged incidents, and the charge involving the younger girl carried a possible life sentence in a conviction. After Hall's indictment in Texas, the police speculated that other young girls in athletic programs may have been victims of his inappropriate sexual advances.

Luis Polonia

In 1989, Luis Polonia was arrested on similar charges of sexually assaulting a minor, while he was an active player with the New York Yankees. After a game in Milwaukee, Polonia engaged in a misguided encounter in his hotel room with a fifteen-year-old fan. Polonia faced a prison sentence of up to ten years, if convicted. To justify his reprehensible behavior and poor judgment, driven by his need for a sexual fix, Polonia claimed that he was unaware of the girl's age.

CONTROVERSIAL WOMEN IN MALE SPORTS ORGANIZATIONS

Ruth Dressen and Charlie Dressen

Only the most diehard of Brooklyn Dodgers fans will remember the circumstances surrounding the sudden dismissal of manager Charlie Dressen after the 1953 season. It was the golden era of baseball in Brooklyn, several years before the lure of California gold was even a twinkle in the eyes of owner Walter O'Malley. Dressen had completed three wildly glorious years as manager, including the winning of two pennants, and he had achieved the most successful record of any manager in the team's history.

The Dodgers' organization maintained a policy of offering only one-year contracts, and although the tenure of major league managers is always tenuous at best, Dressen and his wife bristled over the lack of long-term security. Other managers with poorer records were signing up with two- and three-year deals, which prompted Ruth Dressen to push her husband to be more assertive in challenging the longstanding renewal policy. She taunted him for not taking a more aggressive stance, and she composed a letter, which, in effect, had him demanding an extended term. At his wife's insistence, Dressen overplayed his hand and overestimated how the owners valued him. He may have been a productive manager, but they were not about to be intimidated by his demands; they responded by firing him on the spot. Dressen was apparently imbued by and proud of his managerial success, but given the reality of the contractual tradition, he was coaxed misguidedly by his wife to use poor judgment in pursuing his quest.

Dressen faded into obscurity in assembling a lackluster performance in piloting other teams, and his bucking the system, as it were, probably haunted him for the rest of his life. Ironically, his successor, Walter Alston, led the Dodgers successfully for the next twenty-three years with annual contract renewals.

Anna Benson and Kris Benson

When a sports star marries a celebrity, her actions also receive spotlight attention, and under adverse conditions can do damage to the athlete's career. This seems to be the case with baseball pitcher Kris Benson, and his provocative wife, Anna. It seems that Anna Benson may have used her status as a prominent baseball wife as a platform to gain headlines and notoriety for herself. Unfortunately for Kris, her outspoken and flamboyant machinations in attracting media attention undoubtedly were a distraction and contributed to his premature demise from the New York Mets.

Before marrying Kris, Anna had been a celebrity of sorts in her own right, as a model and stripper. Soon after Kris, an established pitcher, came to the Mets in 2004, Anna posed for *FHM* magazine, and was named baseball's hottest wife. Subsequently, she supposedly sought to further her career by negotiating to pose nude for *Playboy*, in a deal that fell through. While Anna basked in the glow of glamorous adulation, the Mets management quickly viewed her behavior as a source of turbulence and began to consider ways to get rid of Kris Benson.

Anna Benson's other headline-making incidents include freely discussing with the media intimate details of their sex life, and appearing on the *Howard Stern Show* and declaring (in the context of the culture of adultery among sports stars) that, if her husband was unfaithful, she would retaliate by having sex with every member of the Mets team as well as the ground crew. This did not help Kris's standing with the team. She stirred up additional controversy with her provocatively sexy dress at the Mets' 2005 Christmas party, and inappropriately deriding general manager Omar Minaya for assembling an all-Latino team.

Although it has been vigorously denied by the Mets organization, it seems likely that the accumulation of Anna Benson's provocative incidents was instrumental in Kris being traded away in 2006, rather than being given the opportunity to fulfill his expected role as a mainstay of their pitching staff. Later that year, Anna filed for divorce but then changed her mind.

Kendra Davis and Antonio Davis

It is customary for players' wives to attend the team's games, and as such, they can be targets for fan interference, harassment, and abuse. Assertive and outspoken spouses who push back, when they feel their rights are being disrespected or their space is being violated, may get involved in unsavory encounters. Kendra Davis is a case in point.

When he saw a spectator grabbing his wife's wrist in a physical confrontation, Antonio Davis of the New York Knicks bolted into the stands to protect her. The episode occurred in the final minutes of a game in the Chicago Bulls arena in January 2006. Davis, who was the head of the NBA Players Association at the time, was aware that entering the stands was emphatically verboten, but his duty to safeguard his wife from perceived potential danger trumped obeying the rules.

Right or wrong, the NBA, which established a strict prohibition stemming from an ugly brawl between fans and players at a Pacers-Pistons game in 2004, had no choice but to levy a five-game suspension against Davis. In defense of his actions, Davis acknowledged that he would do it again, if a similar situation arose.

Moments before the incident, Kendra Davis, who was at the game with her ten-year-old twins, engaged in an encounter with another (Bulls) fan who she claimed was excessively verbally abusive and was using profanity in berating Antonio. The fan was escorted away by security, but he maintained that Kendra Davis had scratched his face and threatened to pursue a $1 million battery lawsuit unless she apologized.

While public opinion rallied behind Antonio Davis for his actions in defiance of NBA rules, it seems that Kendra Davis played a part in inflaming things by her alleged threatening reactions to these two male fans. Kendra is a self-described nonshrinking violet when she feels she is being mistreated. Shortly after this episode, she was charged with misdemeanor battery in a traffic incident, which occurred three months earlier, in which she threw a cup of coffee at a woman in another car whom she claimed had directed a racial slur toward her.

Anucha Browne Sanders and Isiah Thomas

A favorable outcome regarding women's rights in allegations of misconduct by a sports celebrity occurred in the tempestuous trial of Anucha Browne Sanders versus Isiah Thomas and Madison Square Garden. In a landmark case that demonstrated the legal system's improved readiness to receive complaints and rule against celebrity sexual harassment offenders, a jury awarded Browne Sanders punitive damages of $11.6 million.

The substance of her allegations was that Isiah Thomas had expressed his attraction to her, said he was in love with her, and tried to kiss her. These sexually charged overtures meet the definition of harassment in the workplace. She claimed that this behavior started soon after she was hired in 2003 as a senior vice president for marketing and business operations with a $260,000 salary, and it continued for two years. She maintained that she had no choice but to file her lawsuit, because her complaints that Thomas had made numerous unwanted advances, cursed her, and barred New York Knicks players from working with her on community events were being ignored by Madison Square Garden officials. The legal brief indicated that Browne Sanders was seeking a $6 million payment and total damages of $9.6 million pertaining to two counts of sex discrimination plus two counts of retaliation. An additional precipitating factor was that within a few weeks of initiating her formal complaint to the Garden, James Dolan, the company chairman, fired her.

In justifying her pursuit of this lawsuit, she stated,

> I took this action because I had no choice. My pleas and complaints about Mr. Thomas' illegal and offensive behavior fell on deaf ears. He refused to stop his demeaning and repulsive behavior and the Garden refused to intercede. I am outraged that I was fired for telling the truth.[5]

That is, she was fired as a retaliatory act in response to her going through internal channels to stop the harassment.

The Garden's lawyer asserted that she was fired because of her poor job performance and her interference with their internal probe into her accusations. The defense team sought to discredit her as a conniving woman bent on exploiting the system, and they presented evidence that she had previously filed a sexual harassment grievance while working at IBM.

In response to Browne Sanders' accusations, Isiah Thomas spoke out, against advice from his attorneys, and protested with indignation that he was being unfairly targeted by Browne Sanders "as a pawn for financial gain."[6]

The case came to trial in September 2007, and after two weeks of testimony, the jury agreed that there was evidence of sexual discrimination and that Isiah Thomas and the Madison Square Garden Company were culpable in subjecting her to a hostile work environment. The Garden was ordered to pay punitive damages of $11.6 million: $6 million for subjecting her to a hostile work environment, $2.6 million for terminating her in retaliation, and an additional $3 million from James Dolan, the company chairman, for firing her in retaliation. This sum amounted to peanuts for

Dolan and Madison Square Garden, which is owned by Cablevision Corp. Curiously, Isiah Thomas, although determined to be liable, was not required to pay punitive damages.

In savoring her legal victory, Browne Sanders emphasized that her case represented a larger issue about the treatment of women in the workplace. She stated, "What I did here, I did for every working woman in America. And that includes everyone who gets up and goes to work in the morning, everyone working in a corporate environment. The verdict was more about sending a message to corporate America than the money."[7]

The Garden officials described the verdict as a travesty of justice, and Thomas continued to proclaim his innocence. One of the most important by-products of this case is that it sends a message to sports stars that they need to be mindful of consequences for moral and legal transgressions.

THE FOREMOST SEXUAL ASSAULT CASE OF THE NEW MILLENNIUM: KOBE BRYANT

It takes courage to take on a high-profile sports star, particularly one who has enormous financial resources available to assemble a dream team of attorneys who are skilled at finding ways to discredit the credibility of an accuser. When Kobe Bryant was arrested in July 2003 for sexual assault on a nineteen-year-old front desk employee at an Eagle, Colorado, hotel, it became the primary sports scandal of the year. The charges were felonious, which carried a sentence of four years to life if convicted.

Unlike many NBA players who came from inner-city backgrounds where violence toward women was the norm, Bryant grew up as the privileged son of an NBA player, and flourished with an image of a poster boy with solid values. He came to the NBA directly out of high school and was heralded as the next Michael Jordan. He quickly became a superstar and was rewarded with huge endorsement deals from Nike, McDonald's, and Sprite.

In the complaint, the hotel employee, Katelyn Faber, indicated that she gave Bryant a tour of the hotel when he checked in, and went to his room, where hugs and kisses were reciprocally exchanged. Then, according to Faber, Kobe put his hands around her neck and forced her to have sex with him—that is, he raped her.

Kobe acknowledged the tryst and berated himself tearfully on national television for his adulterous lapse, but he claimed that it had been a consensual encounter that included oral sex, and vaginal penetration that he terminated, after she declined his request that he ejaculate onto her face, an aspect of kinky sex that adds a tone of aggression and humiliation toward the woman. Their sexual liaison ended without Bryant having an orgasm, and he masturbated in his room after Faber left.

In a sports hero culture, in which athletes are besieged by women who are sexually available, this event may have registered merely as a blip on Kobe Bryant's radar screen. Many athletes are known to have numerous one-night stands with admiring groupies, and we have no way of knowing whether Bryant had been involved in similar incidents that had gone undiscovered and unreported. Sports stars generally are treated like studs by accommodating women, and their inflated self-image prompts them to blur boundaries when a woman says no to their sexual demands.

The local district attorney found Katelyn Faber's story to be believable, and he set out to prosecute Bryant, but Faber's tainted background undermined his case. At the legal hearings, Kobe's defense team attacked her credibility and painted her as a promiscuous and mentally disturbed young woman. They presented documentation that when she went for her rape exam, she wore underpants that contained another man's semen and pubic hair. They also indicated that she was taking an antipsychotic drug used in the treatment of schizophrenia, when the incident occurred. Katelyn's roommate asserted that Faber twice had tried to kill herself with sleeping pills, and this cumulative material was used to create a profile of her as mentally unbalanced, which severely compromised her credibility.

She may have been telling the truth about being sexually assaulted, but Kobe had the firepower to destroy her, and under the stressful conditions in which her other sexual activities and background were ruled as admissible testimony, along with two death threats and intense media spotlight, Faber decided to withdraw her criminal lawsuit. Kobe Bryant was vindicated, and his image was partially repaired as he regained several of his lucrative endorsement deals. In 2008, he was named the league's MVP, as he led the Los Angeles Lakers to the NBA championship finals, and was widely regarded as the best basketball player on the planet. Katelyn Faber entered a rehab facility for cocaine addiction in 2004.

The outcome of the Kobe Bryant scandal will sadly reinforce the belief held by many high-profile athletes, who are quick to indulge their sexual appetites indiscriminately—that is, that they can prevail whether they are rightly or wrongly accused of rape. The danger is that possible legal entanglements will be perceived as an irritant rather than as a deterrent. These athletes would be wise to keep in mind that even in consensual promiscuous sex there is a risk of repercussions.

DUKE UNIVERSITY LACROSSE TEAM SCANDAL

The Duke lacrosse team scandal is at the other end of the spectrum of scandals involving women who allege sexual misconduct by athletes. In an episode that spawned racial overtones, community outrage, class divisions, a corrupt district attorney, university heavy-handedness, and traumatic experiences for three student-athletes, Crystal Gail Mangum, a black stripper and exotic dancer, accused three white Duke University lacrosse players of raping her at a team party on March 13, 2006. The media coverage, which trades on scandals, was extensive. Rich white kids versus a poor black woman with sexual allegations in a Southern town is a recipe for ongoing headlines.

In boys-will-be-boys fraternity-like style, the lacrosse team contacted an escort service to send two exotic dancers to entertain at a team party. The players, all but one of whom were white, requested white strippers, but the service sent two black women instead. For openers, one of the players asked if they had brought any sex toys, and one of the dancers countered by asking if his penis was too small. The repartee continued with a player suggesting that they could use a broomstick, and the atmosphere became tense. At this point, the women felt that they were being treated derisively, which would not be unusual in this type of setting, and they abruptly stopped the entertainment and retreated to the bathroom. One or more of the boys followed them, and what happened next is unclear. But what is clear is that the dancers left and one of them, Crystal Mangum, later told the police that she had been raped. She was taken to the hospital for a rape kit exam, and she was interviewed extensively by the police and District Attorney Mike Nifong, who seemed eager to pursue the charges against the lacrosse players.

Accordingly, racial tensions and class antagonisms were incited by this case and a wave of hysteria gripped the college town of Durham, North Carolina. To demonstrate that they took the matter very seriously, and determined to avoid allegations about protecting their students, the Duke administration responded by suspending the accused players (Colin Finnerty, Reade Seligmann, and David Evans) and canceling the remainder of the lacrosse schedule. The coach, Mike Pressler, was forced to resign, and the accused student-athletes were treated like criminals, after they were arrested and indicted on charges of first-degree forcible rape, first-degree sexual offense, and kidnapping.

Over the ensuing months, the case fell apart because Crystal Mangum, the accuser, was not credible, and Mike Nifong withheld evidence and misled the court. Mangum kept changing her story after initially declaring that she had been gang raped by twenty white men, and the stripper who accompanied her refuted the rape story and indicated that Mangum was under the influence of alcohol and medications. Furthermore, laboratory test results revealed that there were DNA samples from multiple non-lacrosse players in Mangum's body, and these findings were unreported at the request of prosecutor Mike Nifong.

In January 2007, after ethics charges were filed against him, Nifong withdrew from the case, and he was subsequently disbarred for fraud, dishonesty, deceit, and misrepresentation. Three months later, the North

Carolina attorney general intervened and denounced Nifong as a rogue prosecutor, and dismissed the charges against the players. To underscore that they were not merely benefiting from prosecutorial misconduct, he declared that the student-athletes were innocent of any wrongdoing.

Isiah Thomas, Kobe Bryant, and the Duke lacrosse players have been subjected to allegations by women who claimed that they crossed sexual boundaries. Once they were ensnared in the legal process, these sports figures assembled high-power legal teams to defend them. Isiah Thomas lost his case, because the jury believed Anucha Browne Sanders's account of sexual harassment. She was a credible witness who drew sympathy and compassion for taking on the old boys' network. Kobe and the Duke players prevailed in their cases without going to trial, because the accuser in the Bryant case had considerable sexual and mental health issues in her background, which would influence her credibility about being raped. In the Duke case, the accuser's inconsistencies were damaging to her credibility, and the corrupt prosecutor exhibited substantial professional misconduct. Additionally, the accuser's promiscuity portrayed her in a negative and unsympathetic light.

CHAPTER SIX

Murder Scandals

There is scant evidence that athletes commit murder or are victims of murder to a greater extent than what takes place in the general population. When these incidents do occur, because of the celebrity status of sports stars, they create headlines and become scandalous. The most serious crimes committed by athletes have involved murder.

In *Sports Heroes, Fallen Idols*,[1] I examined some of the major murder cases centering around famous athletes. The murder charges enveloping professional football heroes Rae Carruth, Ray Lewis, Darryl Henley, Brian Blades, and Raymond Clayborn; professional basketball player Jayson Williams; and MLB players Pinky Higgins, Hank Thompson, and Cesar Cedeno were chronicled.

This chapter focuses on additional murder cases, more recent episodes, and further illegal misbehavior of a previous offender.

O. J. SIMPSON—THE LAS VEGAS CAPER

In September 2007, Simpson and five hired accomplices burst into a Las Vegas hotel room to rob a batch of sports memorabilia from two collectibles dealers. What possibly could have motivated Simpson, who previously was fortunate enough to have avoided a murder conviction, to put himself at such risk? Was it a death wish, as some suggest, or a continuation of an arrogant mind-set that prompted him to believe that he could get away with any transgression? In his defense, Simpson claimed that he was merely attempting to reclaim items that had been stolen from him and that he was unaware that two of his men had brandished weapons in the encounter. The jury was unimpressed with his defense, and, ironically, thirteen years to the day after he was acquitted in his murder trial, they deliberated for only thirteen hours and convicted him on twelve counts, including robbery and kidnapping. He was sentenced to nine to thirty-three years in prison and, under Nevada law, he could have received up to a life term.

There was little interest in this trial by a public that seemed to have grown tired of Simpson's crossing of legal boundaries. In contrast to the extensive support given to O. J. in the 1995 trial by the black community, this time there was a striking absence of any activism within that community or by local journalists on his behalf.

The Issues

In 1995, in what has been termed the trial of the century, former football star O. J. Simpson was acquitted in the murders of his wife, Nicole Brown Simpson, and Ron Goldman. It was widely believed that Simpson was guilty and had been saved by the brilliant maneuvers of his dream defense team. In the subsequent civil suit, Simpson was found to be liable for the deaths, and the court determined that he was to pay $33.5 million to the estates of the victims. Simpson was able to make his assets untouchable, and no amount of the court-ordered payment has ever been made.

Simpson did not seem to learn from his fateful experience in the 1995 case, and he continued to have brushes with the law; the most conspicuous of which was a 2001 road rage incident in Florida in which he was acquitted of battery and auto burglary charges. More recently, he brazenly flaunted a fictional account of the 1994 murders, entitled "If I Did It," which enraged the public and forced the publisher to scuttle the project.

After the 1995 acquittal, Simpson continued to enjoy his celebrity status and operated without accountability. Despite the fact that the vast majority of the American people believed that he was guilty of killing Nicole Brown Simpson and Ron Goldman, it did not seem to modify Simpson's inflated self-image, which dictated that he could do whatever he wanted without restraint or fear of consequences. We can only speculate about the internal workings of his psyche, which at times defied logic in that he appeared to behave with recklessness and poor judgment driven by rage, rather than consideration of how, given the residual public antipathy toward him, he was putting himself at risk. Amazingly, he seemed oblivious to the backlash that could emerge if he crossed boundaries and behaved in ways that ignored society's acceptable standards of conduct.

Thus, after 1995, he was a pariah, but he acted as though he was above the law. So, it was predictable that if he became ensnared in legal transgressions, payback ultimately would come his way. In the Las Vegas case, the jurors maintained that their deliberations were characterized by a total absence of influence from the 1994 tragedies. From a psychological perspective, however, it is likely that on an unconscious level the jury may have wanted to give Simpson his long-overdo comeuppance. This phenomenon is parallel to what has been described as "aversive racism," in which voters who see themselves as believing in racial equality and purport to be comfortable with electing a black person as president, nevertheless, may make a discriminatory choice or decision based on unconscious factors.[2]

Simpson's Las Vegas caper reeks of mental health pathology. Conventional wisdom would suggest that, after you come within a hair's-breadth of being convicted for double murder, you would ensure that you never again placed yourself or anyone else in harm's way; but this way of thinking is not in Simpson's nature. Simpson's pattern of repeatedly performing acts that lead to arrest, his reckless disregard for the safety of others, and a lack of remorse as indicated by an indifference to or rationalization of having hurt, mistreated, or stolen from others are consistent with a diagnosis of antisocial personality disorder.

CHRIS BENOIT

The double murder and suicide of professional wrestler Chris Benoit attracted national headlines in June 2007.

In a gruesome scenario, Benoit, one of the most popular figures in the World Wrestling Entertainment (WWE) organization, killed his wife, Nancy, and their seven-year-old-son, Daniel, before taking his own life. The events occurred over a three-day period in which Benoit, known to his fans as the Rabid Wolverine, began his spree of violence by physically overpowering his wife, tying her wrists and feet together, and strangling her. Police investigators found that she had bruises on her back and stomach and blood under her head, which conveyed that she had put up a struggle. Curiously, Benoit left a Bible alongside her body.

Several hours later, he sedated his son with the tranquilizer Xanax and then strangled him to death. Daniel had been diagnosed with Fragile X syndrome, a form of autism, and the needle marks in his arm led to speculation that he had been injected with a growth hormone because he was undersized. Benoit also placed a Bible next to his boy's body. The next day, Chris Benoit committed suicide by hanging himself in his basement exercise room.

Theories of Benoit's Motivation

Fans and experts alike were stunned by these horrific killings and were at a loss to make any sense out of this situation. Getting inside the mind of Chris Benoit, posthumously, would be a supremely challenging endeavor. Three primary theories emerged regarding the motivation underlying these homicides and suicide. One area of explanation is based on the history of marital discord between Chris and Nancy, and the stress induced by their son's disability. In fact, Nancy had filed for divorce in 2003 and had requested a restraining order against her husband, citing that he had been threatening, abusive, and violent in their home, but she withdrew her suit three months later. It was also reported that recently there had been considerable strife between the couple over how to provide optimal care for Daniel, although his school administrators indicated that his academic skills were adequate. This theory, then, is based on the questionable premise that Chris Benoit acted out his rage toward his wife related to their disharmony over Daniel and that he killed his son to spare him from a tormented future.

An alternative explanation is that this tragedy was driven by changes in Benoit's brain chemistry as a function of his having sustained multiple concussions during his wrestling bouts. Analysis of his brain tissue indicated that he suffered from severe chronic encephalopathy (CTE) and that his brain damage was so extensive that "it resembled the brain of an 85-year-old Alzheimer's patient."[3] Christopher Nowinski, a former wrestler and now president of the Sports Legacy Institute, opined that Benoit had probably endured a series of untreated concussions during his career, which could lead to an unstable mental state and erratic behavior.[4] A study of Benoit's brain revealed degenerative processes that were similar to those found in three former professional football players who had killed themselves. While this might be suggestive of a trend in which severely brain-damaged athletes are prone to depression and self-destructive behavior or violence toward others, the sample of cases is much too small to draw any definitive conclusions. Dr. Robert Cantu, a highly respected neurosurgeon affiliated with the Sports Legacy Institute, conceded that there was no way to know with certainty whether Benoit's history of concussions played a part in the tragedy. To the extent that there is a medically established connection between severe brain damage and compromised cognitive functions, such as good judgment and a checks and balance on the expression of violent behavior, it seems possible that the status of Benoit's degenerative brain process, in which all four lobes of his brain as well as the brain stem showed damage, was a factor that may have triggered his murderous and suicidal actions.

The Sports Legacy Institute has been proactive in drawing public attention to depression and dementia as long-term effects from multiple concussions in the sports world. The Institute has been sharply critical of the WWE and the NFL for their lack of oversight in monitoring the treatment of athletes who suffer concussions.

A third, and more controversial, theory is that the double murders and suicide were fueled by Benoit's involvement with steroids. The notion is that steroid-induced rage and paranoia can lead to uncontrolled violent outbursts. In the Benoit case, the police discovered steroids in his home, and the toxicology report indicated that Benoit's body had ten times the normal level of testosterone. Dr. Kris Sperry, the chief medical examiner in the state of Georgia, acknowledged that testosterone recently had been injected into Benoit's body, but he was reluctant to attribute a causal link between steroids and the murders.

Investigators discovered that Chris had received a ten-month supply of steroids prescribed for his use every three to four weeks between May 2006 and May 2007. Under the WWE drug-testing regulations, Benoit had tested negative as recently as April 2007, only two months before the killings. The WWE, however, declined to make public his three previous test results.

The WWE Spin

The WWE, concerned that a steroids connection to the killings could tarnish its image and hurt its lucrative viewership, was quick to employ damage control and issued a statement of disclaimer. They asserted that the circumstances of the murders and suicide pointed to acts of deliberation—that is, these actions were premeditated by Benoit, rather than impulsive actions driven by steroid rage. Doping experts agreed that the time intervals of over three days made it unlikely that the violence was entirely triggered by what is called "roid rage."

Early Deaths

Professional wrestlers' involvement with steroids is not a new phenomenon. The number of premature deaths among wrestlers is greater than in any other sport, and many of these deaths have been connected to steroids. Eddie Guerrero, a WWE superstar, died in 2005 at age thirty-eight of heart disease linked to steroid use. A year earlier, a similar scenario led to the death of Davey Boy Smith, affectionately known to his fans as "the British Bulldog." Other professional wrestlers have endured serious health hazards from painkillers, alcohol, cocaine, and other illicit substances, which seem to be inherent in the wrestling culture.

A Flawed Drug-Testing Program

As a result of Guerrero's death, the WWE put forth a drug-testing program, but it was implemented poorly. The plan authorized random but not unannounced tests of the WWE's group of 180 performers. The plan also contained an extremely lenient threshold in which a testosterone-to-epitestosterone ratio between four to one and ten to one necessitated follow-up testing. This is in contrast to the World Anti-Doping Agency (WADA) standard that any test that yields a ration of four to one or higher is declared to be a positive test finding. Despite the sham of the lower bar, in which a wrestler can effectively pass a drug test with up to a ten-to-one ratio, eight participants tested positive, which suggests the likelihood that they were steroid users who beat the system. The sanctions are a thirty-day suspension for the first positive test, sixty days for a second positive finding, and a lifetime ban for a third failed test. Thus far, no one has had three positive test findings. The existing policy seems to be mere window dressing, and at the very least, if the organization is to be taken seriously, the threshold must be substantially tightened.

The WWE has been widely condemned for setting in place such a weak drug program and for its general lack of oversight. Phil Mushnick, a respected reporter for the *New York Post*, has declared that "pro wrestling manufactures death" and launched a stinging attack on WWE Chairman Vince McMahon for promoting an entertainment industry that encourages wrestlers to rely on steroids and other substances that jeopardize their health and, in many cases, induce death at a young age. In taking aim at McMahon after the Benoit killings, Mushnick wrote, "Look what it has taken for the mass media to finally begin to report that Vince McMahon has been operating a death mill for the past 25 years . . . pro wrestlers have been steadily dying young since the early 1980s, when McMahon began to rule the industry."[5] Professional wrestlers are shamelessly and dangerously pressured "to develop massive physiques, the kind the industry has demanded and rewarded since McMahon took over."[6]

Fan Reaction

The cadre of Chris Benoit admiring fans who placed him on a pedestal reacted with sadness and disgust to the reality that their anointed hero, with whom they felt so connected, could engage in such violent actions in his personal life. Many felt a sense of betrayal and advocated that his status in the *Wrestling Observer Newsletter* (WON) Hall of Fame be revoked. A 60 percent margin was required to remove Benoit from the WON Hall of Fame. A recall election was undertaken, and 54 percent of the voters opted to remove him, which barely fell short of the criteria for removal.

Fallout from the Benoit Incident

On a positive note, in the wake of the publicity surrounding the double murder–suicide, Georgia Sen. Johnny Isakson pushed for federal investigation and oversight of the wrestling industry with an emphasis on the need for greater control over steroid use.

Dr. Phil Astin, who had prescribed the ten-month supply of steroids to Benoit, was indicted in May 2008 on 175 federal counts for improperly writing prescriptions to nineteen patients. The criminal charges alleged that one of his patients died from the drugs he had dispensed. Dr. Astin pleaded guilty, and in May 2009, he was sentenced to ten years in prison for illegally prescribing painkillers and other drugs.

To a certain extent, some high-profile athletes are at risk for violent encounters that may lead to murder, primarily because of their off-the-field lifestyles in which they put themselves in dangerous situations by frequenting risqué nightclubs. Other scenarios, such as spousal abuse, opportunistic motives, botched robberies, and reckless behavior, also have resulted in murder cases involving athletes. The following cases are representative examples of murder scandals involving athletes in these various categories.

SPOUSAL ABUSE

Tommy Kane

Tommy Kane, a prominent pass receiver for the Seattle Seahawks, pleaded guilty to the brutal murder of his wife, Tammara Shaikh, in November 2003. Kane had been in the grips of depression before the violent eruption in which he stabbed and beat to death the mother of their four children. The couple was separated at the time of the attack, which had escalated from a heated argument. Kane received a relatively lenient sentence of eighteen years for manslaughter, because there was insufficient evidence that he had planned or intended to kill his wife.

Terry Underwood

Terry Underwood, a former football star at Wagner College, was convicted of murdering his pregnant wife, Theresa, while their two young children were asleep in their house, on August 24, 1988.

In a most grizzly murder scene, the police found that Theresa, who was Terry's childhood sweetheart, had been stabbed eighty-eight times. To inflict eighty-eight stab wounds requires an unimaginable magnitude of rage. Underwood confessed to the crime and admitted to investigators that he had "snapped" and started beating her. He also failed a polygraph test. The presiding judge emphasized at sentencing that this was an extremely heinous murder in which his wife "in essence was slaughtered."[7]

At his trial, Underwood maintained that he was innocent and that his confession had been coerced. His attorney contended that he had been subjected to an illegal arrest and a harsh interrogation in which he went thirty-seven hours without sleep and twenty-six hours without food or drink. He pointed out that under circumstances of that degree of deprivation and prolonged interrogation, it was not unusual for someone to incriminate themselves. As for the polygraph evidence, it was argued that such tests are not always reliable. Underwood's best friend testified that Terry had been with him most of the night of the murder and could not have committed the crime. Furthermore, the case was tried in New Jersey, and one of the jurors was the uncle of the Monmouth County, New Jersey, chief prosecutor.

Underwood protested that he had been railroaded into prison for a crime he did not commit and that the jury's dismissal of his defense was a backlash from the Simpson trial. This position is reminiscent of the aftermath of the NFL's Rae Carruth's murder case in which his mother went on national television to plead her son's innocence and to condemn the jury for operating with a Simpson backlash mentality.

There appeared to be a number of possible grounds for appeal in the Underwood conviction, but he lost the appeal. His attorney subsequently filed a motion for DNA testing of Theresa's fingernail and hair samples in the hope that someone else's DNA would be discovered.

An interesting sidelight of this case is that, pending the DNA findings, a movement has begun among Underwood's supporters to get the Innocence Project to take up his cause. The Innocence Project, spearheaded by renowned defense lawyer Barry Scheck, is a nonprofit legal clinic that has gained national recognition as an organization that uses DNA technology to vindicate wrongly convicted people. Their efforts have contributed to 208 alleged criminals being exonerated by DNA test results, including fifteen who were awaiting execution on death row. If they take on the Underwood conviction, it will surely generate headlines.

MOVING IN HARM'S WAY

Charles Grant

Charles Grant, a defensive end for the New Orleans Saints, was among seven men indicted for involuntary manslaughter, stemming from a brawl outside of a Georgia nightclub in 2008. In the fracas in which Grant was stabbed in the neck; a pregnant twenty-three-year-old bystander was shot to death. Grant had been viewed as a potential NFL superstar in 2007, when he was given a seven-year contract extension worth $63 million. Grant's defense was that he did not directly participate in the fight, but it is mind-boggling to observe that star athletes who go out for a night of fun continue to visit these milieus where unpredictability rules the night.

Darrent Williams

At the other end of the spectrum, Darrent Williams, a Denver Broncos star cornerback, was the victim of a drive-by shooting on New Year's Day in 2007 following an altercation at a Denver nightclub between Williams's group and members of another group. In a classic situation in which it takes so little to trigger a violent episode in these nightclub environments, champagne that was being sprayed around by the Williams party hit a participant of another group that included belligerent gang members. A confrontation quickly ensued, culminating in the shooting.

In October 2008, Willie Clark, who was in federal custody in another case, was indicted on thirty-nine counts in the murder of Darrent Williams.

Richard Collier

Richard Collier, an offensive tackle for the Jacksonville Jaguars, was shot and critically wounded just before his team's season opener in September 2008. The circumstances are somewhat vague, but what is known is that the incident occurred at 2:45 A.M., while he was waiting in his car for a woman he had met in a nightclub.

In the past two years, the Jaguars had had eleven players arrested for various offenses, but any intimations that Collier had used poor judgment in seeking out the nightclub environment were dismissed by coach Jack Del Rio as a misguided exercise in blaming the victim. Del Rio defended Collier's right to go out for a fun night before a day off as totally appropriate and responsible, but he seems oblivious to the situational risks inherent in going to these clubs. One year earlier, Collier had received six months of probation time after failing a sobriety test.

VIOLENCE IN NIGHTCLUBS

It is apparent that an epidemic has emerged of athletes who become entangled in violent episodes in a nightclub setting. A partial list of such encounters includes the following:

- 2008—Larry Johnson, Kansas City Chiefs stellar running back, charged with pushing a woman at a Kansas City nightclub and faced a six-month prison term. It was his third charge of assaulting a woman since 2003.
- 2008—J. J. Arrington, Arizona Cardinals running back, arrested in a nightclub fight.
- 2007—Jamaal Tinsley, Indiana Pacers guard, was shot at after leaving a nightclub.
- 2006—Stephen Jackson, Golden State Warriors forward, pleaded guilty to criminal recklessness in a gun-firing incident outside an Indianapolis strip club.
- 2006—Julius Hodge, Denver Nuggets guard, was shot four times after leaving a Denver club.
- 2004—Kwane Doster, Vanderbilt University running back, was shot and killed outside a Tampa nightclub.
- 2003—Joey Porter, Pittsburgh Steelers linebacker, was shot at in a Denver sports bar.
- 2003—Dernell Stenson, Cincinnati Reds player, was shot and killed after being kidnapped in his SUV by two thugs outside a Scottsdale club.
- 2001—Elijah Williams, Atlanta Falcons cornerback, was shot in the leg outside an Atlanta bar in a robbery attempt.
- 2000—Paul Pierce, Boston Celtics superstar, was stabbed eleven times in an altercation at a Boston nightclub.

The pattern is clear that celebrity athletes who frequent the night-club scene are in danger of becoming embroiled in violent episodes. As these circumstances escalate to more explosive proportions, these athletes may become perpetrators or victims of more serious crimes. To some extent, the ubiquitous sense of personal invulnerability, rampant among young sports stars, leads them to underestimate the degree to which they are at risk. The abundance of money that athletes have at their disposal once they have ascended to the professional ranks also makes them targets for predators. As celebrities, they are easily recognized, and by flaunting their wealth, fancy cars, and jewelry in a nightclub setting where drinking prevails, they also are creating a recipe for trouble. In addition, resentment and jealousy about their affluence and robbery motives play a part in the violent incidents affecting sports stars.

Nightclub violence in situations involving sports figures has been happening so often that, in some quarters, it is no longer considered newsworthy. It has become commonplace, and the public has accepted it as a reality that inevitably follows celebrity sports stars. There is something wrong with this picture in which we have become indifferent to athletes committing murder and being shot at or murdered as a result of their having put themselves in dangerous situations.

The major sports leagues have established programs to educate rookies about the dangers they may encounter in off-the-field situations. These seminars usually are presented before the beginning of a new season, and they are intended to raise consciousness and responsibility regarding misbehavior. It would be prudent to expand these education programs by providing ongoing seminars throughout the playing season (and beyond for those players who have gotten into trouble) to reinforce the need to be mindful of the potential vulnerability and responsibility that comes with their celebrity status. Involvement with drugs, drug dealing, and going to shady clubs is a precipitating factor that often leads to violence, and it is tantamount to putting yourself in harm's way. A successful program needs to be launched that punctures athletes' sense of personal invulnerability and helps them to more fully recognize the danger that accompanies frequenting nightclubs and strip clubs where alcohol consumption unleashes inhibitions around violent behavior.

OPPORTUNISTIC MURDER CASES

The pressure on talented young athletes to excel, fueled by aspirations of making it to the professional ranks, and the intensity of overly zealous parents who live vicariously through their offspring, has led to several sports tragedies. In some situations, the blinding desire to succeed leads to a blurring of perspective in which the sport is no longer perceived as a venue for fair play, and the need to derail rivals through malicious aggressive action prevails.

Mitchell Cozad

In September 2006, Mitchell Cozad, an aspiring football player at Northern Colorado University, was distraught over losing the starting punter position to teammate Rafael Mendoza. Cozad was envious of Mendoza's superior ability, and when Mendoza was ambushed and attacked in a dark parking lot by a knife-wielding hooded assailant, the finger of suspicion pointed at Cozad.

Mendoza told the police that his assailant had twice attempted to stab him in the chest after knocking him down on the pavement, but he was able to push him away. He was then stabbed in his kicking leg and sustained a three- to five-inch-deep wound. Because of the attacker's hooded disguise, Mendoza was unable to identify him.

Cozad was interrogated by the police and protested his innocence. He later maintained that he was mistreated by the detectives in the case, who he said pressured him to waive his rights about legal representation and employed other excessively intimidating tactics. Cozad was charged with attempted first-degree murder and second-degree assault. The case went to trial, and Cozad's attorney claimed that aside from the police's procedural misconduct ignoring his client's request for a lawyer, that the real attacker had been Kevin Ausspring, a dorm mate who drove Cozad to and from the crime scene. Cozad passed a polygraph test, which is sometimes unreliable, but the court ruled it to be inadmissible evidence in this case.

The jury did not buy the defense theory and convicted Mitch Cozad of second-degree assault, but acquitted him of first-degree murder. Under the legal guidelines, he could have faced up to forty-eight years in prison, but he received a seven-year sentence. The power of his jealousy and his difficulty in dealing with the reality of not being selected as the starting punter on a team that had a one-and-nine record in the previous season pushed him into a decision that almost led to murder and life imprisonment.

This case often has been compared to the Nancy Kerrigan–Tonya Harding episode ten years earlier. Whereas that situation involved Olympic athletes and had global implications, Cozad stood to gain very little by destroying his rival.

Christophe Fauviau

In a truth-is-stranger-than-fiction scenario, Christophe Fauviau, a former helicopter pilot in the French army, was convicted of spiking the water bottles of his children's tennis opponents, which led to the accidental death of one of his son's rivals. This was a most bizarre and tragic case that highlights the downside of a parent's overinvestment in living vicariously through his children's athletic accomplishments. It further illustrates the extreme lengths such parents will go to give their children an edge.

In describing the blurring of boundaries between himself and his children, which created immense anxiety within him, Fauviau said, "each match was terrible anguish."[8] This anguish prompted him to start using Temesta, an antianxiety medication, which has a side effect of inducing drowsiness.

Soon thereafter he started dropping Temesta into the drinks of as many as twenty-seven rivals of his children in tournaments between 2000 and 2003. The French tennis authorities were delinquent in initiating an investigation after opponents complained of symptoms such as weak knees, dizziness, nausea, and fainting in their matches against his son Maxime and his daughter Valentine. Ultimately, Fauviau's machinations caused the death of twenty-five-year-old Alexandre Lagardere, who is believed to have fallen asleep at the wheel, when his car rammed into a tree after he retired in a tournament match against Maxime earlier that evening.

A jury deliberated for only two hours and quickly found Fauviau guilty, and he was sentenced to eight years in prison. At his trial, a remorseful Fauviau captured the essence of how he indulged his dark side with lethal consequences, under the sway of his passion for victory and his reduced sense of reality. He lamented, "I never realized that by doing this I could harm anyone . . . dropping pills in water bottles became a habit . . . I felt like I was being permanently judged at how well my kids performed."[9]

OTHER SCANDALS

Jim Leyritz

Jim Leyritz, who excelled in the 1999 World Series for the New York Yankees, a high point in his eleven-year major league career, was charged with manslaughter and DUI on December 29, 2007. He had been out drinking with friends in celebration of his birthday and, while driving home at 3:20 A.M., in what the police described as an intoxicated state, he ran a red light and rammed into another car on a Florida street. The driver of the other car was thrown from her car and later died. When he realized the seriousness of the situation, Leyritz panicked and tried to cast blame upon the victim in asserting to the police that "she hit me pretty good."[10] Leyritz's predicament was compounded when he failed a roadside sobriety test and refused a breathalyzer test. Sadly, the victim, Fredia Ann Veitch, was also legally drunk, and she was not wearing a seat belt during the collision. If he is convicted of manslaughter, Leyritz faces fifteen years in prison.

Leyritz had been struggling with postretirement adjustment problems for several years, which was manifested in a messy divorce and a difficult custody battle for his three children. A social work family evaluation concluded that both parents were negligent in some respects, but they awarded custody to Leyritz, who then began to approach his parental responsibilities more earnestly and responsibly. Leyritz had earned $11 million during his playing years, but had squandered it all and was currently reliant on economic assistance from the Baseball Assistance Team. His financial irresponsibility was characteristic of the many professional ballplayers who do not know how to manage their wealth and end up in dire straits.

At the time of the tragedy, Leyritz's driver's license had been suspended for failing to answer a summons for a highway infraction in New York State. Jim Leyritz is yet another example of a sports celebrity who is prone to defy the rules and regulations of society, and thus is at risk for irresponsible or reckless misconduct. He also admitted to using HGH to recover from an injury during his stint with the Yankees.

Ugueth Urbina

Ugueth Urbina stands out as another MLB star who was convicted of reckless attempted murder. Urbina, an eleven-year career relief pitcher, last played for the Philadelphia Phillies through the 2005 season. In October of that year, after returning to his native Venezuela, Urbina along with several men in his entourage attacked a group of workers with machetes. They poured gasoline on them and intended to set them on fire for trespassing on Urbina's ranch. Urbina paid the consequences for this extraordinarily violent reaction. After a speedy trial, he was sentenced to a fourteen-year prison term. Urbina was no stranger to dangerous episodes. Just one year earlier, he was traumatized by the kidnapping of his mother by drug traffickers seeking a huge ransom. It took a stressful period of five months until she ultimately was rescued.

LaVon Chisley

LaVon Chisley was a talented Penn State lineman who believed that his athletic talent would catapult him into the world of professional football. Instead, he landed in jail with a life sentence.

A number of sports agents, eager to have a potential celebrity client in their stable, readily advanced large sums of money to Chisley. The expectation that he would be drafted to the NFL and given a lucrative contract never materialized, and Chisley was at a loss to pay back these benefactors.

In June 2006, in a desperate attempt to find money, Chisley attacked a student at Penn State who was known to carry a large amount of cash.

It was a brutal crime in which the victim, who had been a friend of Chisley's, was stabbed eighty-three times. Chisley was convicted of first- and third-degree murder and sentenced to life in prison.

Montana State University

The pressure to stock varsity college teams with talented athletes has led to questionable recruitment practices in which some schools welcome law-breaking students into their programs. Montana State, which in recent years has had six athletes arrested or charged with murder or major drug violations, is especially visible as a university that has condoned such practices.

The most serious case involved Branden Miller, a basketball player, and John Lebrum, a football player, who were convicted of murder in the 2006 shooting death of a drug dealer. Both Miller and Lebrum had histories of assault incidents, and it was predictable that they might pursue additional violent pathways. Miller was sentenced to 120 years in prison, and Lebrum received a fifty-year sentence.

The epidemic of legal transgressions involving problem athletes at Montana State highlights issues regarding recruitment policies. Firmer standards must be enacted on a national basis to monitor the backgrounds of prospective student-athletes, and the scope of previous illegal misconduct must be given greater weight in the selection process.

CHAPTER SEVEN

Cover-ups

A BRIEF HISTORY

The culture of cheating in sports has always been present, but it has accelerated in recent times in a way that runs parallel to the increasing number of scandals of corruption in our society at large.

The professional sports leagues have repeatedly turned a blind eye toward the damaging scandals within their sport. When their lucrative revenues are at stake, the team owners and even the leagues' commissioners have looked the other way, rather than attempting to protect the public's trust in their game. They subscribe to a culture of deception, and only belatedly do they crack down and implement the necessary policies, regulations, and sanctions to safeguard the integrity of their sports. Until recently, the NFL has been lame in acknowledging the long-term health hazards for players who prematurely return to the game after suffering concussions. It took a rash of former players who revealed a prevalence of depression, dementia, and suicidal behavior before the league addressed the issue of future effects of head injuries, and thereby exposed the magnitude of danger and violence in their sport. MLB never raised a flag of suspicion about the influence of performance-enhancing drugs, when Mark McGwire and Sammy Sosa dwarfed Roger Maris's single-season home run record, and David Stern acted clueless when a crooked referee was exposed after months of an FBI investigation. This chapter explores how baseball, football, and basketball commissioners hide behind a façade of ignorance and duplicitous naiveté in attempting to cover up or defuse brewing scandals that later erupt.

Historically, MLB commissioners like Bowie Kuhn and Bud Selig have been painfully negligent in probing players' misbehavior that threatened to tarnish the image of the game. In 1970, Denny McLain, baseball's premier pitcher, was suspended after it was reported that he had been involved in bookmaking activities in 1967. However, rumors about McLain's association with gamblers had been circulating for two years, and Kuhn, fearful of negative publicity, chose not to address them. After levying the suspension, Kuhn reinstated McLain after only six months, and this lenient banishment was perceived by some reporters as a token penalty prompted by the need for some message of damage control to circumvent a deeper investigation into gambling within baseball.

Kuhn was also at the helm when Pete Rose's gambling activities began to surface in 1977. Kuhn initiated an investigation of sorts, but with Rose as a poster boy for the game, nothing was done until 1989 under the stewardship of a different commissioner. It is now crystal clear that Bud Selig was pathetically slow in addressing the steroids prevalence that has stained the national pastime in the twenty-first century.

In the early years of professional basketball, rumors circulated about players who were accepting bribes to shave points, and conclusive evidence might have doomed the league in its infancy. Attention to these suspicions were diverted by Commissioner Maurice Podoloff when he focused, instead, on Jack Molinas, who was betting on games in which he played during his rookie season in 1954. After Podoloff penalized Molinas with a lifetime suspension, other gambling matters were not investigated, and the NBA remained free of gambling scandals for decades.

THE TIM DONAGHY REFEREE GAMBLING SCANDAL

When the Tim Donaghy scandal surfaced in July 2007, Commissioner David Stern claimed that he had learned about the FBI investigation only one month earlier. Stern deserves credit for the burgeoning popularity of the NBA during his long reign as commissioner, but in as much as Donaghy's crooked actions occurred on Stern's watch, we might also wonder whether he was paying attention.

The league had investigated Donaghy in connection with two off-the-court incidents in 2005 in which he allegedly acted violently toward a neighbor and engaged in a fistfight with another referee in a hotel. Such episodes did not speak well for his character and the desirable image of a referee. Stern supported Donaghy in these incidents and gave him a limp slap on the wrist for allowing himself to be the source of negative publicity for the NBA, but at that point, he should have begun to monitor him as a potential loose cannon. Instead, when the link to gamblers emerged, he offered defensive excuses in taking the position that there are bad apples in every system and that what happened in the NBA is endemic to society at large. In countering his critics, Stern clumsily argued that "criminal activity will exist every place else in the world except in sports is just something that we can't guarantee."[1]

This assessment may be true, but the Tim Donaghy affair heightened other issues that were lying dormant about the integrity of the game. One of the leading concerns is the widespread perception that the league has a different set of standards for its marquee players, who are protected and are treated more leniently on foul calls, than the rest of the players.

The Donaghy episode called increased attention to such issues, and the more Stern tried to marginalize Donaghy as a rogue isolated criminal, the more some observers in the media highlighted other areas of credibility regarding the NBA's image. Reporter Ian O'Connor captured this viewpoint in writing: "The commissioner desperately wants to isolate Donaghy, make him out to be a Frankenstein monster that merely needs to be destroyed and forgotten about. Only putting Donaghy in prison won't eliminate the perception that the NBA operates under an unjust system of justice."[2]

Shortly before his sentencing, Donaghy's lawyer sent a letter to the court targeting the credibility of the NBA, in which Donaghy claimed that league executives had instructed referees not to call technical fouls on star players, which could hurt ticket sales and television ratings, and that referees had been pressured to skew the direction of foul calls in a crucial 2002 playoff game to ensure additional revenues from a seventh game. These assertions were dismissed by the NBA as a desperate ploy by Donaghy to provide information to the court that could create a major scandal of corruption for the NBA and reduce his own sentence for illegally betting on games and providing inside information to gamblers. There is no evidence to support Donaghy's allegations about "broad misconduct in the NBA ranks," but even criminals sometimes tell the truth. Will the league be open to examining its credibility issues under the aegis of an independent investigator, or will its preoccupation with revenues lead to reflexive whitewashing responses?

THE BLACK SOX COVER-UP

The chronology of sports scandals invariably begins with the Black Sox episode in which eight players on the Chicago White Sox were implicated in a scheme to throw the 1919 World Series.

At the time, baseball was rife with incidents of individual players who collaborated with gamblers to fix games. The protocol within MLB to deal with such corrupt athletes was to turn a blind eye or to issue a minor rebuke. Why puncture the fans' belief in innocence and fair play? But the seeds of corruption had been developing for more than twenty years, in a sport that lacked the wherewithal to police itself. Baseball historian Gene Carney, who wrote an entire volume on the 1919 fix and the cover-up, concluded, "It seemed to be in the best interests of baseball—the best financial interest, that is—that the tampering with games by gamblers be covered up—and if discovered, should be quickly portrayed as the rare exception to the rule of honest play."[3]

Rumors of a conspiracy to fix the World Series were omnipresent before, during, and after the Series, but nothing was done about it until the Chicago grand jury initiated an inquiry one year later. The eight players were indicted, and when the case went to trial in June 1921, they were exonerated. In the midst of their jubilation, the next day they were all banned for life by the newly appointed first commissioner, Kenesaw Mountain Landis, who had been hired to clean up the game.

Many books and articles have been written about this dark chapter in sports history. By most accounts, there was a widespread informal conspiracy among players, owners, and league presidents to cover up the scandal. According to Hugh Fullerton, a renowned reporter in that era, the code of silence prevailed. He observed, "The honest players object to squealing and the dishonest ones cover up . . . the fact that organized baseball's settled policy for years of 'keeping quiet for the sake of the sport' has been the very thing which has made crookedness possible and overlooked."[4]

Most of the cover-up focus has been directed at Charles Comiskey, the pernicious owner of the White Sox. Both Comiskey and Ban Johnson, the American League president, had heard the swirling rumors before game one, but neither one pursued the issue. Comiskey, who had a longstanding feud with Johnson, displaced culpability onto Johnson for not putting the Series on hold, or launching an immediate investigation. The consensus of writers on this subject is that when White Sox manager "Kid" Gleason told Comiskey about his suspicions after game two, Comiskey then informed the National League president, John Heydler, about the rumors of a fix. Heydler also contacted Ban Johnson about it and then backed off.

Comiskey later claimed that throughout the Series he had no idea that there was a fix. In fact, he did not attempt to question any of his players during the Series, and, instead, he defended them afterward as being honest; and he disingenuously offered a $10,000 reward for substantiated information about the fix. Eliot Asinof, the author of *Eight Men Out*, the definitive historian of the scandal, wrote: "Comiskey and his lawyer hatching the cover up even as they launch their investigation, believing Ban Johnson and the National commission could be relied on to do absolutely nothing."[5]

It appears that Comiskey, Johnson, and Heydler were all enablers who participated in the cover-up by either turning a blind eye to what they really knew, or dropping the ball and waiting for someone else to pick it up. To expose the crookedness was too threatening to the precarious image of baseball as a sport with integrity.

Of all the participants in the drama it seems that Charles Comiskey was the master of duplicity. Comiskey realized that if the fix was publicly confirmed, he could lose his best players as well as losing substantial future revenue at the gate. So he acted like he was Mr. Righteous in trying to uncover evidence, while simultaneously determined to bury it in deference to his own financial interests. Most sources suggest that while his public posture was to support and protect his accused players, his primary need was to protect his assets, which prompted him to make a token effort for an investigation of wrongdoing. In essence, his real agenda was to avoid, suppress, and conceal any hard evidence from the public, and his $10,000 reward offer was a subterfuge. He already knew the Series was rigged and which players were involved.

Thus, his chief reason for covering up the conspiracy was to safeguard his financial stake as the owner of a highly successful franchise, and, second, perhaps in collusion with other owners, he was motivated to protect the sport from a major scandal at a time when it was already beset by the infiltration of gamblers. To expose the fix would exacerbate the sense of mistrust in the sanctity of the game.

In his analysis of the ingredients of the cover-up, Eliot Asinof concluded that:

> Mostly the secrecy was maintained by the power of the owners themselves. Whatever they knew, or suspected, they concealed, terrified at losing the public faith in the game. At all costs, any suspicious incident would be buried. . . . The official, if unspoken policy preferred to let the rottenness grow rather than risk the dangers of exposure, for all the pious phrases about the nobility of the game and its inspirational value to youth.[6]

It is fascinating to consider how a similar scenario gripped the game some eighty years later. We can see a parallel here to the way the MLB establishment looked askance and significantly underplayed the abundant emerging evidence of steroid proliferation among its players until such time as external pressures (such as Ken Caminiti's revelations in *Sports Illustrated*, President Bush's warning about athletes and steroids in his 2004 State of the Union address, and the congressional hearings on steroids in 2005) forced the owners and the commissioner to initiate the Mitchell investigation.

The Roots of the Black Sox Scandal

The Black Sox scandal can be examined and understood from three perspectives: dispositional, situational, and systemic. A dispositional perspective suggests that certain players who were lacking in moral turpitude were prone to participate in throwing games. Some of them, such as Chick Gandil, the purported ringleader of the fix, seemed more than ready to cross the line of corruption. From a situational perspective, we need to consider two factors: the effect of the players' strained relationship with Comiskey, and the group contagion effect. Comiskey was known to be penny pinching and heavy handed in his treatment of his players, which contributed to a climate in which they might be enticed to cross the line of corruption in response to their mounting anger and resentment toward the owner. When the gamblers, with an assist from Gandil, proposed a way for the players to make some easy money (they were to be paid more for throwing the Series than their entire season's salary), the offer quickly became hard to resist, in the context of their growing animosity toward Comiskey. After the first few players signed on to the plan, the others who were approached crumbled like dominoes under the sway of not wanting to miss out on the payoffs.

From a systemic perspective, the chief factor was that the infiltration of gamblers within professional baseball had increased over many years, as corrupt players like Hal Chase, Lee Magee, and others had played ball with gamblers as well as with their teams. Game fixing on an individual basis had become somewhat endemic to the game. The culture of cheating in sports takes place on many levels. The most prominent headline grabbers involve players who take illegal performance-enhancing drugs to gain a competitive edge or players involved in gambling scandals. However, the arc of transgressions extends to coaches, referees, and even scouts.

In 2008, MLB launched an investigation into scouts who allegedly were skimming the signing bonuses of prospects they were recruiting and pocketing the difference. The practice is most prevalent among scouts in the Dominican Republic, where an increasing number of future major leaguers are found. Scouts employed by the Chicago White Sox, Boston Red Sox, and New York Yankees have been fired or placed on leave in connection with these allegations.

SPYGATE

In their opening game of the 2007 NFL season, the defending Super Bowl champion New England Patriots were discovered filming their opponents' defensive signals. The stealing of signals via videotape surveillance was in clear violation of NFL rules and has come to be known as Spygate.

The League's Response

It was an embarrassment for the league, and Commissioner Roger Goodell slapped the Patriots coach, Bill Belichick, with a $500,000 fine, and penalized the team with a $250,000 fine and the loss of a first-round draft pick in 2008. These were the harshest set of fines levied in league history, an indication of how seriously the commissioner was taking this threat to the perception of the integrity of the game. Goodell had been on a rampage of doling out suspensions to players like Pacman Jones, Tank Johnson, and Michael Vick, whose legal or moral transgressions had further tarnished the image of the players in professional football. Because the implications of the Spygate episode had deeper relevance, even harsher penalties for the Patriots and Belichick would have been in order. In comparison with Goodell's other sanctions, they were treated too leniently.

The Scandal Deepens

It soon became apparent that this was not a singular infraction by the Patriots, and the league requested evidence of similar tapings, but they failed to issue a blanket demand for all of their suspected videotapes. In what later turned out to be erroneous information and that underscores how the media is sometimes guilty of inflaming a scandal, the *Boston Herald* reported that the Patriots had secretly videotaped the final walk-through practice of the St. Louis Rams before defeating them in the 2002 Super Bowl. Curiously, the alleged videotape was not among those asked for by the NFL, and the team submitted material from six other games.

The owner of the Patriots, Robert Kraft, also bears greater accountability, because Spygate took place on his watch. Notably, MLB is held to a different standard than professional football when it comes to the owners' role as enablers in the culture of cheating. In a congressional hearing, MLB Commissioner Bud Selig indicated that he was considering sanctions against the San Francisco Giants for allowing Barry Bonds's trainer, Greg Anderson, to be present repeatedly in their clubhouse, as well as for not reporting concerns about Bonds's alleged steroid use to the commissioner's office. The NFL has thus far remained exempt from similar congressional hearings, and Commissioner Goodell showed no inclination to investigate the Patriots owner's complicity in the Spygate matter. Is Kraft not equally as culpable as an enabler as the owner of baseball's San Francisco Giants?

Sen. Arlen Specter Gets Involved

Goodell further compromised his credibility by quickly destroying the evidence supplied by the Patriots, claiming that he did so to circumvent their being leaked to the public. In an effort to provide a modicum of damage control, Goodell also opined that the taping and stealing of opponents' signals has limited impact on the outcome of games. This led to outcries of whitewashing and accusations of a cover-up from Sen. Arlen Specter. The Pennsylvania senator was piqued at Goodell's lack of response to his inquiry in this matter, and he called for the Patriots management and Goodell to attend judicial hearings. Comparing Goodell's destroying the Patriots tapes to the Central Intelligence Agency's destruction of tapes, Specter highlighted the confiscation of the tapes in stating, "It's the same old story. What you did is never as important as the cover-up. This sequence raises more concerns and doubts."[7]

While Goodell and the NFL franchise owners considered the controversy closed, Specter held firm to the possibility of congressional hearings and strongly urged the NFL to arrange a full independent investigation. Paradoxically, questions have been raised about Specter having his own ax to grind in his bulldog-like pursuit of Spygate. One of Specter's largest campaign contributors, Comcast, had been engaged in a legal dispute with the league regarding the apportionment of games on its cable system. Thus, it is an open question as to whether this connection has influenced Specter to be overly zealous in his crusade against the league and the commissioner.

Goodell's downplaying the potential benefit to the Patriots of the video-taped signals, even if true, intensified concerns about a cover-up. Hypo-thetically, when a defensive play call was deciphered, the Patriots had time to adjust their next play accordingly; and this could lead to a substan-tial advantage. Mike Martz, who was coach of the heavily favored Rams when they lost to the Patriots in the 2002 Super Bowl, maintained that "if you can tell the quarterback what he's going to get defensively, it makes a great deal of difference."[8]

Belichick's Cop-Out

Furthermore, it did not help the NFL's image when coach Bill Belichick offered an explanation that strained the limits of credibility. Belichick supplied a pretense of innocence in claiming that he misinter-preted the league's rules and had believed that it was acceptable to videotape opponents' signals, because he was not using the information in the same game. This was the football equivalent to Barry Bonds's assertion that in using such steroids as "the clear" and "the cream" he believed that he was simply using flaxseed oil and an arthritic cream. Critics took Belichick's lame explanation as confirmation that he had been using this system of signal stealing during his entire tenure as head coach. Sportswriters, most of whom had allowed themselves to be too readily deceived in the steroids era, were now ready to crucify Belichick as a serial cheater. *New York Times* columnist Harvey Araton argued for a one-year suspension against Belichick, claiming that Goodell has the responsibility to crack down harder on a coach who has cheated for a decade than on players who have transgressed.

Ultimately, it was determined from an additional group of eight tapes, submitted by a former Patriots employee in charge of videotaping, that both offensive and defensive play-calling signals used by their opponents had been recorded in six games between 2000 and 2002. Although the allegations concerning the 2002 Super Bowl were retracted, a group of St. Louis Rams players nevertheless filed a $100 million class-action lawsuit against the Patriots for videotaping their pre–Super Bowl practice session.

Specter Presses for Intervention

Arlen Specter has continued to pressure Roger Goodell to appoint a Mitchell-type investigation in response to the evidence from the eight additional tapes submitted, and he admonished the Patriots' "illicit video-taping tactics as more systematic and deliberate than what the NFL has acknowledged publicly" and added, "they owe the public a lot more candor and a lot more credibility . . . If the public loses confidence in professional football it will be like wrestling."[9]

Other members of Congress have shown little interest in pursuing the Spygate scandal. Given the succession of scandals involving cheating in sports, a large segment of the public has become inured and indifferent to athletes, coaches, and others who cheat. Sadly, the public has become numb, and many fans are increasingly buying into the programmed perception that professional athletes are merely entertainers rather than serious role models.

THE IMPACT ON CHILDREN

In pressing his cause, Specter expressed concern about the impact on children from cheating in sports, as exemplified by the Spygate affair. The sustained success of the Patriots could encourage an ethos of cheating, which can have a ripple effect from professional athletes as role models to college, high school, and grade school students.

Indeed, one of the more alarming issues emerging from the Mitchell report on performance-enhancing drugs in baseball was the prevalence of steroids in youth sports. Mitchell's findings indicated that several hundred thousand young people were using steroids, many of whom were identifying with and emulating their sports heroes. In many high schools and colleges, coaches pressure children to get bigger and stronger as a prerequisite for making the team.

One of the most disturbing scenarios is that of parents of athletically gifted children who live vicariously through them, and encourage their use of steroids as a vehicle for greater athletic success.

The Corey Gahan Story

The sad case of Corey Gahan is illustrative. As a thirteen-year-old, Corey Gahan was a champion in-line skater and was earmarked for future success. Under the auspices of his father, Corey was placed in a training regimen that included regular injections of steroids and HGH. Within a year, he had bulked up and his testosterone level had reached twenty times the normal male threshold. Corresponding to his steroid-induced growth, his skating times improved rapidly, and by fifteen, he became the national champion at five hundred, one thousand, and fifteen hundred meters.

His father, Jim, thought that he had provided steroids that were undetectable from the infamous steroids den, Signature Pharmacy, but Corey failed two drug tests and was suspended from competition at the bequest of the U.S. Anti-Doping Agency (USADA), which rescinded his earlier U.S. Indoor Speed Skating championship medals. Corey's father, trainer, and supplier were all implicated and pleaded guilty to conspiracy to distribute steroids to a minor. The father, convicted of supplying steroids to young Corey, received the harshest sentence: six years in a federal prison.

Corey, whose participation in the investigation was central to his father's guilty plea, was left to pick up the pieces of his once-promising career. He feels guilty about his role in his father's imprisonment but also angry and victimized by being pushed into using steroids. He believed he had the talent to be a champion without artificial enhancement, and he captured the essence of being in the grip of steroids use in retrospectively lamenting, "Steroids completely changes your mind-set. They turn you from being an athlete into a monster."[10]

While the prevalence of steroid use among high school students is alarming, there are indications that education programs aimed at this population may be working. A 2007 Michigan University survey revealed that 2.2 percent of the nation's high school seniors acknowledged that they had used steroids at least once, which was down from 4 percent in a comparable 2002 study. With regard to athletes and steroids, several states have instituted a mandatory drug-testing program for high school players, which is administered when they reach postseason play. Skeptics of this program maintain that when athletes know when they are going to be tested, they can discontinue the cycle of steroids and thereby mask being discovered. Other antidoping experts emphasize the value of a testing policy in creating a deterrent effect. It seems likely that a combination of education programs, which includes kids encouraging other kids not to use steroids, and the deterrent effect of a publicized testing policy, offers the best approach to this problem.

THE CULTURE OF CHEATING

In the world of sports, not all cheaters are equal. Different standards of judgment have been in vogue depending on the type of cheating and the era in which it occurred. In baseball, pitchers who have used a spitball to gain an edge have been tolerated for decades, and even have been admired for their cunning ability to get away with it. Many MLB umpires recognized that players were using steroids, but chose not to make an issue out of it and thereby were enablers. In justifying their participation in the cover-up, umpire Ted Barrett explains that he and his colleagues "didn't raise a red flag for them because they saw it as a way for the players to stay on the field. I have some empathy for them, I admit. . . . A lot of these guys, I'm sure they did what they did to recuperate from injuries, or to fight age."[11]

Football Gets a Pass

Nevertheless, when it comes to cheating, professional baseball appears to be held to a higher standard than professional football. The reactions among fans, the media, and even Congress indicates a (newfound) hyper-vigilance regarding steroids use in baseball, in contrast to a selective inattention when it comes to football, in which NFL players who violate the league's drug policy tend to be let off easy in the field of public opinion.

The partiality afforded to football is reflected in the extensive coverage given to suspicions concerning baseball's McGwire, Bonds, and Clemens, whereas in the NFL, Rodney Harrison's four-game suspension in early 2007 for receiving HGH was obfuscated as his team, the New England Patriots, approached the Super Bowl, and Shawne Merriman of the San Diego Chargers headed for the Pro Bowl without mention in the press of his prior four-game suspension for using a steroid precursor.

MLB Commissioner Bud Selig and Donald Fehr, the former executive director of the Players Association, have been chastised by members of Congress in light of the steroids proliferation occurring on their watch, but their NFL counterparts have been given a pass; and neither congressional hearings nor an independent investigation into steroids use, a la the Mitchell inquiry, have been seriously called for.

It is perplexing to attempt to account for the genesis of this differential treatment of the two most popular sports in America. In a sense, we are guilty of a form of cover-up by highlighting our indignation about baseball players who use steroids, while underplaying our condemnation toward cheating football players who entertain us with their violent collisions. Were it not for the outrage that emerged around hallowed records being broken in baseball and track and field, with the assistance of performance-enhancing drugs, the notion of cheating to gain an edge in athletic competition might still be condoned.

HGH Replaces Steroid Use

We are currently in an era of scrutiny, however, and athletes who are driven by the enticement of mega-million-dollar contracts are finding creative ways to stay ahead of the curve of discovery. In the aftermath of the Mitchell report, a stampede of professional athletes appear to be relying on HGH, which for now is undetectable, as an alternative to steroids. In documenting the move away from steroids, there were only five positive findings out of 6,252 tests in MLB for 2006 and 2007.

The Renewed Popularity of Amphetamines

The power of the culture of cheating, however, is not to be underestimated. It seems that a sizeable number of players are working around the rules by receiving medically authorized exemptions for the use of certain drugs. Historically, before they turned to steroids, amphetamines had been the drug of choice for baseball players and such stimulants had been accepted as an adaptive way to deal with the grind of the long season. However, as a backlash from the steroids scandal, amphetamines were banned by MLB, which began a testing program for them in 2006. The terms of the policy directed that first-time offenders were given a warning, and those who tested positive more than once were identified and suspended. As of this writing, only two cases in the latter category have surfaced. It is unclear whether the testing program is working as a deterrent, or whether it is the option of attention deficit disorder (ADD) stimulants that accounts for the shifting trend.

Athletes Who Beat the System

By claiming to suffer from ADD, athletes can qualify for "therapeutic use exemptions," which allows them to use stimulants like Adderall and Ritalin with prescriptions from their cooperating and complicit physicians. Consequently, a sudden abundance of ADD diagnoses among professional athletes underscored their ability to exploit a loophole in the system. To put the issue in perspective, the number of MLB players who received a "therapeutic use exemption" in 2007 mushroomed to 103 from only 28 in 2006. The grapevine for how to beat the system grew rapidly. The 2007 total represents 7.6 percent of active players, which amounts to eight times the adult use of drugs such as Adderall and Ritalin in the general population.

The Plaxico Burress Cover-Up

Cover-ups in sports are not limited to athletes using steroids or gambling transgressions. They also may occur when a player has engaged in illegal activity.

The Plaxico Burress illegal possession of a weapon that discharged in a nightclub and inflicted a wound in his thigh in November 2008 is a case in point. When Burress realized that he did not have a permit to carry a gun in New York—and that the publicity surrounding the incident had career-threatening implications—he panicked and initiated a cover-up that involved and legally jeopardized other people.

Burress was at the nightclub with fellow Giants teammate Antonio Pierce, whom he implored to take him to a local hospital for treatment of his gunshot wound. Fearful of publicity, he admitted himself to the hospital under an alias. Pierce, as a loyal friend, became complicit in an illegal activity by stashing the gun in the glove compartment of his car. The hospital and the emergency room doctor were influenced to remain quiet about a sports celebrity involved in a gunshot episode, which was a violation of the law that required the hospital to report such things to the police. In addition, the Giants and the NFL were negligent in informing the authorities of the event. New York City Mayor Michael Bloomberg was so enraged at this sequence of cover-up attempts that he publicly demanded harsh prosecution for Burress, which inadvertently could have interfered with his getting a fair trial.

CONCUSSIONS AND LATER HEALTH HAZARDS

The most serious area of cover-ups in the world of sports concerns the dangerous consequences of concussions, especially in the collision sport of football. The short-term effects of sustaining a concussion, such as lingering headaches, lethargy, recurrent dizziness, short-term memory loss, nausea, blurred vision, and sensitivity to light and noise, are well known and freely acknowledged. Under pressure from their macho culture in which they are immersed, too many players have returned prematurely to the field, sometimes even in the same game, thereby putting themselves at significant risk for further damage. The most common danger is the appearance of a postconcussion syndrome, in which symptoms occur from a subsequent concussion before the first one has fully healed. Hockey and football are replete with players who suffer from postconcussion syndrome. The premature return to play generally has been condoned or subtly encouraged by coaches and team trainers, who have ignored the common guidelines for concussion management, which mandate that athletes be completely free of symptoms before resuming competition. Most athletes who return early to the game are in denial and convince themselves that they can play through the symptomatic aftereffects of a concussion.

The Long-Term Mental Health Consequences

It is the long-term mental health and cognitive effects of sports-related concussions, however, that have been subjected to a blind eye, a code of silence, and naiveté that is most disturbing. In terms of later problems caused by concussions, athletes are essentially jeopardizing their lives without realizing it. An ostrich-like approach of complicit denial permeates the entire hierarchy of commissioners, team owners, coaches, the NFL-appointed panel on concussions, and the players, who are mesmerized by the glory of playing in the NFL and the appeal of the exorbitant salaries that go with it.

The prevalence of concussions in professional football is undeniable. A study conducted by the players union found that more than 61 percent of retired players had sustained concussions as active players, and that in most cases, they were not sidelined after their head injuries. The report was based on a sizeable sample of 1,100 interviews with former players. The study further revealed that 30 percent of the sample had three or more concussions, and 15 percent had suffered at least five concussions.[12] What was left unanswered by this study and became the subject of further research were questions about the long-range cognitive and mental impairments in connection with concussions, and whether the frequency of concussions was related to these later deficits.

Revealing Research Studies

The University of North Carolina's Center for the Study of Retired Athletes sought to investigate these issues. Based on a survey of more than 2,500 former NFL players, researchers at the Center determined that a correlation existed between a player's history of concussions and later clinical depression, cognitive impairment, and early onset dementia, including Alzheimer's disease. The correlation between concussions and depression in this published study was staggering and alarming. Of the 595 retired players who had three or more concussions, 20.2 percent had been diagnosed with depression, compared with an incidence of 6.6 percent in those who had not sustained any concussions.[13] Despite the clear statistical significance of these results, the NFL, in its best cover-up fashion, utilized selective inattention in ignoring these findings in its concussion pamphlet, which is distributed to all current players. In fact, the league highlighted that "multiple concussions do not leave players more susceptible to future concussions and do not pose long term risks" and "current research with professional athletes has not shown that having more than one or two concussions leads to permanent problems if each injury is managed properly."[14]

This Center for the Study of Retired Athletes research project led by Dr. Kevin Guskiewicz represents the most comprehensive study yet undertaken of football players and future mental health impairment. The weakness of any survey study is that they rely on subjective memories, however, and the league seized on this potential flaw in research design to discredit the findings. Previous papers published by the same Center, which linked football concussions to future mild cognitive impairment and early onset Alzheimer's disease, also were criticized by the league.

In another telephone survey that was actually sponsored by the NFL, the Institute for Social Research at the University of Michigan found that 6 percent of a cohort of 1,063 retired players maintained that they had been diagnosed with cognitive deficits involving dementia, Alzheimer's, or other memory-related diseases. This finding was five times greater than reported in the national population. Once again the league and a spokesman for the NFL concussion committee argued that the study was flawed and they highlighted the unreliability of survey results. In order to gain momentum for their cause, the proponents of the link between concussions and later cognitive impairment will need to present more rigorous research findings since phone surveys are known to contain a margin of error.

The NFL Underplays the Data

Gene Upshaw, the beleaguered former executive director of the NFL Players Association, has repeatedly expressed his belief that no evidence supports the view that the incidence of Alzheimer's disease and other forms of dementia is greater than that seen in the general population. This position has made Upshaw the target of attacks among retired players who maintained that he was insensitive to their cause and concerns. The physical disabilities of Hall of Fame players like Earl Campbell, which are believed to be at least partly induced by years of being pummeled on the field, were instrumental in Tiki Barber, the New York Giants star, opting for early retirement. Campbell has been outspoken about the NFL's indifference toward struggling retired players and has directed his wrath toward Upshaw, who he said, "Should be ashamed. He played the game and he knows."[15] Before his sudden death in 2008, Upshaw's callous retort to his critics was that he is accountable only to the NFL's active players and does not represent the needs of retired players.

Some medical experts have questioned whether concussions absorbed by NFL players lead to subsequent medical and mental impairments. Neurologist James Kelly, a proponent of this view contended, "We have no evidence, none, that there are lingering longterm problems from repeated concussions."[16] However, the dramatic findings of the abovementioned University of North Carolina study have become a source of controversy among neurology experts. On one side of the spectrum is the view registered by Dr. Henry Feuer, a member of the NFL's Mild Traumatic Brain Injury Committee, who lambasted the Center's findings as "virtually worthless" in pointing to the limitations of a survey study.[17] On the other hand, Dr. John Whyte, an authority on neurological research methodology, heralded the study as a meaningful contribution, and declared that it gave us "some pretty solid data that multiple concussions caused cumulative brain damage and increased risk of depression."[18] Dr. Whyte called for additional research studies in this area. Under pressure from the growing body of literature linking football concussions to later in life problems, the league eventually responded to the challenge. Perhaps fearing that the field of public opinion would no longer tolerate turning a blind eye to this issue, the NFL funded a study of its own.

In a letter to the *New York Times*, NFL spokesman Greg Aiello reiterated the league's longstanding position that

> There is no conclusive scientific evidence proving such a connection [between concussions and long-term effects], but we want to know more. That is why we are spending almost $2 million to fund a medical study on concussions with a group of our retired players. The purpose is to determine in a scientifically valid way if there are long-term effects of concussions on retired NFL players.[19]

Despite the limitations of the abovementioned studies, the data were sufficiently compelling for the U.S. Judiciary Committee to initiate hearings on the issue of brain injuries in football. These hearings were held on October 28, 2009 and a number of serious questions were raised about the much heralded proposed NFL study.[20]

The criticisms cluster around sampling problems and conflict of interest issues. The relatively small number of participants in the sample and the absence of a control group represent potential flaws in the research design. The fact that the league is conducting the study rather than an independent research organization is another area of concern. Moreover, it is puzzling that the number of concussions suffered, a key variable purportedly related to later cognitive decline, does not seem to be at the center of the research. Instead, the stated aim of the NFL study is to compare long-term cognitive deficits in a cohort of players who were active for at least two NFL seasons versus a group who played football only through college or up to one year in the NFL. The congressional committee also underscored the danger of long-term effects of football concussions in youth sports and at the high school level.

To put it bluntly, the NFL has been shamelessly remiss in not taking a more active lead in addressing this most serious of issues, and their motivation in not doing so is highly suspect. On a more positive note, the conspiracy of silence and turning a blind eye toward the issue of football-related concussions and short-term, long-term, and later effects has begun to be dismantled in recent years. Public awareness has been accelerating as a cluster of suicides and players' revelations about depression, premature cognitive decline, and early Alzheimer's have come to the fore. The culture of secrecy, fear of being deactivated, and cover-up is gradually being replaced by transparency and accountability.

Combined Sources of Cover-Up

Historically, an unspoken network of collusion has existed in professional football among the league, the owners, the coaches, the trainers, and the players to minimize, obfuscate, and distance themselves from the dangerous and even life-threatening sides of sports that revolve around collision in the core of the game. To the extent that these casualties of the game are increasingly being exposed, attitudes, reactions, and positions that trade on naiveté, feigned cluelessness, or malevolent cover-up will no longer be viable.

Football is our most widely followed spectator sport, but its popularity comes at a high price to its players' health. By the very nature of the game, concussions are inherently entwined in the violent contact and collisions between three-hundred-pound warriors. The fans, until recently, have been kept in the dark about the future effects of concussions.

The NFL administrators and the club owners are culpable, because their primary concern hovers around enhancing revenues by getting the best players to perform on the field at any cost. It is not in their interests to focus on how dangerous and violent the sport is. Administrators do not want concussion publicity because they are motivated to shield the public, who idolize the players, from acquiring an image of their heroes becoming addled and incapacitated. On some peripheral level of awareness, however, people may recognize the implications. They also have a stake in not discouraging the pool of new players from aspiring to an NFL career. The league and the owners need not worry about this variable, because the players themselves are in denial and rarely think about a future with possible depression, cognitive decline, early Alzheimer's disease, and premature death. It is less chilling to invest in thinking that these things can happen to other players but not to me.

Moreover, the players collude in the cover-up, because they are fearful of losing their jobs and their inflated athlete salaries. In addition, they are programmed not to complain about the short-term symptoms of concussions lest they appear to be weak, and the NFL macho culture dictates that players get back into the game as soon as possible. While the average professional football career lasts less than four years, in the minds of the players, the glory, excitement, and financial rewards outweigh the reality. To compound that reality, a recent research study revealed that compared with MLB players, "football players are more than twice as likely to die before age 50."[21]

In brief, the heart of this collusive cover-up involves the owners and the league, which desire money; the coaches and the trainers, who desire victories; and the players, who desire glory.

Belated Breakthroughs

The impressive accumulation of cases that point to a connection between concussions and cognitive deficits as well as depression began with the publicity surrounding the death of Mike Webster. Webster, who was famous for his role in the Pittsburgh Steelers' four Super Bowl victories in the 1970s, died in 2002 at age fifty. He had sustained multiple concussions during his career, and many years later, he was diagnosed as suffering from brain damage and depression. It was widely speculated at the time that his long-term postretirement mental deterioration was a carryover effect from his concussions.[22]

A big step forward in creating public awareness of the problem evolved when former Denver Broncos star Bill Romanowski revealed in an interview with "60 Minutes" the typical course of cognitive decline in athletes who suffer multiple concussions. Romanowski stated that after fifteen to twenty concussions he felt "dazed, confused, losing my memory."[23] And two years later after his retirement, doctors noted a profound slowing of his cognitive functioning.

A similar profile was disclosed by Mel Renfro, a Dallas Cowboys Hall of Famer, who endured nine concussions as a football player. At age sixty-five, Renfro acknowledged that his postretirement physical disabilities had improved, but, in contrast, his depression, cognitive deficits, and fogginess persisted and had worsened over the past seven years.[24]

The Persistence of Denial

Before 2007, the NFL had steadfastly downplayed the dangers of concussions. Several members of the Mild Traumatic Brain Injury Committee, chaired by Dr. Elliot Pellman, the New York Jets team physician, published a paper in the January 2005 issue of the journal *Neurosurgery* and concluded that "there is no evidence of worsening injury or chronic cumulative effects of multiple concussions, and a player returning to the field after a concussion won't sustain a significant risk of a second injury either in the same game or during the season."[25]

Amid intense criticism of the committee's position on concussions, Pellman resigned as chairman, a title he had held since its inception in 1994. Dr. Pellman previously had been discredited for misleading and erroneous information about his medical school training and professional status, and his knowledge of steroid testing was deemed as insufficient when he participated in the 2005 congressional hearings.[26] Given his track record, the underplayed conclusions about concussion dangers issued by the research committee were tainted by a cloud of credibility.

Concussions in Young Athletes

One of the most vexing concerns about football-related concussions involves the very real danger of life-threatening on-the-field collisions to teenagers. Research studies indicate that in the last ten years more than fifty high school or youth players have died or suffered serious head injuries as a result of football concussions.[27]

In the 2005 *Neurosurgery* article cited above, in which the NFL concussion committee members defended the tradition of allowing professional football players to return in the same game, the authors extended this approach to other levels of play in concluding, "It might be safe for college/high school football players to be cleared to return to play on the same day as their injury."[28] In effect, the NFL approach to concussion management sets a dangerous precedent, especially for high school players, "because their brain tissue is not fully developed, and, therefore, it is more easily damaged."[29]

Coaches, parents, and young players have colluded to downplay the prevalence of the concussion problem. Coaches tend to underreport these injuries, and many parents have been excessively proactive in finding doctors who will too quickly authorize a kid's recovery and return.

The greatest danger may emanate from the teenage players who are uninformed, do not understand, or are in denial about concussions. Many operate with the mistaken belief that unless a player is knocked unconscious, it does not qualify as a concussion. Their macho-gladiator identification makes them prone to hide their symptoms, and to keep playing or get back to playing as soon as possible in spite of their symptoms. In so doing, they put themselves at risk for "second-impact syndrome," also known as "postconcussion syndrome," where they suffer a second trauma to the head before fully recovering from the previous concussion. In the most ominous cases, the damage causes a swelling of arteries, increased pressure, and bleeding in the brain that can lead to coma and death.

Essentially, young football players who sustain concussions need to be protected from themselves. The overriding tendency is to minimize their symptoms and prematurely return to play. Much greater oversight and education programs are needed to curtail the risks and derail a trend that threatens to reach epidemic proportions.

Justin Strzelczyk and New Evidence

A major breakthrough in the campaign of the medical establishment to highlight the dangerous effects of football-related concussions developed in June 2007, when Dr. Bennet Omalu, a renowned neuropathologist, examined the postmortem brain tissue of Justin Strzelczyk, a Pittsburgh Steelers offensive lineman who was killed in an auto accident at age thirty-six. Omalu discovered early signs of brain damage that he attributed to head trauma during Strzelczyk's nine-year playing career.

In light of the league's and the Players Association's history of minimizing and discrediting the studies that linked concussions to long-term risks for depression, cognitive impairment, and early Alzheimer's, Dr. Omalu and his associates at the newly formed Sports Legacy Institute began an initiative to study and publicize this issue.

Punch-Drunk Syndrome

The type of damage found in Justin Strzelczyk's brain tissue, called chronic traumatic encephalopathy (more commonly known as "punch-drunk syndrome" or CTE), was also discovered in postmortem examination of the brains of three other former NFL stars, Mike Webster, Andre Waters, and Terry Long. This type of pathology is usually seen in boxers afflicted with dementia or seniors in their eighties, but Webster, Waters, Long, and Strzelczyk were all under age fifty-one. It is frightening to think that they could represent only the tip of the iceberg among retired NFL players.

NFL Suicides

Terry Long, another offensive lineman with the Pittsburgh Steelers from 1984 to 1991, committed suicide in 2005. Initially, the coroner's report stated that CTE related to football head injuries was a causative factor in Long's suicide. A revised death certificate, however, indicated that Long, who had made a previous suicide attempt years earlier, had died as a direct result of drinking antifreeze, and that his football-related brain damage was a contributing factor. Terry Long was only forty-five at the time.

A year later, Andre Waters, a former NFL star with the Philadelphia Eagles, committed suicide at age forty-four. Waters had sustained more than fifteen concussions during his playing days, and upon postmortem analysis, Dr. Omalu ascertained that his brain tissue resembled an eighty-five-year-old man with early signs of Alzheimer's disease. Dr. Omalu concluded that the brain damage was caused and accelerated by Waters's multiple concussions.

This cluster of cases represents a small sample of depression, cognitive deficits, early Alzheimer's, and suicide in retired professional football players who had suffered concussions as active players. Now that the consequences of concussions are coming to light, however, additional studies can be expected to highlight and confirm these alarming connections.

Successive Concussions and Cognitive Impairment

In the somewhat murky area of concussion management, insufficient notice has been given to the issue of exacerbated pathology as a function of successive concussions incurred over a short time span.

After the Andre Waters suicide, Ted Johnson, a ten-year veteran middle linebacker with the New England Patriots, who contributed to their three Super Bowl victories, went public about his symptoms of cognitive impairment and depression following on-the-field concussions. According to Johnson, he sustained a concussion in an August 2002 preseason game, and suffered a second concussion when he was pressured to participate in a high-impact practice drill only four days later. Fearful that if he did not play he could be released and would forfeit his $1.1 million salary, he reluctantly agreed to engage in the practice session.

In retrospect, Johnson returned too soon, and he suffered postconcussion syndrome. One of the major sources of criticism directed toward the NFL has been the tendency for coaches to allow players with concussions to resume playing in the same game. In point of fact, this protocol has been implemented with one-half of such cases.[30] Johnson claims that Patriots coach Bill Belichick later admitted that he had pushed him prematurely to see whether he could play at the required high level.

Beginning in 2003 Johnson maintains that he suffered a series of "mini-concussions" over the next three seasons, which left him feeling progressively unfocused, irritable, and depressed. He retired after the 2004 season, and his symptoms of disorientation and other cognitive problems worsened. The esteemed neurologist Robert Cantu contends that Ted Johnson's depression, cognitive impairment, and signs of early Alzheimer's are connected to his history of concussions, and he predicts that these symptoms will be permanent.

The Ted Johnson saga has highlighted the specific area of dangers associated with recurrent concussions. In assessing an increasing number of cases, Dr. Cantu and other head trauma experts have cautioned that when athletes sustain repeated concussions, especially if they are only days apart, they are at great risk for progressive cognitive difficulties. In addition, the Johnson case shed light on the fact that the rate of recovery from a concussion varies with the severity of the trauma, a point that has not received enough attention.

THE STRUGGLE FOR BENEFITS FOR DISABLED FOOTBALL RETIREES

In recent years, retired football players have become increasingly proactive in demanding greater benefits from the NFL for its cadre of former players who have become disabled. Historically, the league had established a high bar for players to validate (that is, prove) that their disability was precipitated by football-related injuries, which qualifies them to receive full disability payments. Essentially, the league has hidden behind its more accessible partial disability payment program, which entitles players to receive a substandard minimum of $1,500 per month, if their disability makes them unable to work.

Since depression and permanent cognitive impairment generally develop over a period of years following active playing status, players with such concussion-related problems have been at a significant disadvantage in gaining disability benefits.

Brent Boyd

Brent Boyd, who played for seven seasons in the 1980s with the Minnesota Vikings, is a case in point. Years after he retired, Boyd developed cognitive problems and depression, which his doctors linked to his history of NFL concussions.

In processing Boyd's disability application in 2000, the NFL had him examined independently by a neurologist and a psychiatrist. Both doctors indicated on the retirement board's standardized form that Boyd had incurred "an illness or injury resulting from a football-related activity," which confirmed the medical opinion of his own doctors. Nevertheless, the retirement board required Boyd to consult with another neurologist, who reported that "Boyd's physical and mental health problems could not be an organic consequence of the head injury."[31] Based on this opinion, the retirement board rejected Boyd's claim for full disability benefits. Interestingly, the board, which has the final say in disability requests, is composed of three representatives of the league and three from the union; therefore, the players union bears equal culpability in what was a questionable determination. Boyd protested that the board had "doctor shopped" to support its predetermined position, and Gene Upshaw, the executive director of the players union, dismissed this assertion.

Angry and bitter over the process and the ruling, in his testimony before a congressional committee hearing on the NFL's disability plan, Boyd referenced the Terry Long and Andre Waters concussion-related tragedies and accused the board, and indirectly the league, of "using their tactics of delay, deny, and hope that I put a bullet through my head to end their problem."[32]

PUNCTURING THE CONCUSSION COVER-UP

The NFL was painfully delinquent in acknowledging the concussion issue, and some of its high-profile authority figures like Gene Upshaw and Dr. Elliot Pellman and his concussion research committee had been outspoken in discrediting or minimizing the problem, thereby contributing to a cover-up mentality. As a result of the accumulation of research studies, the long list of cognitively challenged retired players coming forth, and a probable concussion link with several suicides, a cover-up approach is no longer a viable option. Accordingly, the league has pledged to conduct its own large-scale study, and their research results are expected to be revealed in 2010.

The magnitude of potential cognitive problems associated with football concussions is poignantly captured by Pittsburgh Steelers safety Troy Polamalu, who has incurred six concussions. In Polamalu's view,

> Concussions are weird in the sense that you don't know the severity of it. You can't really measure it too much. Not only that, it's the worst injury you can sustain in sports. You can live without legs, your arms, but it's hard to go on in life without your mind.[33]

THE 88 PLAN

The wives of former players Ralph Wenzel and John Mackey, a Hall of Famer, have been advocates of publicizing the connection between a concussion history and their husbands' current dementia. Both players show signs of extensive mental deterioration and have no memory of being teammates, nor of even playing for the 1972 San Diego Chargers. Mrs. Mackey had been in ongoing contact with ten football wives whose husbands were struggling with early onset dementia. In 2007, when the image of the NFL was tarnished by its stonewalling the connection between concussions and later cognitive decline, she persuaded Commissioner Paul Tagliabue to establish the 88 Plan. The Plan, named in honor of John Mackey's jersey number, designated that former players who are afflicted with dementia problems can receive benefits of up to $88,000 a year for their care and treatment. The 88 Plan coexists alongside the league's traditional disability plan, and the applicants are reviewed by the same league and players union representatives who serve on the retirement board panel. Although the NFL in its official position continues to maintain that there is insufficient scientific evidence to establish a connection between football-related concussions and later cognitive decline, it has identified 103 former players with dementia or Alzheimer's disease who could qualify for assistance from the 88 Plan.

NEW NFL GUIDELINES ON CONCUSSIONS

In a reversal of its earlier stance that players who sustain concussions may return to the same game without additional risks, the NFL, before the 2007 season, recommended that teams refrain from allowing players who become unconscious after a concussion to play again in the same game. The position seemed to represent a concession to placate the concussion and later-in-life cognitive decline hawks. However, Dr. Henry Feuer, a member of the league's concussion research committee, opined that "guidelines focusing on loss of consciousness were misdirected, and that loss of consciousness was 'about the least important' of all factors in assessing severity of a concussion."[34]

On another positive note in 2007, the league established a "whistle-blower" system encouraging the anonymous reporting of any incident in which a doctor was pressured by coaching personnel to authorize a player's return to the game. This move may have come about in response to the Ted Johnson situation. In finally being more proactive, Commissioner Goodell established seminars on concussion management and treatment for team physicians and trainers. Goodell denied that the negative publicity surrounding the Andre Waters and Ted Johnson incidents had compelled him to initiate these moves. He stated, in fact, that the league had been studying these issues for fourteen years. We can only wonder why it has taken so long to address these issues definitively.

A GLANCE AT THE FUTURE

In a most innovative step forward, a research project has been funded to study the brain tissues of deceased athletes. The Center for the Study of Traumatic Encephalopathy at Boston University's School of Medicine in collaboration with the Sports Legacy Institute is administering the program, and thus far, twelve former and current athletes who have sustained concussions, including six NFL players, have signed on to donate their brains to the Center after their deaths. The goal is to examine the brain tissue of athletes to clarify the presumed connection between on-the-field concussions and long-term effects of cognitive impairment. It is a tribute to those who have been relentlessly proactive in pursuing this issue, in spite of prolonged denials on the part of the NFL, that these athletes are agreeing to participate in this groundbreaking research study.

In support of its mission, the Center revealed in September 2008 that it had examined the brain tissue of John Grimsley, a former Houston Oilers linebacker, who accidentally shot and killed himself. The findings confirmed that Grimsley's brain, at age forty-five, showed similar damage (traumatic encephalopathy) to that found in Mike Webster, Terry Long, Andre Waters, and Justin Strzelczyk. It seems likely that there will be many more John Grimsleys along the way, and the Center expects to develop a brain bank of one hundred specimens.

Hopefully, their data will put this most egregious of sports cover-ups to rest.

EPILOGUE

As a teenager, I was attracted to the rough-and-tumble excitement of roller derby. I wanted the "sport" to be on the level. A big part of me knew it was fake, but I wanted it to be real, so I avidly rooted for my favorite team (the Brooklyn Red Devils) and my favorite players (Ken Monte and "Toughie" Brasuhn), and I allowed myself to be fooled into believing that the competition and rivalry in roller derby were authentic.

It was a necessary illusion for me to hold onto for a while in my youth, a time when I was not yet ready to deal with the realities and disappointments in life. In the current era, this would no longer be possible. The degree of scrutiny given to today's sports figures and the media's stark and unrelenting exposure and revelations about sports stars' flaws, transgressions, and other venues of corruption deprive our youth of holding onto their heroes in unalloyed form; and it forces them to prematurely see and address the dark side of life.

As part of healthy development, children need to have an extended period in which they admire and connect with important authority figures in their lives. This begins with their early relationships with their parents and other loved ones, which establishes the template for trust and the capacity for love.

As they begin to recognize the limitations of their parents, they may turn to external heroes, which provides them with figures to believe in and something good to connect with. Sports heroes often become special figures, real and symbolic, that our youths attach themselves to. Once these structures are embedded within children, they are better able to tolerate the disappointments that may follow when the flawed aspects of their "heroes" become apparent.

The chief danger of being exposed to news about the criminal behavior or other forms of corruption entangling our sports stars is that it can lead to an abrupt loss of a cherished hero, an object of love, so to speak. This attachment to a sports hero contributes to the child's ability to feel good about him- or herself for experiencing these loving feelings and the feeling of security through the affiliation with someone "good." And deflation can follow from such a sudden loss when the much-needed hero is shown to have clay feet.

In the ongoing parade of famous athletes falling prey to scandals, Olympic gold medal swimmer Michael Phelps tarnished his reputation because of a photo linking him to marijuana smoking in 2009 (which led to a three-month suspension); baseball's premium star Alex Rodriguez was reported to have tested positive for steroids in 2003 (before there were penalties); and Manny Ramirez was suspended for fifty games for a positive drug test, also in 2003. These news briefs have further eroded the belief that our superstars are pure, untainted, and worthy of unyielding adulation. It is increasingly apparent that many sports celebrities are not what they seem to be.

These scandals compel us to see the truth, which is that talented athletes, like most other people, also have a dark side with lapses in integrity, which coexists alongside all of their other positive attributes. As a society, we are now obliged to prepare our children to deal with the true nature of things, sometimes before they are emotionally ready to absorb them, as the scope of childhood innocence becomes truncated.

NOTES

CHAPTER 1

1. Steve DiMeglio, "Opinions Mixed on Ephedra Use in Baseball," *USA Today Sports Weekly*, February 26, 2003, 5.

2. Bobby Ojeda, "Extreme Baseball," *New York Times*, February 23, 2003, section IV: 11.

3. Mike Schmidt, *Clearing the Bases* (New York: Harper Collins, 2006), 3.

4. Michael Sokolove, "The Scold," *New York Times Magazine*, January 7, 2007.

5. Johnny Davis, personal communication, May 14, 2007.

6. George Will, "Barry Bonds's Enhancement," *Newsweek*, May 21, 2007, 82.

7. Mark Fainaru-Wada and Lance Williams, *Game of Shadows* (New York: Gotham, 2006), xii–xiii.

8. George Vecsey, "For Two a Day of Recognition; For One a Day of Reckoning," *New York Times*, January 10, 2007, D1.

9. Ibid., D2.

10. George W. Bush, State of the Union Address, January 20, 2004.

11. Congressional Hearings, March 17, 2005.

12. Mark Fainaru-Wada and Lance Williams, *Game of Shadows* (New York: Gotham, 2006), 246.

13. Jeff Pearlman, *Love Me, Hate Me* (New York: Harper Collins, 2006), 203–4.

14. Ibid., 213.

15. Ibid., 200.

16. Mark Fainaru-Wada and Lance Williams, *Game of Shadows* (New York: Gotham, 2006), 194.

17. Stanley Teitelbaum, *Sports Heroes, Fallen Idols* (Lincoln: University of Nebraska Press, 2005), 102.

18. John Heilman, "Let Juice Loose," *New York Magazine*, April 17, 2006.

19. George Will, "Barry Bonds's Enhancement," *Newsweek*, May 21, 2007, 84.

20. Jeff Pearlman, *Love Me, Hate Me* (New York: Harper Collins, 2006), 3.

21. Ibid., 275.

22. Rick Reilly, "No Doubt About It," *Sports Illustrated*, December 13, 2004, 118.

23. Bob Klapisch, "Slugger Must Come Clean about His Past Dirty Deeds; McGwire Gets Slap in the Face by Hall of Fame Voters," *The Record*, January 10, 2007.

24. William C. Rhoden, "Baseball's Ugly Side Just Got Uglier," *New York Times*, October 2, 2006, D2.

25. Tom Verducci, "Hard Numbers," *Sports Illustrated*, May 15, 2006, 39–43.

26. George Will, "Barry Bonds's Enhancement," *Newsweek*, May 21, 2007, 84.

27. Bob Klapisch, "Hank Strikes Out," *The Record*, August 9, 2007, S1.

28. Jeff Pearlman, *Love Me, Hate Me* (New York: Harper Collins, 2006), 320–21.

29. Ibid., 319.

30. Christian Red, "Van Slyke: I'm Certain that Bonds Used 'Roids," *New York Daily News*, May 5, 2004.

31. Sam Borden, "Jackson Said His Frustration Led to Speaking Out on Steroids," *New York Daily News*, March 12, 2004.

32. "Baseball Testing a Joke, Pound Says," *Ottawan Citizen*, March 5, 2000.

33. "Report: Bonds Failed Amphetamine Test," Associated Press, January 11, 2007.

34. Jack Curry, "Baseball Asserts Fewer Players Failed Drug Tests," *New York Times*, August 11, 2006, D5.

35. Tom Verducci, "Hard Numbers," *Sports Illustrated*, May 15, 2006, 39.

36. "Giambi Says Major League Baseball Should Own Up to Presence of Drugs," ESPN.com, May 18, 2007.

37. "Poll: 62% Believe Clemens Should Be in the Hall of Fame," Associated Press, March 21, 2008.

38. Selena Roberts, *A-Rod: The Many Lives of Alex Rodriguez* (New York: Harper Collins, 2009).

39. Ibid., 34.

40. Ibid., 41.

41. Michael Schmidt, "A First Step toward Drug Testing Next Year Is Taken," *New York Times*, September 21, 2007, D6.

42. Adrian Wojnarowski, "Landis Testing Faith in Heroes," *The Record*, August 2, 2006.

43. Gina Kolata, "Some Athletes' Genes Provide License to Outwit Testing," *New York Times*, April 30, 2008.

CHAPTER 2

1. Pete Rose, *My Prison Without Bars* (Emmaus, PA: Rodale, 2004), 188–89.

2. Mike Schmidt, *Clearing the Bases* (New York: Harper Collins, 2006), 156.

3. Fay Vincent, "The Problem with Forgiving Pete Rose," *New York Times*, December 8, 1999, A23.

4. Jim Bouton, "How Baseball Grew a Gambler," *New York Times*, October 26, 1999, A27.

5. Mike Schmidt, *Clearing the Bases* (New York: Harper Collins, 2006), 163.

6. "Rose Admits to Betting on the Reds Every Night," Associated Press, *New York Times*, March 15, 2007, D6.

7. Jay Leno, *The Tonight Show*, March 26, 2007.

8. Loren Feldman, "The Long, Slow Fall of a Gridiron Great," *Gentlemen's Quarterly* 58, no. 12 (December 1988): 299.

9. Ibid., 299.

10. "What Hooks Us," *Time Magazine*, July 16, 2007, 44.

11. Charley Rosen, *The Wizard of Odds* (New York: Seven Stories Press, 2001), 16–17.

12. Stanley H. Teitelbaum, *Sports Heroes, Fallen Idols* (Lincoln: University of Nebraska Press, 2005), 69.

13. Ibid., 98.

14. Eric Konigsberg, "Double Dribbling," *New York Times Book Review*, March 3, 2002, 22.

15. Charley Rosen, *The Wizard of Odds* (New York: Seven Stories Press, 2001), 284.

16. Ibid., 19.

17. Denny McLain, *I Told You I Wasn't Perfect* (Chicago, IL: Triumph, 2007), 150–51.

18. Denny McLain and Mike Nahrstedt, *Strikeout: The Story of Denny McLain* (St. Louis, MO: Sporting News, 1998), 15–16.

19. Denny McLain, *I Told You I Wasn't Perfect* (Chicago, IL: Triumph, 2007), 153.

20. Ibid., 14.

21. Ibid., 14.

22. Ibid., 21.

23. Ibid., 121.

24. Ibid., 283.

25. Ibid., 383.

26. Ibid., 165.

27. Roscoe Tanner, *Double Fault* (Chicago, IL: Triumph, 2005), 148, 153.

28. Ibid., 206.

CHAPTER 3

1. Steve Adamek, "League Says Ref Is One Bad Apple," *The Record*, July 25, 2007, S1.

2. Liz Robbins, "The NBA Learned of the FBI's Referee Inquiry Last Month," *New York Times*, July 25, 2007, D1.

3. Ibid., D3.

4. "Jagr Gambling Revelations," *The Ottawa Citizen*, October 25, 2007.

5. Ibid.

6. Dave Anderson, "Gretzky Is Taking Some Hits Off the Ice These Days," *New York Times*, February 10, 2006, D1.

7. Mitchel Maddux, "Gretzky Knew Wife Was Betting," *The Record*, February 10, 2006, A1.

8. Adrian Wojnarowski, "The Grate One Is an Annoyance," *The Record*, February 12, 2006.

9. Joe Drape, "Talk of Efforts to Fix Matches Rattles the Pro Tennis Circuit," *New York Times*, November 25, 2007, 1:1.

10. David Leonhardt, "Sad Suspicions about College Basketball," *New York Times*, March 8, 2006, C1.

11. Justin Wolfers, "Point Shaving: Corruption in NCAA Basketball," *Amer. Economic Review* 96, no. 2 (May 2006).

12. Ron Reno, "The Dirty Little Secret Behind March Madness," *Citizen Magazine*, March 30, 1999.

13. Richard Hoffer, "Goodbye, Mr. Chips," *Sports Illustrated*, May 15, 2006, 18.

14. Carlos Monarrez, "Daly Reveals Major Gambling Losses in Book," *Detroit Free Press*, May 3, 2006.

15. Charles Barkley, "I Do Have a Gambling Problem," http:sports.espn.go.com/nba/news/story?id=2432043, last accessed 9/4/2009.

16. Ibid.

CHAPTER 4

1. "Bears Done with Tank," Associated Press, June 26, 2007.

2. "Tinsley Is Happy to Be Alive," Associated Press, *New York Times*, December 11, 2007, D5.

3. Lynn Zinser, "Tinsley Is More Careful Since Escaping Attack," *New York Times*, December 18, 2007, D2.

4. Joe Lapointe, "Giants Say Burress's Season Is Over," *New York Times*, December 3, 2008, B12.

5. Boomer and Carten, WFAN, December 4, 2008.

6. Jack McCallum, "Fed Up Yet?" *Sports Illustrated*, August 6, 2007, 44.

7. Ibid., 43.

8. Michael S. Schmidt and Judy Batista, "Plea Deal Complete, Vick Speaks of Mistakes," *New York Times*, August 28, 2007, D1.

9. Ibid., D2.

10. Chris Berman, *SportsCenter*, ESPN, August 29, 2007.

11. Ibid.

12. Michael S. Schmidt and Judy Batista, "Plea Deal Complete, Vick Speaks of Mistakes," *New York Times*, August 28, 2007, D2.

13. Michael S. Schmidt and Judy Batista, "After Plea, Vick Is Barred Indefinitely by the NFL," *New York Times*, August 25, 2007, D2.

14. *New York Times*, Aug. 15, 2009, D1.

15. Bob Cook, "Big Ben's Wreck Won't Scare Other Athletes," MSNBC.com, June 13, 2006, http://nbcsports.msnbc.com/id/13285770/ns/sports-nfl/, last accessed 9/1/09.

CHAPTER 5

1. Lynn Zinser, "Sending a Message, Judge Sentences Jones to 6 Months in Prison," *New York Times*, January 12, 2008, D3.

2. Lynn Zinser and Michael Schmidt, "Jones Admits to Doping and Enters Guilty Plea," *New York Times*, October 6, 2007, D1.

3. Jere Longman, "Letter Urges President Not to Give Jones Pardon," *New York Times*, July 23, 2008, D1.

4. "In Sexual Assault Cases, Athletes Usually Walk," *USA Today*, May 28, 2004.
5. "Thomas Defiant in Face of Harassment Claims," Associated Press, January 26, 2006.
6. Ibid.
7. "Jury Rules Thomas Harassed Ex-Executive; MSG Owes Her $11.6 M," Associated Press, October 7, 2007

CHAPTER 6

1. Stanley H. Teitelbaum, *Sports Heroes, Fallen Idols* (Lincoln: University of Nebraska Press, 2005).
2. Nicholas D. Kristof, "Racism Without Racists," Week in Review, *New York Times*, October 5, 2008, 10.
3. "Benoit's Brain Showed Severe Damage from Multiple Concussions, Doctor and Dad Say," ABC News, September 5, 2007.
4. Brenda Goodman, "Wrestler Killed Wife and Son, Then Himself," *New York Times*, June 27, 2007, A15.
5. Phil Mushnick, "Benoit Tragedy Wakes Up Media," *New York Post*, June 29, 2007, 91.
6. Ibid.
7. Wayne Coffey, "Ten Years Later, Terry Underwood Still Looking for Daylight," *New York Daily News*, October 7, 2007.
8. CBS.com, March 10, 2006, http://www.cbsnews.com/stories/2006/03/07/world/main1376475.shtml, last accessed 9/8/09.
9. ABCNews.com. March 10, 2006, http://abcnews.go.com/international/story?id=1680047&page=1, last accessed 9/8/09.
10. Katie Thomas, "For Leyritz, Future in Balance after a Fall," *New York Times*, November 3, 2008, D3.

CHAPTER 7

1. Michael S. Schmidt, "League Finds Donaghy Was Sole Referee Culprit," *New York Times*, October 3, 2008, D2.
2. Ian O'Connor, "Stern Will Always Be Tied to Scandal," *The Record*, June 12, 2008, S11.
3. Gene Carney, *Burying the Black Sox* (Washington, DC: Potomac, 2006), 293.
4. Hugh Fullerton, "Are Baseball Games Framed? The Inside Story of What Led Up to the Major League Scandals," *Liberty*, March 19 and 26, 1927.
5. Gene Carney, *Burying the Black Sox* (Washington, DC: Potomac, 2006), 271.
6. Eliot Asinof, *1919: America's Loss of Innocence* (New York: Donald L. Fine, 1990): 301–02.
7. Greg Bishop and Pete Thamel, "Goodell May Have to Explain Actions in Spying to Congress," *New York Times*, February 1, 2008, D1.
8. John Branch and Judy Batista, "NFL Says Tapes Add Nothing to Inquiry," *New York Times*, May 14, 2008, D1.
9. Greg Bishop, "Senator Calls Patriots' Spying Wider Than the NFL Admits," *New York Times*, May 15, 2008, A1.

10. Luis Fernando Llosa and L. Jon Wertheim, "Sins of a Father," *Sports Illustrated*, January 21, 2008, 33.

11. Bruce Weber, "Cheating Matters (Sometimes)," *New York Times*, Week in Review, December 16, 2007, 3.

12. Mike Freeman, *Sunday, Bloody Sundays: Inside the Rough and Tumble World of the NFL* (New York: Harper Collins, 2004), 75.

13. Alan Schwarz, "Study of Ex-NFL Players Ties Concussions to Depression Risk," *New York Times*, May 31, 2007, D7.

14. "For Jets, Silence on Concussions Signals Unease," *New York Times*, December 22, 2007, A22.

15. "Former Oilers Star Campbell Criticizes Upshaw," Associated Press, *New York Times*, July 1, 2007, D5.

16. *Sunday, Bloody Sundays: Inside the Rough and Tumble World of the NFL* (New York: Harper Collins, 2004), 76.

17. Alan Schwarz, "Study of Ex-NFL Players Ties Concussions to Depression Risk," *New York Times*, May 31, 2007, D7.

18. Ibid.

19. Greg Aiello, "NFL's Concussion Study," *New York Times*, June 10, 2007, D10.

20. Alan Schwarz, "NFL Is Scolded over Care on Injuries," *New York Times*, October 29, 2009, B12.

21. Daniel Gross, "The NFL's Blue-Collar Workers," *New York Times*, January 21, 2007, Section IV: 5.

22. Mike Freeman and Linda Villarosa, "The Perils of Pro Football Follow Some into Retirement," *New York Times*, September 26, 2002, D1.

23. *60 Minutes*, Interview, October 15, 2005.

24. Alan Schwarz, "An Answer to Help Clear His Fog," *New York Times*, May 31, 2007.

25. Selena Roberts, "The Many Perils of Unqualified Hypocrisy," *New York Times*, April 13, 2007.

26. Ibid.

27. Alan Schwarz, "High School Players Stay Silent on Concussions, Raising Risk," *New York Times*, September 15, 2007, A1.

28. Alan Schwarz, "Concussion Panel Has Shakeup as Data Is Questioned," *New York Times*, March 1, 2007, D7.

29. Alan Schwarz, "High School Players Stay Silent on Concussions, Raising Risk," *New York Times*, September 15, 2007, A1.

30. Alan Schwarz, "Dark Days Follow Hard-Hitting Career in NFL," *New York Times*, February 2, 2007, D2.

31. "Fighting for Benefits," ESPN.com, February 10, 2007, http://sports.espn.go.com/nfl/columns/story?id=2760591, last accessed 9/1/09.

32. Alan Schwarz, "Congress Scolds NFL and Union," *New York Times*, June 27, 2007, D5.

33. Alan Schwarz, "Nerve Center For Head Trauma," *New York Times*, January 2, 2009, B7.

34. Alan Schwarz, "New Advice by NFL in Handling Concussions," *New York Times*, August 21, 2007, D1.

INDEX

About the Author

STANLEY H. TEITELBAUM is a psychoanalyst specializing in individual, group, and couples therapy. He is affiliated with the Postgraduate Center for Mental Health and the Training Institute for Mental Health, both in New York, and the Center for Psychotherapy and Psychoanalysis in New Jersey. Teitelbaum has written numerous articles in leading mental health publications and is the author of two books: *Sports Heroes, Fallen Idols* and *Illusion and Disillusionment.* He has appeared on more than fifty national television and radio shows, including ABC's *Nightline* with Ted Koppel, *Good Morning America, 20/20,* and Court TV. Over the last twenty years, Dr. Teitelbaum has been interviewed frequently for newspaper and magazine articles on human motivation on such diverse topics as "Preventive Strategies in Dealing with Sports Rage," "Women As Targets of Athletes' Violence," and "The Importance of Athletes as Role Models and Leaders."